FORTIFIED WINE

THE ESSENTIAL GUIDE TO AMERICAN PORT-STYLE AND FORTIFIED WINE

KENNETH YOUNG

WINE APPRECIATION GUILD
SAN FRANCISCO

FORTIFIED WINE

THE ESSENTIAL GUIDE TO AMERICAN PORT-STYLE AND FORTIFIED WINE

Fortified Wine
The essential guide to American Port-style and fortified wine

Wine Appreciation Guild
Text © 2016 Kenneth Young

Managing Editor: Bryan Imelli
Special Editor: TIPS Technical Publishing, Inc
Book and Cover Designer: Diane Spencer Hume

Wine Appreciation Guild
is an imprint of
Board and Bench Publishing
www.boardandbench.com

Library of Congress Cataloging-in-Publication Data
Names: Young, Kenneth (Writer on wine), author.
Title: The essential guide to American port-style and fortified wine /
  Kenneth Young.
Description: San Francisco : Wine Appreciation Guild, 2016. | Includes bibliographical
references and index
Identifiers: LCCN 2016041554 (print) | LCCN 2016042367 (ebook) | ISBN
  9781935879572 (
Subjects: LCSH: Fortified wines--United States. | Fortified wine
  industry--United States.
Classification: LCC TP557 .Y685 2016 (print) | LCC TP557 (ebook) | DDC
  663/.2260973--dc23
LC record available at https://lccn.loc.gov/2016041554

Printed in the USA

CONTENTS

ACKNOWLEDGMENTS

I'm not really sure what sparked my adult life-long fascination with wine. It probably had something to do with being a physical science major at Chico State University and classes in organic chemistry. I recall hearing commercials about wines from "Napa, Sonoma, and Mendocino" so to satisfy my curiosity, I would take the four-hour trek to Napa in the days when you could make a left turn on Highway 29. Those occasional trips to wine country fashioned my fundamental wine appreciation and spurred me to learn more. I was hooked on the art and science of wine but rarely could afford to indulge my infatuation. Over the years, I continued to superficially study California wines and became somewhat proficient at selecting wines for personal and professional occasions.

I met my future wife in 1992 and found we shared a common interest in wine. She told me she wanted me to meet friends who owned a vineyard and winery. It was warm spring Saturday when we drove east—not west—to meet her winery friends. Imagine my disappointment that her friends' winery was not Napa or Sonoma but in the unheard of Shenandoah Valley in the foothills of the Sierra Nevada. Driving through rolling hills dotted with relatively small vineyards we finally arrived at a barn-like structure fronted by a vast green lawn boarding an idyllic lake surrounded by grape vines. This is where I met the Deaver family. Deavers had been farming in Amador County since the late 1850s and grown Zinfandel and Mission grapes dating to the 1880s. Ken Deaver was an imposing but gentle man clad in denim and topped by his signature floppy tan Stetson. While Ken was the vintner, sister Joey was in charge of the tasting room. It turned out they needed someone to work in the makeshift tasting room on weekends and I jumped at the change to "work" at a winery.

For the next year I spent most of my weekends pouring four Deaver wines; White Zinfandel, Red Zinfandel, Chardonnay, and Zinfandel Port. Back then, the Sierra Foothills was a largely anonymous wine region and 20–30 visitors over a weekend was a crowd. I spent my time between customers reading about wine, winemaking, and the history of California wine. Before long, Ken Deaver became my mentor and one of my closest friends. I am truly grateful for Ken's tutelage, which eventually led to this book. Ken was best man at our wedding and with his wife Jeanie, are life-long friends. Thanks Ken and Jeannie - I wouldn't be here without you.

I became Deaver's week-end part-time wine educator in 2001 after a career in non-profit organization management. When I had the opportunity, I would accompany Ken in the vineyards and visit our winemakers eager to learn more about grape growing and winemaking first-hand. I spent a couple days during the 2001 crush working with Windwalker Vineyards winemaker Rich Gilpin to whom I am grateful for the hands-on experience. This experience turned out to be a blessing when in late October, Ken said he wanted to make port from late harvested Barbara and Sangioivese, and I was going to be the winemaker. Armed with just enough knowledge and coached by Rich, we made a pretty good wine that eventually won a Bronze medal in the Orange County wine competition.

Among of my duties as wine educator was writing about Amador wines in general and Deaver wines in particular. I wrote several articles for the various wine publications and somehow came to the attention of Jim and Deana Hansen, publishers of d'Vine Wine and Visitors Guide. That association, for which I am most appreciative, led to a decade of monthly feature and wine-education articles eventually becoming wine editor. Their enduring commitment and support guided my development as a writer and I am thankful for their cherished friendship.

While researching a piece on California Port, I contacted renowned Napa port maker Peter Prager for an interview. During our conversation, one thing led to another and the Sweet and Fortified Wine Association (SFWA) was revived after several years of dormancy and I became the part-time staffer for Association. SFWA's purpose is to educate the American public regarding sweet and fortified wine.

This book is a tribute to the contemporary fortified wine makers of America - several of whom contributed its content. First and foremost, I want to thank SFWA President Peter Prager for his unwavering commitment to the fortified wine industry and his ongoing leadership as spokesperson for American fortified wines. He and bother-in-law Richard Lenney mentored me on many of the fine points of port production. The Prager family came to St. Helena in 1979 to make port and they continue to be a shining example of premium California port wine.

I am eternally grateful to all the members of SFWA who contributed to this book but especially appreciative of three remarkable members and friends. Michael Blaylock is the winemaker for Quady Winery in Madera, California and certainly one of foremost technical experts on fortified wine production. I truly appreciate his technical review of this book and his suggestions that kept me from making some really dumb errors.

I am indebted to veteran port maker Peter Ficklin whose family pioneered making port-style wines from traditional Portuguese grape varieties grown in California. His historic and technical contributions were immensely important to his book.

Raymond Haak is a highly regarded Texas fortified wine producer whose expertise was of great value to the book. Thanks Ray and thanks as well to Ray's chef Tyler Henderson for his thoughts on fortified wine and food.

Marco Cappelli is an acknowledged authority on making Angelica and his crucial contribution to the segment on Angelica production is deeply appreciated.

A special thanks to Bill Reading of Sonoma Port Works for his sherry expertise and my favorite sherry and ginger ale cocktail.

While I have not personally met the "flavor maven", I sincerely want to thank Tim Hanni for sharing his unique perspective on food and wine with me for this book. His thoughts are particularly valuable in understanding the versatility of fortified wines.

Many thanks are due to a number of supporters for this tome including SFWA Board member Julie Pedroncelli-St. John, and the Wine Institute's Tom LaFaille for their expertise on the political challenges of international trade. Thanks as well to Sun-maid's Charles Feaver for his technical contributions on brandy and wine spirits production. Finally, thanks to SFWA port-maker members Bob Routon, Bart Barthelemy, Don McGrath, Matt Meyer, Dr. Marc Schrader, and Greg Holman for advice and support.

It is my sincere desire that this book will contribute to the validation of modern American fortified wines as respected world-class wines.

—Kenneth Young

DEDICATION

To my wife Nita for her faith, persistence, support and love. She kept me going with "what's taking so long?"

PREFACE

PORT AND AMERICAN FORTIFIED WINE: IT'S NOT A QUESTION OF QUALITY, JUST A MATTER OF DIFFERENCE

Let's set the record straight from the outset: American wines produced by the addition of wine spirits or brandy during the fermentation process (fortification) are not and never have been intended to be exact replicas of fortified wines from Portugal (Port and Madeira), Spain (Sherry), or Italy (Marsala). The Port purists vehemently claim that "the only REAL Port comes from Portugal." Technically, they have a valid claim. This doesn't mean, however, that American fortified wines are somehow inferior to European fortified — they are simply *different*.

There are number of factors that affect the differentiation between American and classic European fortified wines. Therefore, it would be constructive to briefly summarize the most influential of these elements before embarking on the true story of distinctly American fortified wines.

Terroir

The term *terroir* relates to the environmental factors, including climate, soil, and geography, that affect the specific habitat of wine grape vineyards. Classic port wine grapes are grown in the roughly 180-square-mile Douro Valley region of northeastern Portugal. The region is subdivided into the Baixo Corgo, Cima Corgo, and Douro Superior. Straddling the Douro River, each subregion terroir differs somewhat in soil, climate, and sun exposure. Temperatures in the Douro Superior can reach well over 100°F, with as little as 12 inches of rain annually. However, the Cima Corgo, in the heart of the region, has a slightly more moderate terroir and is the home of Portugal's finest port wine grapes. There is a definite terroir associated with the Spanish Sherry region of Jerez. The tiny region on the southwestern tip of Spain has a distinctive Mediterranean climate and chalky soils that are ideal for Sherry grapes.

In contrast, there is no typical terroir for American fortified wine grape vineyards. Classic varieties are grown on the granitic soils of the Sierra Nevada foothills, while native and hybrid varieties thrive in the loams of Missouri and the rocky soils of Arkansas's Ozarks. Vineyard climates range from the dry, hot summers in the Central Valley of California to the warm, humid growing seasons in the southeast states of North Carolina and Virginia and the chilly winters of New York and Michigan. Annual seasonal rainfall in vineyards can range from nearly zero to well over 30 inches.

Terroir is often used to describe the character of a specific wine type. This certainly applies to the Ports of Portugal's Douro Valley and Sherries of Jerez but has no real application when describing American fortified wines.

Vineyards

There are approximately 101,000 acres of vineyards in the Douro Valley region and roughly 40,000 port wine grower/producers. This is a ratio of 2.5 acres of vineyard per grower/producer. In California alone, there are about 606,000 acres of wine grapes and nearly 5,900 producers for a ratio of 103 acres per grower/producer. Of course, nearly all the Douro's vineyards produce port grapes while only a small fraction of America vineyards produce grapes that go into fortified wine. Since the ratio of vineyards to fortified wine grower/producers varies widely from state to state, no meaningful comparison can be made between vineyards and production in Portugal and the United States.

A particularly sharp contrast between European and American vineyards is found in the Portuguese system of vineyard classification. The Instituto dos Vinhos do Douro e Porto (IVDP) classifies Douro region vineyards on an alphabetic letter system (A–F) based on a numeric score for vineyard characteristics. This annual classification dictates production levels and grape prices. Most Ports are made from grapes grown in A- and B-rated vineyards.

Clearly, no such vineyard classification exists in the United States, and there is no domestic control over vineyard production and grape pricing.

Grapes

Portugal is said to have the greatest number of grape varieties in the world. Of the approximately five hundred varieties, only ninety are allowed to be planted in the Douro region. Of these, only twenty-nine are "recommended" for the production of port wines, while the remainder are merely "authorized." All of the recommended varieties are *vinifera* with long histories of wine production. Often, the most prominent port varieties (Tinta Roriz, Tinta Cão, Tinta Francesca, and Touriga Nacional) are grown together in a "field blend" vineyard where the grapes are harvested and processed together.

American producers have no restrictions on the grape varieties used for fortified wines. Over sixty red and white varieties are tapped for domestic port-style, sherry-style, and Madeira-style wines including ten Portuguese and twenty-six classic *vitis vinifera* gapes. Producers across the country utilize several native American varieties like muscadine, as well as hybrid varieties such as Frontenac, Chambourcin, and Niagara. While fairly common prior to Prohibition, field blend vineyards and co-fermentations are rare in contemporary fortified wine production.

White grapes Palomino and Pedro Ximenez are the predominant varieties in Spanish Sherry. Both varieties are quite rare in the United States so *vinifera*, including Grenache, Orange Muscat, and French Colombard, are used, while in the east, hybrids including Chambourcin, Niagara, Delaware, and native muscadine produce American sherries.

Fortifying Spirits
Aguardente is the fortifying agent in Portuguese Port wines. This is a 77 percent alcohol wine spirit distilled from the grape solids left after pressing. Aguardente is a neutral, colorless, flavorless spirit that must be approved annually by the IVDP for Port production.

In the United States, wine spirits or brandy for fortification can be made from any wine grape and can vary from 70-95 percent alcohol. The only restriction, according to the US Alcohol and Tobacco Tax and Trade Bureau (TTB), is that the fortifying distilled spirit be produced from the same fruit as the base wine—in this case, grapes.

Production Process
The Portuguese have been making Port wines essentially the same way for centuries. As a result, the "standard" production practices are closely monitored by the IVDP to ensure uniformity of product quality.

No such organization exists in the United States and probably never will. Even though Americans have been fortifying wine almost as long as the Portuguese and Spanish, there are practically no regulations on the production of American fortified wines. In fact, "fortified" is not even defined in present law or regulation.

Traditions notwithstanding, there are significant differences in the methods used by Iberian and American fortified wine producers including:

- Portuguese application of "foot treading" in "largars" versus mechanical crushing in the United States.
- Cofermentation of port varieties in Portugal versus single variety fermentation in American production.

- Fortification of juice in Portugal versus the American option of fortifying on or off the skins.
- Exact use of a 1:4 fortification ration for Portuguese Port versus variable fortification ratios of American fortified wines depending on the final desired alcohol and sweetness levels.
- Aging, blending, and bottling in Portuguese nonwinery facilities ("lodges" in Vila Novade Gaia) versus aging, blending, and bottling in the American producer winery facility.

There are several other "technical" and regulatory differences between European and American fortified wine production that clearly establish the differentiation between foreign and domestic products.

Styles

Nowhere are the differences between Portuguese and Spanish fortified wines and American fortified products more evident than in the styles fashioned by vintners.

The Portuguese have a highly structured, patently defined if somewhat baffling Port classification system closely monitored by the IVDP. Briefly, these uniquely Portuguese styles include:

Ruby: young, bright colored, everyday port aged two to three years with no or little time in wood.

Tawny: a blend of different vintages with darker red/brown color, aged in oak six to seven years. Fine Tawny ports can comfortably age twenty to forty years in bottle.

Single Quinta: Ports made from a single quinta or "farm."

Colheita: Ports made from a single vintage in years not declared as vintage. Usually dense and concentrated, this port is aged for eight years or more entirely in wood.

Vintage: considered Port's greatest wines, these are single-year wines aged for no more than two years in wood to preserve youthful fruitiness for the length of time the wine is in the bottle. Port Lodges declare a "vintage" in only the best growing years — about three times a decade.

Late-Bottled Vintage (LBV): a vintage port from a year that did not reach the standard for vintage declaration. Aged in wood for four to six years before release.

Vintage Character: A blended port made in the "vintage style."

There are no mandatory style classifications for American port-style fortified wine. In 2007, the Sweet and Fortified Wine Association (SFWA) established suggested definitions for only three port-related terms. These are:

Ruby: Port-style wine released with fewer than six years of barrel aging.

Tawny: Port-style wine released with a minimum of six years of barrel aging.

Vintage: Port-style wine declared "vintage" by the producer, showing the vintage date on the label in compliance with TTB label regulations *and* aged in barrel for no more than three years.

A minority of American producers actually refer to these terms on their labels or in their marketing and there is no method for determining whether producers using these terms follow the "suggested" standards.

The fine Sherries of Spain are classified in an impressive variety of styles including Fino, Manzanilla, Oloroso, Cream, and Amontillado. Production methods, blending techniques, aging regimes, sweetness levels, and grape varieties all contribute to the classification of Spanish Sherry.

In the United States, sherry-style producers label their products based primarily on sweetness. Domestic sherry-styles progress from dry—less than 2.5 percent residual sugar (RS)—to Cream Sherry at around 10 percent RS. Again, there is no specific standard for the production and classification of American sherry-style wines.

Sales and Distribution

For over three centuries, a few British firms had a virtual lock on the distribution of Portuguese Port wines. While the grapes were grown and wine fermented in the Douro Valley, the wines were finished and shipped from facilities in the port city of Vila Nova de Gaia, just across the river from Oporto. As a result, these "Port houses" had a near-monopolistic centralized control of the Port trade. Things have loosened up a bit but the worldwide distribution of Portuguese Port is still centered at the mouth of the Douro.

Most American fortified wines are intended for domestic consumption. Very few American producers are involved in the international fortified wine market. Distribution outside a producer's state or region is rare except for a half dozen or so "large" vintners. Most American fortified wines are sold through the winery tasting room, online, or in selected local retail outlets. Some vintners may sell to local or regional restaurants.

The contrast in sales and distribution of European and domestic fortified wine is dramatic and leads to an even more significant disparity in consumer perception.

Consumers

Fortified wine consumers can be divided into three general camps. There are the "Port /Sherry purists" (or nearly purists), the knowledgeable but open-minded consumer, and the rest of us that either like or dislike sweet, higher alcohol wines.

Port/Sherry purists will seldom if ever acknowledge that true Port and Sherry can ever be produced outside Portugal and Spain. They have a history of studying and drinking European fortified wines and their palates are conditioned to recognize these traditional wines. American fortified wines will almost always come up short in comparison tastings by the purists. We acknowledge and value the perspective of these dedicated Port and Sherry aficionados.

A significant fraction of wine consumers are the enthusiasts that have a basic understanding and appreciation of domestic port- and sherry-style fortified wines. They include fortified wines in their drinking portfolio as an aperitif and/or dessert wine. These consumers are open to exploring different fortified wine styles and are regular buyers, usually from the winery or local wine shop.

The final group is the casual wine consumer who enjoys a variety of wines for a variety of reasons. These folks are most often under-informed about fortified wine but have a definite position with regard to sweetness. Those who like sweet wines are more likely to embrace port- and sherry-style wines than those more accustomed to dry wines. Casual consumers are prone to evaluate fortified wines on the overall perception of taste and flavor rather than some predetermined criteria or standard. They are infrequent purchasers of fortified wines they like.

Government Regulation

The European wine industry overall—and the fortified wine industry in particular—is highly regulated. European governments have established and enforced grape-growing and wine-production standards and regulations for almost a millennium.

In contrast, the American wine industry was virtually unregulated until the repeal of Prohibition in 1933. Even now, while there are regulations regarding the production and labeling of domestic wines, few standards relate to American fortified wine. In fact, there is no federal regulation referring the production of fortified wine. Federal regulation 27 CFR Part 4-4.21 has only this to say: "*Dessert wine* is grape wine having an alcoholic content in excess of 14 percent but not in excess of 24 percent by volume."

Where the government regulation becomes a concern for the American fortified wine producer is the matter of labeling. This is a complicated issue having to do primarily with international trade and is discussed in some depth in chapters 2 and 4 of this book. The essence of the issue is the effort by European wine producers to protect what they believe to be proprietary semi-generic geographic designations including "port" and "sherry." As a result of agreements with the European Union in 2006, federal regulations prohibit the use of "port" and "sherry" on domestic fortified wine labels except for those labels covered under the "grandfather" clause.

The label restrictions on semi-generic terms places the American fortified wine industry in a bit of dilemma. Because of Repeal-related regulation (Federal Regulation Title 27, Part 4, Subpart D, Section 4.39(7) in TTB.gov), domestic producers are prohibited from using "any term which tends to create the impression that a wine contains distilled spirits." Terms like 'fortified" and "wine spirits/branded added or blended" cannot appear on labels.

While a long tradition of governmental standards and regulations tend to favor European fortified wines in the international market, American regulations are severely restricting the domestic fortified wine market.

This preface opened with a statement that European and American fortified wine are *different*. The paragraphs that followed outlined and summarized the various factors substantiating this thesis. Now that the distinction has been established, this book provides a comprehensive guide to how we make and enjoy fortified wine in the good old U S of A.

A Note on the Fortified Wine Producers Found in Chapter 5 (And Why They're "Paradigmatic" of the American Wine Style)

It's an exciting time in American fortified wine production. Clear of its recent disreputable past and free from the constraints of a rigid stylistic expectation, winemakers are testing their skills with new grape varieties and innovative production methods. Ironically, the purists' claim to Port superiority, its defining features, is exactly what makes American fortified wine so interesting: its envelope-pushing variety.

The producers profiled in chapter 5 are an example of this diversity. Each state has at least one producer committed to delivering premium value fortified wine. It is my hope that wine lovers world-wide explore the rich, sweet wines America has to offer.

HISTORY OF FORTIFIED WINE IN AMERICA

PART 1. BRIEF HISTORY OF FORTIFIED WINES

Port

The story of port wine goes back to when the Anglo-Portuguese Commercial Treaty of 1308 was superseded by the Treaty of 1353, which granted Portuguese fishermen the right to fish off the coast of England. The Treaty of Windsor established a more lasting alliance between England and Portugal in 1386. This led to the exchange of Portuguese wine for British goods.

When the British blocked French ports in 1678, the English turned to Portugal to fill the wine void. What they found was almost intolerable. The wines were in rotten casks and stank from transport in goatskins. In an effort to improve quality, English, Dutch, and Scottish wine merchants set about organizing

The Portuguese have been shipping wine from the Atlantic port city of Oporto since the late 17th century. Oporto Portugal.

the Portuguese wine trade. The first true Oporto wine in England was an un-fortified Portuguese table wine called "portoport" (Johnson 2002). However, the wine was not widely accepted and when peace came in 1686, shipments of Portuguese wines decline sharply.

Determined to find a reliable alternative to French claret, tenacious English wine prospectors came across a pleasurable wine developed by monks in a monastery in Lamego, northern Portugal. The wine was made by adding agua ardente (a distilled spirit) to the local red wine of the Douro valley. By the early 1700s, English shippers found that adding a little brandy to natural-strength wine from the rocky slopes of the Douro improved flavor and reduced spoilage of crudely made wine during transport.

Disaster struck Portugal in 1755 when an earthquake virtually destroyed Lisbon, the nation's capital. To finance the reconstruction of the devastated cap-ital, the king's chief minister Sebastiao de Carvalho—the Marquis of Pombal—revived the monopoly concept by establishing the Alto Douro Wine Company, which effectively seized control of the Portuguese port trade. As a result of the government-backed company's almost dictatorial policies, doubtful wine pro-duction methods were eliminated and the best wine growing areas delineated. It was the Marquis's Alto Douro Wine Company that established the original delineation of the Douro District. In addition, Pombal made Oporto the special-ist wine port of Portugal. The Alto Douro Wine Company lasted until 1833 but it wasn't until 1888 that Portugal gave up absolute control of the wine trade and extended leases to British wine shippers (Johnson 2002).

Sherry

To mark the discovery of the "new world," Christopher Columbus and his crews likely celebrated by dipping liberally into the ship's stores of saca, a sweet for-tified wine from the southwest of Spain. Some two decades later, Portuguese explorer Ferdinand Magellan spent more outfitting his around-the-world expe-dition with Spanish sherry wine than he did arming his 237 crewmen (Johnson, 2002).

The Phoenicians introduced viticulture to the southwestern area of the Ibe-rian Peninsula around 1100 BCE and was continued by the Romans when they took control of the region around 200 BCE. When the Barbarians invaded Spain in 409 CE, the Vandals occupied an area that came to be known as Vandalu-sia—what we now know as Andalusia. After the Moors conquered the territory in 711, the center of Andalusia was the town of Xerez, which the Arabs pro-nounced as Jerez or Scheris. By 1608, the British had adopted the term "sherry" to distinguish the wine from Xerez, which developed a European reputation as the world's finest wine (Sandman 1955).

Following Sir Francis Drake's sacking of Cadiz in 1587, sherry became a highly popular wine in England. Since sherry was a key Spanish export to the United Kingdom, several British families established English companies to produce and ship Jerez sherry. Among Great Britain's most prolific markets for sherry were her colonies in America.

Madeira

The year was 1802 and the USS Constitution, flagship of America's fledgling navy, was back to sea to complete her mission to protect American merchant vessels from raids by Algerian pirates. Stopping briefly for provisions in Funchal, the capital of the Portuguese island of Madeira, her bilges were loaded with what would become a great treasure—several pipes of Madeira wine. On her return to Boston, her valuable cargo would be decanted into glass carboys then bottled as young America's most popular wine. Ironically, it was a bottle of this sweet, fortified wine that launched "Old Ironsides" in 1797.

Madeira is an Atlantic island some 500 miles west of Portugal that was "accidentally" discovered by Portuguese explorer Gonslaves Zarco when he was blown off course by a violent storm in 1418. The island was so tree-covered that he named it "wood" or in Portuguese, madeira. In the mid-1400s, Prince Henry the Navigator of Portugal ordered the Malvasia vine to be planted on Madeira and ordered the production of wines to compete with wine commerce dominated by Venice and Genoa.

During the sixteenth century, a well-established wine industry on the island was supplying ships sailing for China, India, and Japan by way of the Cape of Good Hope with wine for the long voyages across the sea. The earliest examples of Madeira were unfortified and had the habit of spoiling at sea. Madeira producers soon found that adding a little alcohol distilled from the island's abundant sugarcane protected the wine from extreme temperatures as the boats crossed the equator while rocking the casks back and forth. Some wine that was not sold returned to Funchal on Madeira. When tasted, these "returned wines" were found to be superior and Madeira wine labeled as vinho da roda (wines that have made a round trip) became the customer preference. By 1794, Madeira vintners realized that shipping pipes (112 gallon casks) back and forth over the equator was time consuming and expensive, so a technique was discovered for artificially heating the wine in large ovens or wine hot houses called estufas.

Madeira wine was shipped to the American colonies from the port city of Funchal.

Madeira is perfectly situated in the Atlantic shipping lanes and was a natural port of call for ships traveling to the Americas. Almost all friendly ships dropped anchor in the harbor of Funchal, the trading port and regional capital of the island. Madeira gained exclusive trading rights with the British colonies through the marriage of Portuguese princess Catherine of Bragança to Charles II of England. The king granted Madeira the right to sell the island's

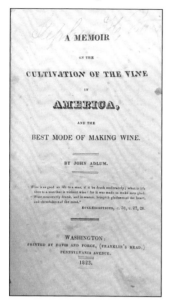

wines directly to the colonies in 1663. In the coming years, King Charles would allow only English ships from English ports carrying only English goods to trade in English ports and territories. However, Madeira was exempted from the decree and could be shipped directly to American ports.

Madeira was an important fortified wine in the history of America. The 1768 seizure of John Hancock's sloop, *Liberty*, loaded with 25 pipes of Madeira wine was a major contributor the increasing fervor of revolution. The British Boston Harbor commissioners had concocted a new tax that prevented offloading Hancock's cargo, infuriating the Madeira-loving colonists adding fuel to their discontent over British rule. Madeira was a favorite beverage of many of America's founding fathers including Thomas Jefferson, Alexander Hamilton, Benjamin Franklin, and George Washington. It is said that the signing of the Declaration of Independence was celebrated with a toast of Madeira.

John Adlum addressed the issue of fortification in his 1823 treatise on early American winemaking. (From the Rare Book Collection of the Lenhardt Library of the Chicago Botanic Garden.)

PART 2. AMERICA BEFORE PROHIBITION

The Colonies

The saga of American wine begins with the legend of Leif Erickson landing in the New World around 1001 CE. According to the story, Erickson was so taken by the expanse of vines congesting the shoreline forests that he named the new land "Vinland." Most likely, what Erickson—or his peers—actually saw were wild cranberry vines that had a natural tendency toward tree climbing.

Even though the Norsemen may have mistaken cranberries for grapes, early European explorers and settlers looked to the vast land across the Atlantic as the source of a new and endless supply of wine. The earliest reference on record of grape growing in North America is by Italian explorer Giovanni da Verrazzano who explored an area along what is now the North Carolina coast near Kitty Hawk in 1524. He called the region Arcadia and commented that if properly "dressed," grapes from the vines crawling up the trees would "undoubtedly … yield excellent wines" (Pinney 2007, p.11). But these were not the *vitus vinifera* wine grapes of Europe. Instead, these were native *vitis rotundiflia* vines producing muscadine grapes, a large, tough-skinned round fruit with a sweet favor and strong musky odor. Further down the coast, the Spanish established a settlement on Santa Elena Island (Parris Island, South Carolina) in 1568 and, using abundant muscadine grapes, became the first attempt at American wine-growing.

Half a century later, the English took interest in the potential of the new colonies to provide an economic alternative to European goods essential to the British lifestyle. It became the objective of early English colonization to provide England with "silk, wine, and olive oil" (Pinney 2007, p.12). As early as 1609, Jamestown, Virginia, settlers tried winemaking from native grapes. This "Rath" or young wine was probably made from large black, white, or red *vitis labrusca* known as the northern fox grape. The term "foxy" is derived from labrusca's distinctive flavor and fox-like aroma. For the next century, French, English, Greek, Portuguese, and Dutch colonists made vain attempts to produce merchantable American wine from native grapes. None of these wines, however, measured up to the clarets of France, the sherries of Spain, or the Madeiras and ports of Portugal (Pinney, 2007).

The colonials' solution to poor colonial wine from native grapes was to import and plant European vines. The turn of the eighteenth century found colonists from Massachusetts to the Virginia struggling in a futile effort to grow European vines in the harsh new world environment. Climate extremes from snowy cold to hot, humid temperatures, along with fungal diseases including powdery mildew, black rot, Pierces Disease, and Phylloxera, all conspired to frustrate even the most knowledgeable and ardent American winegrower.

Among the more zealous American viticulture pioneers was Thomas Jefferson. For more than thirty years, beginning in the early 1770s, Jefferson tried unsuccessfully to cultivate European vines in his Monticello vineyards. By 1817, Jefferson had given up on growing European vines and conceded that native grapes could make a wine with the fine aroma that could be "distinguished on the best tables of Europe." However, he went on to say, "unhappily that aroma, in most of samples I have seen, has been entirely submerged in brandy" (Pinney 2007, 128–29).

Jefferson's statement is some of the first evidence that native American wines were distilled into brandy then blended back with the original wine. This "fortification" with brandy may have been the secret to the drinkability of many native American wines. More evidence of early American fortified wine is recorded by Reverend Hugh Jones who wrote in the early 1700s of a "strong wine" made by prominent Virginian Robert Beverly. Jones wrote that he often drank strong wines of good body and flavor, the red reminding him of the taste of claret and the strength of port (Pinney, 2007, p.67). The reference to port implies that it may have been a regular early American winemaking practice to fortify native wines with brandy. None other than Benjamin Franklin established verification of the practice of fortification. In Franklin's *Poor Richard Almanack* of 1743, he advises winemakers that "If you make Wine for Sale, or to go beyond Sean, one quarter part must be distill'd and the Brandy put into the three Quarters remaining" (Pinney 2007, p.86).

Americans were making fortified wines when it became a free, independent nation.

The New Republic

The turn of the nineteenth century saw rapid expansion of the nation. Explorers charted roads through the mountainous boundaries of colonial America and soon settlers of all stripes flooded to the fertile hills and valleys of Pennsylvania, Ohio, Kentucky, Indiana, and Missouri. Among these adventurers were farmers, nurserymen, and winegrowers determined to fulfill the promise of marketable American wines. Learning quickly that European vines fared no better in the nation's interior than they did in the east, winegrowers turned again to native vines. Innovative growers in the southern states began experimenting with crosses between native American vines and the few surviving European vines. Many of these new American "hybrids" were the result of natural cross-pollination.

John Adlum (1759–1836) is widely considered the "Father of American Viticulture." Following service in the War for Independence, Adlum retired to a farm on Maryland's Susquehanna River where he planted European vines which promptly died. Some years later, Adlum moved to Georgetown on 200 acres above the Potomac River where he planted vines he called "Tokay." Since his days in Maryland, Adlum had a long correspondence with Thomas Jefferson. In 1822, Adlum sent Jefferson one of his bottles of "Tokay" and a second bottle to James Madison. In reality however, the wine was not true Tokay but an accidental *labrusca/vinifera* hybrid called "Catawba." Adlum got his original cuttings from a Mrs. Scholl in Clarksburgh, Maryland (Pinney 2007). The name comes from a river in western North Carolina and the grape is said to have been first found near present-day Ashville.

Catawba, however, was not Adlum's greatest contribution to the neophyte American wine trade. In 1823, Adlum authored the most comprehensive book on American viticulture and winemaking to that time. Adlum's seminal publication was based on his practical experience and knowledge as a winegrower and winemaker, plus the published work of Swiss John James Dufour. In his book, *Memoir on the Cultivation of the Vine in America, and the Best Mode of Making Wine*, Adlum addressed fortification: "For those who put brandy to their wines, it is best to do as the practice is in the Island of Madeira, that is, to put brandy in the cask first, and then fill the wine or must on it." (Pinney, 2007, p.86). He went on to explain the difference between adding spirits or brandy during and after fermentation. He postulated that adding brandy to impede fermentation could result in unwanted impurities in the wine and did little as a preservative. On the other hand, Adlum postulated that adding various levels of spirits or brandy to finished wine could provide some medicinal benefits attributable to the alcohol.

In the South, the scuppernong muscadine of North Carolina was the staple wine grape upon which fledgling winemakers most depended. Benjamin Waring made wine in Columbia, South Carolina, in 1802 from native grapes but had to add one gallon of brandy for every 12 gallons of juice to make the wine palatable (Pinney 2007). James S. Guignard made wine from a grape called Norton, as well as Catawba, and "Guignard." General Thomas McCall made wine from a native varities including Warrenton and Herbermont, a hybrid grape named for Frenchman Nicholas Herbermont. All of these early American wines from native vines and hybrids were low in natural alcohol and too high in acid. Invariably, they required the augmentation of sugar, and fortification by adding spirits or brandy.

By the mid-nineteenth century, winegrowing was a significant product of many American states and a thirsty nation eagerly consumed wine from native as well as newly hybridized grape varieties. However, an event in a foreign country 3,000 miles from the cultural centers of Boston and New York would alter American wine commerce forever.

California

In 1847, California—or "Alto California" as it was then known—was a sleepy backwater wasteland that had just been wrested from Mexico during the Mexican War. While a small contingent of American forces occupied California, the territory hadn't yet been paid for as part of the United States $15 million restitution to Mexico under the terms of the Treaty of Guadalupe Hidalgo.

On January 24, 1848, the cry of "GOLD" rang from a small sawmill on the banks of the American River about 100 miles east of the tiny port town of San Francisco. By year's end, tens of thousands of ardent gold seekers from across the nation and world would comb the foothill streams of the Sierra Nevadas in search of the elusive treasure. Few could predict that within a decade, the color of California's future prosperity would transform from gold to purple.

Southern California

Winegrowing and making were not new to California by the time of the gold rush. The Spanish were the first Europeans to explore and settle the vast southwest region of North America. An integral element of every Spanish settlement was a mission founded by Jesuit or Franciscan friars. Among the first duties of these zealous missionaries was to plant grapes for the production of sacramental wine. Some historians claim the first wine grapes in "new Mexico" were planted in 1626 at the Socorro mission on the Rio Grande River. By the mid-eighteenth century, the Spanish settlers and their missions had moved west. Alto California's first mission was founded in 1769 in San Diego by Franciscan priest Junipero Serra. There is little doubt that the San Diego mission had a vineyard but the first clear reference to planting grapes at a mission comes from San Juan Capistrano in 1779. The earliest known California wine vintage from the mission was 1782.

A day's journey east by foot or mule from the diminutive pueblo of Los Angeles, Father Jose Zalviea was in charge of the Mission San Gabriel vineyard and winery. Between 1806 and 1827, Father Zalviea developed the largest and most prosperous of the mission vineyard and wine ventures. His vineyard produced between 400 and 600 barrels of wine and 200 barrels of brandy by 1829. He produced four wines: a dry red table wine and sweet red wine, as well as two white wines. One of the white wines was a table wine and the other a brandy-fortified wine called Angelica (Pinney 2007).

Mission Grapes and Angelica

No one knows just when the name "Mission" was given to the vines brought from Mexico to the American southwest. The grape had been in the new world for 150 years before it came to Alta California in the 1770s. The vine took to the California climate like a native and by the 1830s, three varieties of Mission vines were grown in most of California's pueblos and ranches. By the gold rush of 1848, Mission grapes were also known as "California," "native," or "Los Angeles" and was to become most popular wine grape in the gold country.

Mission has its origin as a Spanish wine grape variety called *listan negro* (Garza, 2015) with relatives in South America including the *Criolla negra* of Venezuela and Argentina and the *Pais* of Chile. The popularity of Mission grapes came not from their ability to produce fine wine but from their productivity and ease of propagation. Wines produced from Mission grapes were either coarse, high-alcohol, poor-quality table wines with low acid and little varietal character or heavy sweet wines. Enter Angelica.

Los Angeles, "City of Angels" circa 1869. (Wikipedia commons.)

The classic Angelica (named for the city of Los Angeles) is a historic sweet fortified wine made typically from the Mission grapes and often served as a dessert wine. Some versions of early Angelica consisted of the unfermented grape juice fortified with grape brandy immediately after pressing. Others were made like port, where only partially fermented wine, still retaining a large amount of sugar, was infused with brandy. The relatively high alcohol of the brandy arrested the fermentation, leaving a fortified wine high in alcohol and high residual sugar (usually about 10 percent to 15 percent). Angelica was usually made from 50 percent mission wine and 50 percent mission brandy.

Commercialization of Angelica took place sometime prior to 1857 when pioneer Los Angeles vintner William Wolfskill sent President James Buchanan "some Angelica." (Pinney, 2007, p.249). Los Angeles's first commercial wine house, Kohler & Frohling, listed sherry, port, and Angelica in their product list sent to New York and Boston wine buyers in the late 1870s (Pinney, 2007). In the early 1880s, Angelica produced by the Anaheim Colony was marketed in San Francisco and on the East Coast.

In 1873 Matthew Keller ("Don Mateo") entered an Angelica into the California State Fair made of grapes from his Los Angeles vineyard adjacent to that of William Wolfskill. According to Keller's description, the Angelica was made from "Panse Musquie, the Muscat Noir de Jurd and the Mission grape, equals of each, dessicated and the juice concentrated" (Teiser and Harroun, 1983, p.65).

In 1871, Los Angeles banker Isaias W. Hellman, future California governor John G. Downey, and wine man Benjamin Dreyfus bought 5,000 acres of Rancho Cucamonga, where Mission grapes had been growing since the 1830s. In 1873, Jean Sansevain produced Angelica from Rancho Cucamonga, which, for a time, was the largest vineyard in the state.

In 1930 (during Prohibition), there were a million gallons of Angelica in storage in California.

Northern California

There was no centralized winegrowing area or effort in northern California for the second half of the nineteenth century following the gold rush. Early on, grape growing and winemaking came to the Sierra foothills in the wake of the dash to find California gold. Nearly three hundred thousand gold hunters came to gold country from a diversity of ethnic and geographical backgrounds. While most either went boom or bust, many found the area so appealing that they chose to practice former skills in the new west. Men and families of Italian, Irish, French, German, and English descent settled in the Sierra foothills to farm in support of the miners. Many of these men had backgrounds in grape growing, winemaking, and cooperage. The first vineyard in gold-rich Amador County was planted in 1852 by Massachusetts school teacher Benjamin Bert. By 1857 Bert and his brother had planted two thousand Mission, Catawba, and Isabella grape vines from cuttings most likely obtained from pioneer New England nurserymen in Sacramento. By 1868, 250,000 gallons of wine were being produced annually by 139 wineries in Amador County, much of which was Angelica (Costa, 1994).

Northeast of San Francisco lay two fertile valleys occupied by beneficiaries of pre-California Spanish land grants. The region was governed by General Mariano Vallejo whose presidio was adjacent to the Sonoma mission. When the mission was secularized in 1835, Vallejo took over the 300-square-foot vineyard that produced 540 gallons of wine in 1840. While there is no record of what the wine was, it was probably made from Mission grapes. Therefore, it is likely that some was Angelica. Perhaps of greater import than its status as

SONOMA.

Sonoma, the domain of General Mariano Vallejo, circa 1850. (Johnson, Theodore T. Wikipedia Commons.)

a wine source, Vallejo's vineyard was the source of cuttings for pioneer wine-growers including William and John Rowland in Solano, Dr. Edward Bale in St. Helena, and George Yount, who first planted grapes in Napa County.

South of San Francisco Bay, the emphasis was on the importation and planting of European vines. The Mediterranean climate of northern California was uniquely comparable with many of Europe's wine regions, and growers and nurserymen including Pierre Pellier and Antoine Delmas imported vines and cuttings from France between 1852 and 1854. By 1858 Delmas advertised he had 350,000 vines of 105 varieties (Pinney, 2007),

In the valley between the coast range and the Sierras, the first vines were planted in the Lodi/Stockton area in 1850, and Stanislaus and Yolo counties in 1852. John Sutter made brandy on his 6,600-acre New Helvetia (Sacramento) land grant. Further up the valley, Dane Peter Lassen set out a small landmark vineyard in Tehama in 1846 that would become the town of Vina. Perhaps most notable of the pioneer California nurserymen was A. P. Smith, whose Sacramento nursery had hundreds of varieties of *vinifera* for sale in 1859 including Black St. Peters—Zinfandel.

In 1860 California made 246,518 gallons of wine, including 162,980 from the Los Angeles area, 19,000 more from other southern California regions, and 64,000 gallons from the Sierra Foothills and Bay area (Pinney 2007). A significant portion of this wine was Angelica and other wines to which abundant brandy was added for flavor and alcohol boost. By the turn of the century, the numbers would shift dramatically.

Rise and Fall

The four decades between 1860 and the turn of the century saw brisk expansion of viticulture and winemaking in northern California and shifting fortunes in southern California. Perhaps the most dramatic example of a fading southern California wine trade is the rise and fall of the Anaheim Colony.

Los Angeles County surveyor George Hansen bought 1,165 acres from the Juan Ontiveros Rancho San Juan Cajon de Santa Ana land grant in 1857. Hansen established the Los Angeles Vineyard Society by offering German immigrants a share of a fully developed cooperative winegrowing community on the property he named Anaheim. Investing $60,000 to dig a six mile irrigation canal to bring water to four hundred thousand newly planted Mission vines, Hansen ensured that all was in order when the first German settlers arrived on their 20-acre parcels in 1859. None of the new winegrowers had winemaking or farming experience. It quickly became evident that the cooperative concept was not going to work, and by 1869 there were forty-seven private wineries in the colony. Anaheim reached its peak in 1883 when ten thousand acres of vines produced 1.25 million gallons of wine, including a significant portion of Angelica that was marketed nationwide. Then, disaster struck in the form of Pierce's disease and by 1885 most of the vines were dead. The estimated loss to the southern California economy was over $10 million, from which the wine trade never recovered.

The Anaheim Colony is a story of boom and bust in the annals of southern California wine. Pierce's disease ended the colony at a cost of over $10 millon but a century later, Disneyland is Anaheim's biggest revenue producer. (Orange County Historical Society: History Articles, www.orangecountyhistory.org.)

To the north, Napa, Sonoma, Santa Clara, and the Central Valley were experiencing an influx of well-to-do wine entrepreneurs and winegrowers. German immigrants, among them Jacob Gundlach and Charles Bundschu, established large vineyards and wineries in Sonoma County, as did the infamous Hungarian count Agoston Haraszthy. Across the Mayacamas Mountains to the east, more

German visionaries, including Charles Krug, Jacob Beringer, and Gustave Nie-
baum, were establishing legendary wine empires. Even though these pioneer
wine men were to leave their mark forever on California wine, trouble was
on the horizon. In 1875, fully 80 percent of California wine was made from
Mission grapes and a significant amount of wine was distilled for brandy. Sud-
denly, overproduction of mediocre wine and overplanting, as well as the import
of superior European wines, led to the wine depression of 1876–79. To make
matters worse, phylloxera was found on grapevine roots in the Craig vineyard
on the west side of Sonoma Creek in August, 1873. The microscopic root louse
that had devastated French vineyards laid waste to 75,000 acres in California
between 1873 and 1895.

The story of Vina is a compelling tale of the fortunes of northern California wine commerce. In 1869, former governor and Central Pacific Railroad
president Leland Stanford bought 75 acres of mostly Mission grapes at Warm
Springs in Alameda County near Mission San Jose. By 1891, the Stanford vineyard had 182 acres of Mission vines that were the source of the widely acclaimed Stanford Angelica.

Stanford was a man of big ideas and great dreams. His 1880 trip to the
grand chateaus of France was likely the inspiration for his desire to become
a great wine producer. Between Red Bluff and Chico, 150 northeast of San
Francisco, Henry Gerke had planted 75 acres of vines and built a winery on
Rancho Bosquejo where he made Angelica. Gerke purchased the property in
1852 from Danish pioneer Peter Lassen who was granted the land around 1834.
Stanford bought the Vina ranch in 1881 and planted the first 1,200 acres of
Charbono, Burger, Zinfandel, Blau Elben, and Malroisie vines. He constructed
a modern three-story winery and produced the first Vina vintage of 200,000
gallons of wine and 1,200 gallons of brandy in 1885. The profits from this first
vintage were applied to the endowment of Stanford University in November of
that year. By 1890, Vina had grown to 59,000 total acres, 3,825 of which were
planted with wine grapes. Stanford built a great wine cellar that covered two
acres and included a "Sherry Room." He spent $9,000,000 on Vina and could
produce 1.2 million gallons of wine and 450,000 gallons of brandy per vintage.
It was the largest vineyard and winery in the world (Peninou, n.d.).

On June 20, 1893, Leland Stanford died and so did the vision of Vina. By
the turn of the century, the title to Vina was transferred to Stanford University
and it was becoming clear that the winery and vineyard had peaked; decline was
evident. Some of the older vines were showing signs of phylloxera. In 1908, the
majority of the 6,700-ton crop was used to make port, sherry, Angelica, muscatel, and brandy. Vina Port was used to "blend up" the thinner valley ports of the
California Wine Association. The winery building burned, either by accident or
by arson, just prior to the 1915 harvest and the remaining 2,000 acres of vines
pulled. Vina Ranch was subdivided and sold in 1919 but remnants of the great
Stanford winery still exist. In 1955 an order of Roman Catholic monks purchased 590 acres of the old Stanford Ranch property and established the Abbey
of New Clairvaux where they currently make "Abbey Angelica."

From the 1880s to Prohibition, the California wine industry experienced a series of economic booms and busts. European winemaking was surviving the phylloxera plague and the cost of imported wines escalated. As a result, eastern wine merchants wanted only cheap California wine. The majority of these California wines came from Central Valley. Here, winegrowing was carried out on a grand scale. The rich, deep, fertile land from Lodi to south of Fresno fostered vast irrigated vineyards producing enormous yields of low-acid, high-sugar grapes. As a result, Central Valley wines were sweet and most were fortified.

Most California wines left the wineries in bulk. Eastern wholesalers would blend and label as they wanted. Wholesalers, retailers, and saloonkeepers adulterated many California wines to meet the tastes of their customers. In addition, over-production caused major marketing problems for California growers and wineries in the late nineteenth century. For example, California produced 10 million gallons of wine in 1880 and 18 million in 1886. By 1892, Zinfandel grapes—then California's most important red wine grape—sold for $10 a ton.

The story of J. De B. Shorb and his San Gabriel Wine Company serves as a vivid illustration of the ups and downs of the California wine industry in the last two decades of the 19th century. Marylander James De Barth Shorb came to California in 1863 looking for oil. His attention soon turned to other interests, namely wine man Benjamin Wilson's daughter. Wilson had come to California in 1841 and acquired an 1815 Mission vineyard in the Pasadena area of southern California. Wilson's Lake Vineyard was well known for its distinctive sweet fortified wines— port, sherry, and Angelica.

Shorb married Sue Wilson in 1867 and went to work making Lake Vineyard the "largest

J. De Barth Shorb on the steps of his San Marino home with a part of his large family around 1880. The site where the house stood is now occupied by the Henry E. Huntington Art Gallery. (The Huntington Library, San Marino, California.)

wine manufacturer on the Pacific Coast" (Pinney, 2007, p.299) by 1875. In 1882, Schorb had transformed Lake Vineyard into a completely new enterprise, the San Gabriel Wine Company. Financed with half a million dollars from wealthy English and Californian investors, San Gabriel Wine Company became the "largest in the world," (Pinney, 2007, p.303) with a capacity of one million gallons of wine a year. However, by 1884, things were beginning to unravel. When Shorb began shipping San Gabriel wine to agents in New York, problems developed by the time the wine arrived on the east. Complaints persisted of spoiled wine that had not survived the train journey through the sizzling deserts of the Southwest and the humid Midwest plains. An eastern merchant called San Gabriel's staple port wine "trash" that he would not give away much less sell. Shorb and his investors countered that the complaining agents were lying adulterators.

Mission San Gabriel de Arcangel about 1900. The historic Commandant's Quarters are at left. (Photo Courtesy of the City of San Gabriel.)

Problems persisted not only with the wines but with the new winery facility as well. The winery building was too dry and caused excessive evaporative loss, while the storage building was too hot to allow the wines to fully develop. Then there was the fatal Pierce's disease that raised its ugly head in the vineyards in 1888.

The economic struggles of the San Gabriel Wine Company came to a head when in 1892, the company could no longer make and sell wines and turned to the exclusive manufacture of brandy. In order to concentrate on the brandy trade, San Gabriel Wine Company stock was sold for 35 cents a gallon, including 90,000 gallons of port and 25,000 gallons of Sherry. Shorb officially went out of business with his death in 1896.

The industry's solution to the wildly fluctuating price of wine was the California Wine Association. CWA was organized in 1894 by the seven largest California wine merchants. At its peak, CWA had fifty-two wineries and controlled the bottling and shipment of a majority of wines from its huge Winehaven facilities in Richmond on the San Francisco Bay. The majority of CWA production was red and white table wines but the proportion of fortified wines increased until Prohibition. The flood of cheap, fortified CWA wines to the Midwest and East was in direct contrast to the aims of the rapidly expanding temperance movement and the changing focus of alcoholic beverage consumption from rural to urban.

The New Century

Storm clouds were on the horizon for the American wine industry as the 1900s rolled into view. "Demon rum" and any even remotely alcoholic beverage was being increasingly vilified as the temperance movement gathered steam across the nation. In California, however, winegrowers and winemakers blissfully disregarded the warnings that threatened the industry. Proponents of early American wine—like Jefferson who said "No nation is drunken where wine is cheap"—saw wine as an agrarian product and "the only antidote" to the nation's "bane of whisky" (Pinney, 2007, p.435). The temperance movement didn't see wine that way. To the "Drys," the proliferation and popularity of fortified wine was a major contributor to the image of wine as booze.

There was some effort by California producers to distance wine from liquor interests but to no avail. Large wine producers made almost half their profits from fortified wine and brandy. Much of the fortified wine was consumed in saloons and taverns owned and operated by large distillers. On the eve of Prohibition, newspaperman and politician Chester Rowell proclaimed that "There has never been any excuse for fortified wine except as a booze excuse" (Lukacs 2005, p.96). Nonetheless, by the time the Eighteenth Amendment was ratified, California had 90,000 acres of vines and an annual crop valued at $25 million. Wine was crucial to the state's economy.

"THE RIGHT OF WAY"

During the late nineteenth century a temperance movement was active in California, and George Frederick Keller produced a series of color lithograph cartoons satirizing the movement for The Illustrated Wasp. The practitioners of the movement were always represented as ducks. Here in The Right of Way, the temperance fanatics are chased away by Bacchus, who arrives on the front of a locomotive named Common Sense. (Courtesy of the Unzelman Collection.)

Prohibition

There is no doubt that Prohibition had a tremendous impact on the American wine industry in general and fortified wine in particular. The Eighteenth Amendment was ratified in January 1919 and went into effect in January 1920. American wine production went from 55 million gallons in 1919 to 20 million gallons in 1920. By 1925, commercial wine production reached its lowest level of 3.5 million gallons. However, in that same year, Americans drank 150 million gallons of legal "homemade" wine

The National Prohibition Act (Volstead Act) was the enforcing authority for the Eighteenth Amendment. The so-called "fruit juice clause" amendment to the Volstead Act allowed each American head of household to make up to 200 gallons a year of "non-intoxicating cider or fruit juice in the home" (Okrent, 2012, p.176) for the use of family members. Grape juice fell under this definition. As a result, Zinfandel and Mission grape prices went from $10–$20 a ton in 1919 to $125 a ton in 1920. Central Valley vineyard land went from $100 an acre in 1919 to $500 an acre in 1921 and $1,000 an acre in 1923 (Muscatine, Amerine, and Thompson, 1984). Home winemakers wanted a hardy, thick-skinned grape with lots of color to meet the demand of eastern foreign-born families. Soon, growers were replacing vineyards of classic grapes with durable, high-yielding Alicante Ganzin and Alicante Bouschet that withstood shipment to the East Coast.

Another key provision of the Volstead Act was the allowance, by permit, for production and sale of sacramental wine, wine for medicinal purposes, and wine used in cooked food as flavoring. Here was an opportunity for industrious vintners to thrive in the hostile environment of Prohibition. One such persevering wine man was Beaulieu Vineyard's Georges de Latour. As a devout Catholic, Latour was able to strike a deal with the Archbishop of San Francisco to produce altar wine for the dioceses. By 1922, Latour had expanded his sacramental wine distribution to seven eastern states with offerings including port, sherry, Angelica, muscatel, and Madeira.

In other sections of the nation, however, Prohibition curtailed much of the wine business. A few hardy and determined vintners continued a mild production of sacramental and "medicinal" wines in the southern states. The Drys virtually shut down the Midwest wine industry, which had being doing well at the turn of the century: Sandusky, Ohio, and the islands of Sandusky Bay in western Lake Erie had 39 operating wineries when Prohibition went into effect. New York found itself second only to California in wine production by the time of Prohibition. Concord was New York's most prolific variety and proved to quite adaptable to making grape products like jams and jellies during Prohibition.

The story of eastern viticulture and winemaking would be incomplete without the mention of Captain Paul Garrett. Born in North Carolina in 1863, Garrett (the father of Virginia Dare Scuppernong wine) developed a great wine empire throughout the South and established a network of vineyards and wineries from New York to Southern California by 1919. With the approach of Prohibition, Garrett moved to Canandaigua in 1913 to manage his vast holdings. He refused to believe that Prohibition would be permanent so he devised ways to keep his empire afloat until repeal. His most creative idea was the introduction of Vine-Go in 1929. The concept was to sell concentrated grape juice in cans along with complete winemaking and bottling services in the buyer's home. Garrett organized a number of the remaining California wineries into Fruit Industries Ltd and sold five and ten gallon barrels of "port," "muscatel," and other blended concentrates throughout the nation. The Drys, however, created a political storm that eventually led to the demise of Vine-Go in 1932.

Prohibition did far more damage than good to American wine commerce. While the American public became more familiar with wine because it was cheap, fairly easy to get, and they could make it themselves, Prohibition almost irreparably damaged the American wine industry. It took forty years to start to recover from the poor reputation of American wine.

PART 3. FORTIFIED WINE IN POST PROHIBITION AMERICA

Repeal

Prohibition ended December 5, 1933, when Utah was the thirty-sixth state to ratify the Twenty-first Amendment—repeal. There were 268 bonded wineries by the end of 1933 (repeal) and 20 million gallons of wine were produced. Before Prohibition, there had been more than 900 bonded wineries in the United States and 694 bonded California wineries. In mid-1933 there were only 177 surviving wineries in the state (Pinney 2005). The majority of American vineyards were planted with inferior wine grapes. Rexford Guy Tugwell, a member of Franklin Roosevelt's post-Prohibition brain trust, envisioned a wine future of cheap, plentiful, unregulated wine as an agricultural product after repeal. However, in 1935 Congress killed a federal plan to research enology and viticulture nationwide as a means to revive America's wine industry. In 1934 there was an effort to develop winemaking in the southern states through large scale planting of muscadine grapes under the Federal Emergency Relief Administration. This project failed in 1937.

Three-quarters of the 32 million gallons of wine sold in 1934 were consumed in five states: California, Louisiana, New Jersey, New York, and Michigan. Before Prohibition, dry table wines dominated the market by a ratio of 3:2. By 1937 the ratio had switched to 5:1 sweet-to-dry (Pinney 2005). Post-repeal Californian wine was either peasant wine made in a rough-and-ready way by a small proprietor, or industrial wine made without any concern beyond cheapness and volume. Wineries in Arkansas, Michigan, and Washington were almost exclusively devoted to the production of fortified wines.

Unfortunately, the repeal coincided with the height of the Great Depression—the source of many of today's obstructive regulations and heavy taxation. The Liquor Taxing Act of 1934 set table wine tax at 10 cents per gallon and fortified wine at 20 cents. The taxes were decreased by 50 percent in 1935 but the precedent had been set. The American government ceased to see wine as an agriculture product, and federal policy on wine since Repeal views wine as either a commodity restrained by taxation or a luxury open to sumptuary taxation.

Winegrowers in many areas of California were quick to realize that their fortunes in the post-Prohibition wine trade depended on their ability to organize as well. Thus, grower co-ops like the Lodi's Woodbridge Vineyard Association, Bear Creek Vineyard, and East Side Winery produced large volumes of bulk wine in the latter half of the 1930s. The fifteen large, mostly co-op wineries in Lodi produced 25 million gallons or one-fifth of all California wines by the end of the decade.

However, the majority of California's grape and wine production was centered in the vast Central Valley, where Prohibition-era overplanting of inferior grape varieties, including the prolific Thompson Seedless raisin grape, kept grape prices unstable. Here, too, cooperatives like the Central California Wineries and California Cooperative Wineries were organized and backed by the Bank of America to stabilize grape prices. The result was a steady stream of railroad tank cars flooding eastern markets with cheap bulk wine. It was during this hectic post-Prohibition chaos that future wine industry giants like Gallo, Cella, Rossi, and Petri first came to light.

To deal with the avalanche of rules and regulations related to repeal, veteran dry-wine vintners organized the Wine Producers Association in 1935. In Central Valley, predominantly fortified wine producers formed the California Sweet Wine Producers in 1933. This differentiation clearly defined longstanding conflicts of interest in the state's wine production that would persist for the next four decades.

There were four basic wine types produced in California following repeal.

- Muscatel was almost always made from the raisin grape muscat of Alexandria and fermented on the skins for flavor. Much of this sweet wine had muscat brandy added.
- California sherry was made from practically any grape but primarily Thompson seedless or Flame Tokay. Wines were fermented to dryness then fortified with sherry material or shermat, then heated to 125°F for three to six months in redwood tanks. To soften the rough Madeira-like process, sweet white wine was added to sweeten sherry.
- Angelica became a generic fortified white wine made from any variety by adding brandy.
- Tokay was blend of port, sherry, and a neutral white wine such as Angelica. Tokay, Angelica, and white port often came out of the same same barrel.

The most significant result of Prohibition, however, may, in fact, have been the repeal and the crazy quilt of laws, regulations, and taxes that the wine industry is trying to live with to this day.

War

The war years (1939–45) brought significant changes to the American wine industry. For starters, wine grape production was diverted to raisin production. Wine contributed to wartime industries by producing tartrates from the pomace or inside of storage tanks for rayon, photographic chemicals, and medicine. In addition, wartime price control allowed wineries to charge higher prices for higher quality wine.

Perhaps the most dramatic impact of the war on California wine was the arrival of four big distillers to California as a result of the diversion of distilled spirits for munitions. Schenley distillers based in New York bought Cresta

Blanca from Lucien Johnson who bought it from Clarence Wetmore. Then the big distiller bought Roma from the Cella family and Greystone winery in Napa. By 1944 Schenley was California's largest wine organization.

Meanwhile, Kentucky's National Distillers bought Italian Swiss Colony in 1942, while Seagrams, then headquartered in Montreal, bought Paul Masson in 1942 from Martin Ray. Finally, Hiram Walker purchased De Turk Winery in Santa Rosa and a winery in the Cienega district of San Benito County in 1943. These four companies controlled 25 percent of the wine production during the 1940s.

The Postwar Years

The emerging pattern of postwar wine industry renovation and expansion that began at Repeal was for large scale production of standard, blended wines—most of which were fortified. The postwar question was whether Americans would continue their preference for sweet fortified wines rather than dry table wines. New, sweeter wines could be made from cheaper Central Valley grapes since the sweetness masked defects in flavor and acid.

Postwar speculation brought on a flurry of winery and vineyard transactions. However, when grape prices tumbled to $25 a ton, new interest was generated in cooperatives. Some 140 growers built the Del Rey Winery near Fresno in 1946, while groups of a hundred or more growers developed Yosemite Winery in Madera, and Lockford Winery near Lodi. Together, these co-op wineries had the production capacity of over one million gallons—almost all of which was devoted to fortified wine.

Prior to the war, there were some 45,000 acres of mostly Zinfandel and Mission vines in Southern California's Cucamonga Valley. Pioneer-era families like Galleano, Filippi, DeMateis, and Riboli had been making popularly acclaimed port, sherry, Madeira, and Angelica since repeal. However, in late 1940s and early 1950s, the baby boom heralded steady urban encroachment that

Cucamonga Winery in the early 1950s. Houses soon become a better crop than wine grapes in Southern California.

19

replaced rows of Zinfandel and Mission with rows of suburban track houses. By the early 1970s only a small island of vines survived, but the historic Galleano, Filippi, and San Antonio wineries continue to produce world-class fortified wines to this day.

The wine sales collapse of 1947 was almost entirely felt by large producers of fortified and jug wines. Premium producers were largely unaffected. From 1946 to 1948, fortified wines were produced at a ratio of 5:1 over table wines. In 1948, fortified wine retailed at less than 40 cents a gallon—well below the cost of production (Pinney 2005).

Back east, New York, Pennsylvania, Ohio, and Michigan dominated postwar wine production. Most Michigan wine produced from Concord grapes was lightly fortified to bring alcohol to 16 percent to make "light port." In Arkansas, wines were sweet and fortified. Nelson Wine and Distilling Company made 24-percent-alcohol apple and Concord wine labeled with the Cocktail, Razorback, Eight Ball, and Pink Elephant brands. Between 1951 and 1975, sweet, mostly fortified wine accounted for about 70 percent of all American wines.

Cheap and Fortified

A 1955 survey of Americans commissioned by the Wine Advisory Board found that (Pinney 2005):

- Two-thirds of those polled drank alcoholic beverages,
- Half of the above occasionally drank wine,
- Port, sherry, Kosher, Sauterne, and Burgundy are the most often named, and
- Port and sherry were regarded by a large proportion as mealtime wines.

In 1954, federal regulations allowed "special natural wine"—wines to which various flavors had been added. In 1957, Gallo added concentrated lemon juice to white port to create Thunderbird, which sold for a mere 60 cents a quart. Thunderbird became America's best-selling single wine and the favorite choice of skid row. Gallo's Ripple was a lightly carbonated fortified sweet wine with lower alcohol that was attractive to younger drinkers. Because of its low price, Ripple also became the preferred wine for destitute drinkers and alcoholics. Gallo went on to produce Boon's Farm Apple wine in 1961.

During the 1940s and 1950s, Taylor Cellars (Canandaigua) became New York's biggest winery by producing cheap fortified wines from labrusca grapes. The 20-percent-alcohol, pink, flavored blend called Richard's Irish Rose became extremely popular in the slums of eastern cities.

United Vintners Italian Swiss Colony made Silver Satin a flavored fortified wine. Other popular flavored fortified wines included Ariba, Golden Spur, Red Showboat, and Zombe. By 1960 these cheap fortified wines had earned some interesting and descriptive designations including gutter-punk champagne, street wine, block party breakup, goon, bum wine, bag wine, hobo juice, and poverty punch.

The arrival and consumption of the flavored fortified wines marked the low point in American wine history.

Change in the Wind

In 1947, the unregulated industry stubbornly persisted in producing undistinguished sweet fortified wines for an unstructured and largely indifferent American public. The slightly sweetened red, pink, and white wines of the 1950s and 1960s were made to suit what was imagined to be the American taste in wine. The number of American wineries declined from 414 in 1945 to 374 in 1950 to 271 in 1970 (Pinney 2005).

At the beginning of the 1960s, the American public was beginning to become familiar with increasing quantities of decent table wine, distinctively identified by type and origin. Consumption of table wines had been steadily but slowly growing since the 1950s. There were several reasons for this shift in American wine taste. Perhaps the most significant was the escalation of American economic and social affluence. The jet age ushered in an era of unprecedented travel to Europe resulting in more familiarity with the wines of the classic European wine regions. In conjunction with this new affluence, Americans became interested in the role wine played in the pleasures of more sophisticated foods.

It was becoming evident by 1960 that the American wine industry had to make vast improvements in viticulture and enology in order to survive in the world market. In California, winegrowers ripped out the Prohibition-era Alicante, Mission, and Flame Tokay in favor of classic *vinifera*, including Cabernet Sauvignon, Zinfandel, Merlot, Chardonnay, and Sauvignon blanc. Grafted to disease-resistant rootstocks, vast new vineyards of fine wine grapes compatible with specific environments grew on wire trellises spaced for efficient management.

At University of California, Davis (UC Davis), Professor H. P. Olmo and his team of scientists developed new grape varieties including Ruby Cabernet, a cross between Cabernet Sauvignon and Carignan, and Emerald Riesling, a cross between White Riesling and Muscadelle. These new grapes were cultivated to improve the quality of Central Valley jug wines previously made from inferior varieties.

In the east, French hybrids dominated wine grape growing from New York to Missouri. These new complex hybrids were own-rooted (meaning the vines grow from the original roots, not grafted root stock) and named for hybridizers including Chelois, Chamborcin, and Seybal. They were created with the resistance of American varieties and fruit quality of French varieties.

In wineries that survived the struggles of the postwar years, a new breed of vintner was emerging with innovative approaches to quality winemaking. For example, James Zellerbach started Hanzell in 1952 and was the first to use stainless steel temperature-controlled tanks for fermenting Chardonnay. In Napa, industry pioneers like Robert Mondavi were experimenting with smaller 60-gallon oak barrels to age small lots of both red and white wines. There were also improvements in fining, filtering, and stabilization that resulted in wines with greater quality and aging potential.

In the 1960s, Almaden, Christian Brothers, and Paul Masson found a niche between the vast undifferentiated fortified wine market dominated by the industrial producers of Central Valley and the small, highly individualized table wine market belonging to a handful of prestige wineries. By the early 1960s, Gallo recognized the slow shift from fortified to table wines and went outside the Central Valley for grapes for hearty Burgundy based on Petite Sirah from Napa and Sonoma. Gallo became the leading American wine producer in 1966.

The last year that fortified wine sales exceeded table wine sales was 1966, when 165 million gallons of wine total were produced in California. Of this total, fortified wine accounted for 85 million gallons (51.5 percent), while table wine tallied 80 million gallons made by 231 wineries. Sales of table wine exceeded fortified wine in 1967 (Pinney 2005). A decade later the numbers had reversed dramatically, with 345 wineries making 300 million gallons of table wine and only 13 million gallons (4 percent) of fortified wine. Granted, table wine production included the so-called "mod/pop" (sweetened, flavored, and carbonated) wines, but the trend was decisive. The future of California and indeed the national wine industry was irreversibly devoted in unfortified dry or slightly sweet table wines.

While the winds of change whistled through the California dry wine industry, there was a slight breeze rustling in the fortified wine segment of the trade. Maynard Amerine and E. H. Twight of UC Davis describe domestic ports from the Central Valley as "cheap, common" (Pinney, 2007, p.87), insufficiently aged, and made from the wrong grape varieties. They think it is possible to produce good wines from the region if the proper grape varieties were found to withstand the brutal summer desertlike conditions. Their explorations took them to Portugal where they found a number of grapes used to make traditional port wine. Cuttings of these promising varieties were obtained and planted in the university's experimental vineyard.

After the war, Walter Ficklin and his sons Walter Jr. and David looked to expand their Madera ranch by growing grapes and making wine. The senior Ficklin contacted UC Davis experts Albert Winkler and Maynard Amerine for advice on which grape varieties would be best suited to their area. The professors showed the Ficklins samples of port dessert wines made from the Portuguese grape varieties in the Davis vineyard. The visitors were sold and in 1945, the first Portuguese vine cuttings were grafted on Ficklin's existing rootstock. They chose Tinta Madeira, Tinta Cao, Touriga, and Alvarelhao as the most promising varieties to produce quality California port.

The Ficklins completed their unique adobe brick winery in 1948, just in time for crush. For the next six decades, three generations of Ficklins would produce one of California's most respected port wines made exclusively from Portuguese grape varieties.

By the mid-1970s, the breeze of change in California fortified wine quality reached Napa. The Prager family moved from southern California to St. Helena with the sole purpose of making world-class port wines from Portuguese as well as classic grape varieties. Since 1979, Prager Winery and Port Works has produced nationally acclaimed red and white ports of exceptional quality and value. Prager is also credited with making the first California port from Petite Sirah grapes.

Angelica's nineteenth-century ghost still roamed the sparse vineyards of the Sierra Foothills in the mid-1970s, when young UC Davis enology graduate Andy Quady made his first Zinfandel port. He realized that quality California port could be produced by blending traditional Portuguese varieties grown on the hot, rolling hillsides. He was able to convince Frank Alviso to plant five varieties of Duoro grapes in his legendary Madera County Clocksprings Vineyard. Quady established his winery in Madera in 1979 sourcing port grapes from Alviso's vineyard. Andy continues to use Sierra Foothills Portuguese varieties in his highly acclaimed "Starboard" port.

The early 1980s saw small wineries in the Sierra Foothills take a renewed interest in the production of fortified port-style wines as an opportunity to fully utilize their late-ripening, high-sugar grapes. Led by Sonora Port Works in Mariposa County and Deaver Vineyards in Amador County, foothills winemakers found a unique niche by producing classic and Portuguese variety fortified wines. Angelica herself reappeared in limited vintages of fortified wines made from the few remaining stands of Mission grapes in the state.

The number of new California fortified wine producers climbed slowly as the close of the twentieth century found just under 50 throughout the state. Since 2000 however, there has been a steady increase in interest in American fortified wine production. The Sweet and Fortified Wine Association has identified over 450 California fortified wine producers and an equal number of fortified wine producers across the nation. While specific production levels are difficult to identify, California vintners produced an average of just over three hundred cases of fortified wine annually with the largest individual port houses producing three thousand to five thousand cases. However, these figures do not reflect fortified wine production by the wine giants including Gallo, Bronco, the Wine Group, and Constellation brands.

While the future looks rosy for small-volume American fortified wine producers, there are major challenges ahead. Most of these issues involve the use of label terms including "port" and "fortified." These terms have significant implications for truth in advertising, nutrition, and content disclosure, as well as international trade. There are also issues regarding standards for types and classification of fortified wines and, of course, sweetness, and alcohol. However, few, if any, of the challenges faced by the American premium fortified wine industry involve product quality. American premium fortified wine will never again be associated with a cheap drunk for the down-and-out as in the 1950s.

2

MAKING AMERICAN FORTIFIED WINES

Webster defines "fortify" as a verb meaning to "impart strength or vigor to." This definition is appropriately applied to winemaking since Webster goes on to define "fortified wine" as "a wine, as port or sherry, to which brandy has been added to arrest fermentation or increase alcohol content."

American vintners have been making fortified wines for over two centuries. However, unlike the traditional practices now codified in Portuguese and Spanish law, there is no customary standard for American fortified wine. In fact, the terms "fortified" or "fortified wine" are not defined in federal regulation and the term "dessert wine" is generally applied to wines with no less than 14 percent and no more than 24 percent alcohol by volume (ABV). As a result, American winemakers are relative free to create a broad spectrum of grape, berry, and fruit "fortified" wines.

For our purposes, we are going to focus only on grape wines, starting with port-style fortified wine.

PORT-STYLE

In deference to our Portuguese friends who judiciously claim "port" as a proprietary term only applied to fortified wine from the upper Douro Valley region of Portugal, we shall use "port-style" to describe this broad category of American fortified wine. In truth, the vast majority of domestic vintners have no desire to exactly replicate Portuguese port. Even using Portuguese grape varieties, differing climates, geographies, viticultural practices, and production methods make duplication of Portuguese ports highly unlikely. Subtle differences will always exist.

Another significant difference between domestic and Portuguese fortified wines lies in their respective marketing distribution. While Portuguese ports are distributed worldwide, few American port-style producers engage in overseas trade. With the exception of America's largest wine producer, domestic vintners tend to produce relative small quantities of distinctive port-style wines specifically crafted to satisfy their unique styles and please their customer base. It is because of this stylistic distinctiveness that the discussion of domestic port-style wine production is focused on smaller, emblematic American vintners.

Harvest

All good wines start in the vineyard and the time-tested adage "good wines come only from good grapes" could not be more pertinent when applied to port-style wines. Picking at the right time is key to American port-style wine-makers who look for balance and maturity in the grapes at harvest. Maturity is a function of grape physiology, the primary components of which are sugar, acid, and phenols.

Grape sugars consist mostly of glucose and fructose that increase as grapes ripen. Sugar levels are expressed in degrees Brix (or degrees Balling), which is the percent by weight of dissolved sugar solids in 100 grams of juice. Brix levels correspond to roughly 57 percent of the potential alcohol in unfermented grape juice. For example, juice from grapes harvested at 24.2° Brix will have a potential dry wine alcohol level of 13.8 percent.

Acidity is what gives crisp brightness to wines. Tartaric acid is the most prominent grape acid, followed by malic acid and small amounts of citric and succinic acid. The amount (TA) and level of acid (pH) are equally important in determining grape maturity. TA or "titratable acidity" is a measure of the total acid in both unfermented and fermented grape juice expressed as the percent of tartaric acid content. This figure can be anywhere from 0.50 percent to 0.85 percent for most wines, depending on grape variety and viticultural practices. In chemistry, pH is the range of acid intensity based on the number of free hydrogen atoms in a solution. A solution with 1.0 pH is strongly acidic while a solution with 6.9 pH is as nearly neutral as pure water (pH 7.0). White grape juice has a slightly lower pH (around 3.3) than red juice (roughly 3.5).

Phenols are a group of organic compounds in grapes that affect the taste, color, and structure of wine. These compounds include pigment anthocyanins (color) and tannins that strongly influence wine structure including astringency, color stability, aging ability, and mouthfeel. Resveratrol, the antioxidant often associated with the health benefits of red wine, is a natural phenolic compound. The bulk of phenols are found in grape skins and seeds. The color of red wines is a product of slow extraction of anthocyanins from the skins of red grape (including "black" and "blue") varieties. White grape varieties have lower total phenol concentrations but colorless anthocyanins are often synthesized from skins.

The search for the perfect sweet spot of ripeness begins weeks before pick-ers descend on the vineyard as vintners walk among the vines to monitor berry development. While examining grape physiology, they will occasionally pop a berry in their mouths to taste the relationship between sugar and acid as well as skin thickness and seed hardness. While most vintners will also employ modern tools to measure sugar and acid numbers, they rely extensively on their years of tasting experience to read grape maturity. Only when skin color is appropriately

Many American fortified wine producers will use half-ton bins for fermentation after the grapes have been sorted, destemmed and crushed. (Photo courtesy of Jim Hansen.)

dark, stems are firm, seeds are dark walnut or chocolate brown, and taste has the correct sugar-acid balance do vintners alert picking crews.

In warm-climate growing regions like southern California and the Southwest, physiologically mature vinifera grapes for red port-style wines are harvested at between 24° and 26° Brix with TA ranging between 0.5 and 0.8 (5 and 8 grams per liter). Harvesttime sugar levels for white port grapes from these regions are a point or two lower, with TA in the 0.60–0.75 range.

In the cooler, moist regions of the South and Southeast Coast, where muscadine is the predominant wine grape variety, fruit tends to ripen at lower sugar levels and a bit higher acidity. Muscadine grapes are usually picked at 16°–20° Brix with a TA rarely above 0.70. Hybrid grapes grown in the Midwest and Northeast rarely achieve the sugar-acid ripeness of warm-climate classic varieties even with extended hang time.

Some years ago, UC Davis devised a simple formula for determining ripeness. Research indicates that grapes with a sugar-to-acid ratio of 30–35:1 were in the preferred ripeness zone (Cox 1985). For example, grapes measuring 20° Brix with a TA of 0.80 have a sugar-to-acid ratio of 25:1 and thus are not quite ripe. Grapes at 24° Brix with a 0.70 TA have a sugar-to-acid ratio of 34:1 and are ready for harvest.

Another approach to quantify ripeness involves multiplying the pH of the grape by itself then multiplying this product by the degrees Brix. The theory is that prime white grape ripeness will have a value of 200 while the ideal red grape ripeness value is 260. An example would be a red grape with a pH of 3.4 and 24° Brix. The result would be 277—a bit above perfect but definitely ready for harvest.

The concern with simple ripeness indicators like the sugar-acid ratios is that they are quite variable across different varieties and growing conditions.

These significant variations and indiscriminately applied universal rules of thumb have limited value for predicting wine quality. Moreover, it is unclear to what degree ideal sugar-acidity balance coincides with optimal maturity of grape flavorants.

Crush

The early stages of red and white port-style wine fermentation differ little from those of dry wine. Grapes arrive on the crush pad in the early morning hours when vineyard temperatures are low. This is especially important to white port-style makers since they prefer lower fermentation temperatures in the 45°F–60°F range. Harvest temperature is not as important for red port-style varieties since fermentation temperatures are higher, in the mid-80°F range. However, vintners would prefer to have grapes arrive for crush at moderate temperatures to minimize pre-fermentation cooling or heating.

Most vintners will hand-inspect and sort grapes prior to crush to remove under- or overripe fruit, any unsound berries, and MOG—material other than grapes. Larger producers may employ an optical scanner to remove any undesirable fruit or material. With few exceptions, grapes are crushed and destemmed with careful attention paid to avoiding crushing seeds that could add bitterness to wine. Crushing equipment capacity can vary from a few tens of pounds per hour to multiple tons per hour. Crushers/destemmers most often consist of a receiving hopper that feeds an auger into either adjustable rollers or rotating drums that break the skins and release the juice, skins, and seeds

Punching the "cap" of skins back into the fermenting juice two or three times a day maximizes the extraction of color pigments. (Photo courtesy of Jim Hansen.)

as "must" into a receptacle. Stems are collected at one end of the crusher and returned to vineyard as mulching material.

The must is usually pumped from the crusher to any of a variety of fermentation containers, depending on availability and the vintner's preference. Some producers prefer half-ton open top plastic or stainless steel bins while others use open or closed stainless steel tanks of varying capacities. Many vintners will add 50 to 100 ppm (parts per million) of sulfur dioxide (SO_2) to retard unwanted indigenous yeast in the new must.

At this point, producers begin to apply individual winemaking techniques and styles. Some producers will cold soak the must for 24–48 hours prior to yeast inoculation. This pre-fermentation practice begins the process of extraction that results in the transfer of flavor, aroma, color, and phenolic organic compounds from the grape skins to the juice. The rate of pre-fermentation extraction varies with each grape variety and is more often employed when making red port-style wines. Since white grapes marginally contribute color, flavor extraction is the purpose of pre-fermentation skin-to-juice contact for white port-style wines. Other winemakers will yeast inoculate shortly after crush and rely on the fermentation process for color, flavor, aroma, and structure.

Not all domestic wineries have the good fortune of having their fruit source within a couple of highway hours away. This is particularly true of vintners in the Midwest, Northeast, and some regions of the South and Southeast where it is difficult to grow and fully ripen classic vinifera. However, thanks to modern technology and a plentiful supply of classic wine grape varieties, primarily from California's Central Valley, winemakers across the nation have alternatives.

Perhaps the most convenient source for winemakers without direct access to fresh fruit is wine grape concentrate. Most grape concentrates are made by boiling grape juice to eliminate two-thirds to three-quarters of the water naturally present. Heating might give the juice a cooked flavor, so concentrate is made under reduced pressure, which lowers the boiling point and minimizes loss of fragrance, color, and varietal character. A potential shortcoming of juice concentrate is shorter-lived wines than fresh grapes would yield. This is not a concern when using concentrate to make fortified wines since the blending of wine spirits during fermentation and long aging enhance the wine's life.

Concentrates can be made from any grape variety and are available fresh or frozen in a variety of container sizes. Most classic wine grape concentrates are produced by large grape-processing operations in Central Valley, California.

Concentrates destined for commercial wines are usually made with the same quality grapes that wineries compete for so prices are comparable to what a winery would pay for fresh grapes. Concentrates of American and hybrid grape varieties are also produced in the eastern United States, as evidenced by the popularity of Welch's Concord and Niagara juice concentrate. Reconstituting grape juice prior to fermentation is a simple process and individual producers will usually provide customers with detailed instructions and recommendations.

A second alternative for vintners is to purchase fresh grapes direct from growers or brokers who ship fruit by refrigerated truck to the winery. This is certainly not a new approach, as many California grape growers survived Prohibition by shipping railcar loads of fresh grapes to eastern terminals in Chicago and New Jersey. Fruit brokers would then sell all or portions of the grape load to both legitimate (home winemakers) and illegitimate (bootleggers) customers. The trip across the country required regular stops to replenish ice in the railcars to prevent spoilage. Today's refrigerated big rigs traveling on America's super-highways make the trip in 48–60 hours.

A substantial portion of the fresh grapes sold to Midwestern and Eastern winemakers comes from the Lodi region of California. Fresh Syrah, Cabernet Sauvignon, Zinfandel, and Sauvignon blanc grapes are favored by these fortified winemakers. Fresh grapes arriving by truck from remote vineyards are handled and crushed in the same manner as any other fresh grapes.

Fermentation

Up to this point in the process, we only have a must of grape juice mixed with seeds and skins. Fermentation only takes place when the must or juice is subjected to the action of tiny single-cell fungi call yeast. These organisms are quite common and thousands of species are found in the natural environment. Yeasts feed on sugars. They metabolize hexose sugars, such as glucose and fructose, as an energy source and do not need sunlight for development. Yeast species either require oxygen for aerobic cellular respiration or are anaerobic, requiring no exposure to oxygen. Both species however, have aerobic methods of energy production. Fermentation, then, is the process of yeast converting sugars to carbon dioxide and alcohol while releasing heat.

Saccharomyces cerevisiae is the yeast species used in winemaking. This yeast occurs naturally in the environment and can be seen as a component of the thin white film on the skins of some dark-color grapes. However, different natural or native strains of S. cerevisiae have differing and often unpredictable effects on wine grape fermentation. While some long-time portmakers prefer to use native yeasts or have developed "house blend" yeasts, the majority of port-style winemakers employ commercially cultured yeast strains. Many use the same yeast stains for dry as well as port-style wines.

Yeasts come to the winemaker as dehydrated powder that requires careful re-hydration to ensure strong, healthy fermentation. An initial yeast inoculation following product rehydration specifications will result in 3–4 million viable cells per milliliter of must. Under favorable conditions, the cell population will increase to 100–150 million cells/milliliter before fermentation begins. As living organisms, yeast can survive most winemaking environments. When they run into unfavorable conditions, such as a lack of nitrogen, stress is put on their performance. Winemakers can address these stressful conditions with yeast nutrients to correct the problem. Since port-style wine fermentations are relatively short, rarely are yeast nutrients need to reach the desired alcohol-sugar levels. Some winemakers will, however, use nutrients to ensure a smooth, trouble-free fermentation.

Dry wine fermentation procedures vary between white and red wines. Fermentation of red wine must almost always proceeds with juice in contact with skins while white must is pressed with only juice undergoing fermentation. In general, these standard procedures also apply when making port-style wines. However, since most of the flavor components of grapes reside in the skins, some white port-style wine producers elect to ferment "on the skins." Even though there is relatively little color in white grape skins, vintners may elect to extract some yellow or light gold color by on-skin fermentation.

Red port-style fermentation goes quickly—between two and four days at temperatures in the mid-80s. The trick is to maximize color, flavor, and phenol extraction early during fermentation. The process produces substantial amounts of carbon dioxide that carries the skins and seeds to the top of the fermentation vessel. This is called the "cap." Since the skins in the cap contain the majority of desirable color and flavor components, the goal is to optimize skin-to-juice contact. The longer the skins are in contact with the juice, the deeper the color of the juice. Pumping juice from lower levels of the fermentation tank over and through the cap three to four times a day is a method preferred by larger producers to maximize extraction. Small lot producers may optimize extraction by "punching" or submerging the cap into the juice at least twice daily.

Enological enzymes are a resources developed by modern enology to assist vintners with more efficient fermentation. Enzymes are natural protein catalysts that facilitate and increase the rate of chemical reactions. Some white fortified wine producers will use a pectic enzyme to enhance color and increase filtration efficiency. Pectins are a gelatinous glue that holds plant cells together. Pectic enzymes help to break down the fruit's fiber to make the pulp less thick. This allows more of the fruit's character to be released during fermentation and pressing. In addition, pectic enzymes help make sure the wine is clear by breaking down pectin chains, which enhances filtration without affecting wine color and flavor components.

Fortification

Fortification is the process of adding alcohol spirits to arrest fermentation. Alcohol spirits are derived from distilling products of fermentation. Therefore, fortified grape wine is the result of blending grape spirits with grape must or juice to stop fermentation at a predetermined level of residual sugar and alcohol.

When to fortify and how much alcohol to blend are the major decision points for fortified wine producers. Winemakers must consider a number of options prior to fortification including what type of spirits to use, final sweetness and alcohol levels, and final wine style. Economics also play a role in the fortification decision.

Arguably, the selection of fortifying wine spirits or brandy may be the most important of the vintner's decisions. Federal regulations require winemakers to use only spirits derived from the same fruit as used for the production of fruit wines. Thus, only spirits derived from grapes can be used to fortified grape wines. The use of other fruit spirits or gain alcohols for the production of forti-fied grape wines is strictly prohibited.

The "brandy" used by fortified wine makers is not the same brandy we as-sociate with the large snifter of warm, brown liquor sipped in front of a glowing fire. Vintners use the terms "Brandy" or "Neutral Spirits, Fruit Grape" (NSFG) to describe the alcohol used in wine fortification. According to federal alcohol regulation, "Brandy (Federal Regulations Title 27 Chapter 1 Subchapter A, Part 5, Subpart C,Section 5.22(d)) is spirits distilled from the fermented juice, mash or wine of fruit or from its residue at less than 95 percent alcohol by volume (190 proof) having the taste, aroma and characteristics generally attributed to brandy." The regulations go further to specify "Brandy" as grape brandy stored in oak containers for two or more years. Other types of fruit brandy must be further identified, such as "Plum Brandy."

Nearly all the domestic grape brandies produced in the United States are distilled in Central California. Brandy is usually derived from California wines using a variety of grapes, depending on the location of the distillery and the producer. Thompson Seedless, Burger, French Colombard, Muscat of Alexan-dria, and occasionally the ancient Mission are the most popular brandy-pro-ducing varieties. Few domestic fortified wine producers choose to distill their own brandy or wine/spirits. Federal regulations require wineries to obtain a separate license to produce distilled alcohol products. Further regulations spec-ify complex requirements for production and storage of distilled products in facilities separate from the winery. Complicated rules for handling, accounting, and taxation can make winery-owned-and-operated distilleries a challenging proposition.

Brandy or wine spirits are produced by either batch distillation from a pot still or fractional distillation using a column still. Batch distillation starts with a single batch of starting material that is heated in a pot still and the wine distillate of between 26 and 50 percent alcohol is collected then further concentrated by a second distillation to a higher strength brandy of up to 80 percent alcohol.

Fractional distillation relies on a fractionating column to separate compo-nents with different volatilities found in the starting material. The separation along the height of the column can be viewed as a series of batch distillations, concentrating the more volatile component at the top and leaving behind the less volatile component at the bottom. Fractional distillation can be set up as a continuous process by removing the separated components from the different positions along the column (alcohol at the top) and then replacing the removed components with more of the starting material. Fractional distillation can effi-ciently produce a neutral, high-strength spirit of between 94 and 96 percent al-cohol, called High Proof or SVR (Spiritus Vinum Rectificatum). High Proof is widely considered the most suitable spirit for fortification purposes where min-imal dilution of or interference with the wine/grape flavors is intended.

Individual vintner preference ultimately determines the style of brandy ap-plied to fortification. A significant portion of domestic fortified wine producers prefer to use 190 proof (95 percent alcohol) "clean" neutral wine spirits with no trace of flavor or aromatics. Blending clean brandy is more likely to result in a fortified wine that retains varietal flavor and aroma characteristics. This material is usually shipped to the winery in inert food-grade plastic containers. Other producers exercise a variety of approaches to fortification, including the use of lower alcohol brandies (140–160 proof) to retain fruitiness and a lighter structure. Some vintners prefer to age their fortifying brandies in nearly neutral oak barrels to impart a touch of woodiness in the finished product. Regardless of the specific brandy or wine spirits employed, the ultimate goal of the fortified winemaker is to produce a balanced wine where the alcohol does not overpower distinctive varietal flavor and aroma.

Once the decision on the style of fortifying brandy/wine spirits is made, the vintner must determine whether to fortify the fermenting juice on or off the skins. Here again, individual preference and style is the primary determinant although economics is a consideration. Both methods are commonly employed in making red and white port-style wines.

Winemakers who favor fortifying on the skins contend that brandy or wine spirits act as a solvent that enhances extraction of color and flavor components. This method is a bit more labor-intensive, requiring thorough mixing to ensure uniform distribution of spirits throughout the must. On-skin fortification can be significantly more expensive than off skin, since up to 30 percent of the spirits can remain with the skins after pressing.

Fortifying off the skins means that the fermenting grape must is pressed, removing the seeds and skins, prior to adding brandy. Off-skin fermentations tend to result in a "cleaner" fortification that retains fresh fruit flavors while maintaining color. While mixing is still required, this method also ensures a more complete integration of juice and spirits with no loss of fortifying material.

The next step in the fortification process is to determine the amount of brandy or wine spirits to blend. Veteran port-style winemakers have an intuitive feel for the right amount of fortifying material to blend based on grape variety, length of fermentation, desired final sugar and alcohol levels, and overall wine style. However, there is a formula for determining the optimum quantity of fortifying spirits necessary to reach a specific final alcohol value in the finished wine. The Pearson Square is a practical tool for calculating the volume of wine with a given alcohol content that is required to bring the alcohol content of another wine to a desired level. The winemaker only needs to know the alcohol level of the fortifying material, the alcohol level of the base wine, and desired final concentration to make an accurate calculation.

When to fortify may be the most crucial decision the port-style winemakers must make. A universally accepted fable of the port-style vintner is that the perfect time to fortify always occurs at three o'clock in the morning. While a bit of an exaggeration, the parable does illustrate the importance of fortification at the ideal fermentation sugar and alcohol stage. While there is no absolute "ideal" number, port-style winemakers generally agree that a sugar value of 10°–13° Brix with 7 to 8.5 percent alcohol is the best range for blending brandy or wine spirits. The precise sugar-alcohol value is, again, a factor of the grape variety, blending spirits, finished wine style, and individual vintner experience.

Whether fermentation occurs on or off the skins, the fermenting juice is separated from skins, seeds, and stems by pressing. Typically, pressing involves two steps. Whole grapes or fermented must go into the press, releasing some juice to freely run into a container. This "free-run" juice is a result of little or no pressure and has more sugar and less acid and tannin than the later press fractions. As pressure increases, the "press-run" juice contains decreasing levels of sugar and increasing levels of acid, color, and tannins.

Deciding between two basic press types is usually a matter of winemaker preference and economics. Traditionally, American port-style wines were made using the old-fashioned but effective manual basket press. This press operates by ratcheting a wood or metal plate down on the grapes or must and extracting the juice into a catch pan at the bottom of the press. The amount of pressure exerted by the manual basket press is a function of the desired intensity of the juice and the strength of the press operator. Having been on the business end of a manual basket press, the author has experienced its challenges firsthand.

Modern enological technology has eased pressing labor substantially. While boutique wineries may still use a small manual basket press, medium and large basket presses are now pneumatically operated and feature digital readouts for applied pressure. The "basket" of a basket press can be made of dense wood (oak or redwood), fiberglass, or stainless steel.

The bladder press is the more contemporary pressing alternative for larger producers. Grapes or must are loaded into a cylinder, closed at each end. An elastic bladder expands and pushes the grapes against the sides of the stainless steel cylinder. The juice then flows out through small openings in the cylinder. The cylinder rotates during the process to help regulate the pressure. Most pneumatically operated bladder presses include electronic systems that automate a preprogrammed pressing process. Pressed juice is run off through holes in the cylinder into a catch tank, where it is pumped into settling or storage containers.

Every winemaker has a preference regarding the proportion of free-run and press-run juice in the finished wine. Some vintners prefer wines containing as much as 90 percent free-run juice while others will blend different fractions of press-run juice to achieve a specific stylistic balance. Press-run juice not destined for finished port-style wines is often blended with other fortified wines, sold to other wineries, or sold to distillers to produce wine spirits.

When fermentation has completely stopped, most domestic ports finish with alcohol levels between 18 and 21 percent with residual sugars between 7.5 and 10 percent. At this point, the new wine is usually racked into stainless steel tanks or wooden vats and allowed to settle for at least two months. However, some winemakers will rack directly into barrels for aging. Others let the new wine settle a couple of months in the tank then rack into barrels followed by three or four more rackings to clear the wine.

Barrel Storage

Once the wine has settled, the majority of producers rack the young port-style wine into barrels or casks for storage and aging. Port-style wines can be broken down into two broad categories. Wood-aged port-style wines are aged in wood (usually oak) barrels, casks, or vats while bottle-aged port-style wines mature in bottle. As port-style wines mature, the firm tannins and intense fruity flavors of youth gradually give way to the velvety smoothness and mellow, nuanced character that develops with age. At the same time, there is a change in the wine's appearance. The initial deep violet or red color slowly becomes paler, evolving into the subtle amber tone. The speed at which port-style wines mature depends on the how the wine is aged.

An example of the "solera" aging system. (David Bird, Understanding Wine Technology. Board and Bench Publishing: San Francisco.)

Oak has been used to make wine barrels and casks for over two thousand years because of its extremely tight grain, which prevents leakage. As still table wines mature in oak barrels, organic compounds are extracted from the wood and dissolve in wine. These phenols affect color, taste, mouth feel, and aroma, what we call the "bouquet" of the wine. However, most vintners want to avoid the influence of oak in their port-style wines, so they use well-maintained, older, neutral barrels to allow the wine to slowly develop character by aging. Other winemakers may want a subtle woody character in the wine and will age their wines in three- to four-year-old barrels.

Oak barrels act as semipermeable membranes that allow water and alcohol to evaporate through the pores in the wood. Depending on a number of factors, including humidity, oak species, and barrel age, a typical 60-gallon barrel may lose between 1.5–2.5 gallons of wine to evaporation per year. Dry storage conditions result in more water evaporation and increase the alcoholic concentration of the wine. Gradually, evaporated alcohol and water is replaced by oxygen passing through the wood and is absorbed by wine. This is not necessary a good thing when making table wines but is highly desired by the port-style vintner. Deliberate oxidation results in decreased astringency and increased color and stability. Port-style wines aged in wood are in contact with the air and will evolve more rapidly than wines aged in bottles, which have almost no air contact. In a small cask or barrel, where air contact is greatest, the wine will age faster than in a large vat where it is more limited.

Blending

Blending wines of different varieties and ages is a long-held winemaking tradition. Vintners can blend fortified varietal wines prior to aging in order to subtly adjust color, flavor, and structure, which results in the specific finished port-style wine that achieves their stylistic objectives. Approximately 18 percent of domestic red port-style wines are blends of traditional Portuguese port grape varieties while another 19 percent are blends of classic vinifera or native American and hybrid varieties.

Varietal blending is usually accomplished prior to aging. Some vintners will harvest all the port-style varieties at the same time and "co-ferment" them together. This process is most often applied to port-style wines produced from traditional Portuguese varieties. Other winemakers elect to ferment individual varietal lots then rack and blend before barrel aging.

Many American port-style vintners fashion their distinctive wines by blending two or more wines from different production years. Once more, it is the unique slant to the vintners art that determines the final blend of multiple vintages. The goal is to achieve a consistent port-style character and average age in every wine released to the consumer.

The solera system is a well-established method of wine blending and aging developed by the Spanish and Portuguese to achieve consistent house-style aroma, taste, and quality. The complicated endeavor involves barrels of different vintages stacked on top of each other, the oldest on the bottom and the youngest on the top. Each year, a predetermined quantity of the bottom (the oldest) barrels' volume will be drawn off to be bottled as that year's product. The headspace created by the removed wine will be filled with wine from the level above, and those barrels will be filled with the level above them, while the last year's barrels on the top level will be topped up with current year's wine. Each year, as a limited amount of finished product is drawn from the bottom level of barrels, the average age of the wine in the bottom barrels will continue to increase until it reaches a constant average age. While the solera system is a fascinating approach to producing port-style wines of consistent age and quality, it is somewhat labor intensive, takes time to develop, and requires the vintner's commitment to limited and consistent annual production.

A recent trend in American port-style wine production is the incorporation of nongrape concentrates such as chocolate or berry flavoring. This so-called "infusion" involves the addition of flavored powders, essences, or highly concentrated natural juices to finished port-style wines prior to aging. The intent is to give the wine a uniquely identifiable flavor character that consumers can connect with familiar foods and desserts.

There is no standard for the addition of flavoring in port-style wines and each producer adds sufficient material to achieve his or her stylist objective. However, the addition of infusion products to a "natural wine" constitutes a "formula wine," according to the Federal Alcohol and Tobacco Tax and Trade Bureau (TTB). Therefore, federal regulations require producers of infused wines to have their flavor additive formulas approved before production. Since it is highly unlikely any two production formulas are the same, vintners view the specifics of their infusion process as proprietary and rarely share their formulas.

Aging

Wine aging is the process of changing wine with the intent of improving certain characteristics including favor, aroma, and overall mouthfeel. These changes occur due to the complex chemical reactions of phenolic compounds. In processes that begin during fermentation and continue after bottling, these compounds bind together and aggregate. Eventually these particles reach a certain size where they are too large to stay suspended in the solution and precipitate out forming the sediment found in barrels and bottles.

The desired style of the finished wine determines where and for how long the fortified wine is aged. While Portuguese port producers have a somewhat mystifying litany of terms to define port wine styles, American port-style vintners have simplified the terminology to three basic styles.

American "ruby" is the term for a port-style wine released with less than six years of barrel aging prior to bottling. Most domestic ruby port-style wines spend only two or three years in barrel before bottling in order to preserve a fresh, fruity character and retain the wine's bright ruby color. Tannins in ruby port-style wines tend to be a bit more solid and distinctive but the initial barrel aging usually provides sufficient time for these phenolic compounds to be well-integrated before bottling. Because of their structure and relatively short aging regime, ruby port-style wines tend to not benefit from additional home cellar aging and are meant to be enjoyed shortly after being made available to consumers.

American "tawny" is the term for a fortified port-style wine released with a minimum of six years' barrel aging prior to bottling. There is no restriction on the amount of time a domestic tawny port-style wine must age in bottle prior to release. However, many American vintners will age their tawny port-style wines a total of eight to ten years. Tawny port-style wines derive their identity from the deep amber or mahogany color that evolves as they mature in the barrel. The color change in port-style wine is the result of various phenolic compounds that create wine colors. Anthocyanins are specifically categorized as contributing to the variability of these colors. Various natural chemical reactions occur among different anthocyanins present in wines, resulting in the formation of more stable, denser pigments that create deeper, darker color. As the aging process continues, chains of organic compounds (primarily anthocyanins and tannins) continue becoming denser, to the point that they are no longer dissolved in the wine and settle in the bottle as sediment or "crust." This sediment is not harmful and does not adversely affect the favor, aroma, or bouquet of the wine. However, decanting will leave the sediment in the bottle and clear wine in the decanter. Tawny's flavor will become nuttier and the flavors will develop a richer character as the wine matures.

"Vintage" is a term for an American fortified port-style wine declared vintage by the producer. It shows the vintage date on the label and is aged in a barrel for no more than three years. By declaring a vintage, vintners are recognizing that the grapes for that particular harvest are of exceptional quality and that only those grapes are used to produce the wine. There is no hard and fast rule for declaring a vintage for domestic port-style wines. Grape quality involves a variety of aspects but climate and growing conditions are often the most important factors in declaring a vintage. In some regions of the country, such as California, annual variations in growing conditions are relatively minor and declaring a harvest exceptional can be infrequent. In other areas of the country with more variable growing conditions, declaring a vintage harvest may be more common. On average, American vintners declare a vintage port-style wine only a few times a decade.

Finishing
Fining and Racking
Once fermentation is complete, the new fortified wine is usually transferred to barrels to rest and allow the lees (deposits of dead yeast and other particles) to settle out. A primary goal of fortified wine vintners is to produce wines with clear, brilliant color. Fining and racking wines to remove any material that might inhibit clarity often achieves this objective. As with most other domestic fortified winemaking procedures, there is no standard when it comes to fining and racking. Fining involves the introduction of an agent such as bentonite, gelatin, or egg whites to remove specific suspended materials in the wine. Since alcohol aids clarification, some vintners find no need to fine their fortified wine. Other winemakers fine their wines a short time following fermentation while others will do a final fining just prior to bottling

In addition to, or in lieu of, fining, winemakers will rack the wines off the lees as a method of clarification. Racking is the moving the wine from one container—usually barrels—to another, leaving the lees in the original container. Some vintners will rack within a month or two of completing fermentation while others may wait a year or more to rack. Rarely are the fortified wines racked more than once a year prior to bottling. As the wine ages, the volume decreases through evaporation leaving what is called "head space." Table wine makers minimize head space by "topping" or filling the barrel back up with wine to control oxidation. This is not much of an issue for fortified wine makers since the oxidation induced by air in the head space is desirable for slow aging.

Stabilization

Ever open a bottle of wine to find tiny crystal-like particles adhered to the bottom of the cork? These tartrate crystals are harmless and have no effect on flavor or aroma but consumers often view these particles as a wine flaw or fault. Wine grape juice is often supersaturated with potassium bitartrate following crush. As the wine ferments, the solubility of bitartrate decreases and stimulates slow, spontaneous precipitation. Incomplete precipitation of potassium bitartrate (KHT) results in the offensive tartrate crystals. Since tartrate crystal formation most often occurs in unstable young wines, aged fortified port-style wines seldom have to deal with this problem. However, consumers demand wine free of any real or perceived flaws so even fortified wine vintners must take steps to ensure consumer confidence.

There are several methods of achieving KHT crystal stability in wine. The method preferred by most fortified wine vintners is cold stabilization. This process involves chilling the wine in temperature-controlled stainless steel tanks to near freezing for a few days. A refrigerant is circulated through a jacket around the tank that lowers the temperature, causing any remaining KHT to settle out on the bottom of the tank as cream of tartar. Cold stabilization is usually carried out a few weeks before bottling.

Other methods of KHT crystal stabilization include reverse osmosis and spinning cone/centrifuge technology. These high-tech schemes are expensive and very rarely used by American fortified wine vintners. In fact, many fortified winemakers seldom if ever experience tartrate instability and shun the stabilization process.

Filtering

Filtration has been a controversial issue since the emergence of the modern American wine industry in the 1960s. Proponents of filtration claim that the process ensures stable, technically correct wine free of any flaws, faults, or impurities. On the other hand, detractors suggest that filtration interferes with the natural development of wine and can remove or alter elements in wine that affect flavor, aroma, and structure.

Technically, filtration involves the removal of particles, macromolecules, and colloidal matter on or within a fibrous or porous material. Filtering material ranges in pore size from 100 microns for removing large particles, down to less than one micron for "polish" filtration to eliminate undesirable molecules and microbes. Wine is usually pumped through a series of plates containing the filtering material. The number and size of plates in the filter frame are determined by the desired degree of filtration.

There is no unanimity among domestic port-style vintners regarding filtration—some do, some don't. A common factor, however, is that aging and the high alcohol level in fortified wine affect the scope of filtration. Barrel aging allows larger particles and undesirable components to settle out of the wine over time. This residue is left behind when the wines are racked and clarified prior to bottling and usually requires minimal particle filtration. Similarly, the high alcohol in fortified wines overwhelm almost all microbes and bacteria that could have long term effects on the wine. To be on the safe side, however, many port-style vintners will do final polish filtration just prior to bottling.

Bottling

Bottling American port-style wine is both a process and an art. The process of bottling is fairly standard, while the bottle itself is often an expression of the vintners art.

Unlike table wine bottles that tend for conform to the traditional Bordeaux, Burgundy, and Hock/Alsace styles, there is no "typical" bottle style for American fortified wines. Vintners are free to express their individuality by packaging wines in an infinite variety of glass containers. Fortified wine bottles range from tall and thin to short and stubby, from sleek and sensuous to common and traditional. Vintners may further distinguish bottles with artful etchings or molded designs.

Often producers will utilize bottle size and shape to distinguish fortified wines from other wine products. While table wines are commonly packaged in standard 750 milliliter (ml) bottles, fortified wine producers typically employ three different bottle sizes. According to data from the Sweet and Fortified Wine Association, only half of American fortified wine is packaged in 750 ml bottles, while 35 percent of vintners market their product in 375 ml bottles. The final 15 percent of American fortified wine makers offer their product in 500 ml bottles.

The selection of bottle size is a function of economics and fortified wine consumption. In general, fortified wines tend to be expensive because of the relatively higher cost of production due to the price for brandy/wine spirits, and expenses related to aging. Producers using larger bottles suggest that consumers are willing to pay for a fortified wine that they can enjoy on any occasion over a relatively long period of time. Consumers will often pour the contents of a 750 ml bottle into a decorative decanter that tastefully displays wine's dramatic color as they leisurely sip small measures over a few weeks or months. Fortified-wine vintners favoring the smaller bottle format champion the concept that the cost of larger bottles may be outside the price range of many consumers. These vintners conclude that they can recover costs and realize greater returns by marketing moderately priced, smaller bottles to a wider consumer base. A second aspect of support for the smaller format is consumer perception that wine in a different bottle is distinctive or "special." Small bottles with unusual or unique shapes, contours, and colors often draw consumer attention and appeal to an inherent interest in the contents.

Practically all domestic port-style wine producers use cork as their closure of choice. While there are a variety of alternative closures available to the industry, fortified wine vintners elect to stay with cork because it is still viewed by consumers as the traditional mark of wine quality. The problem of cork taint (2,4,6 trichloranisole), widespread some years ago, has largely been overcome by cork producers who claim to have reduced the occurrence of taint by 90 percent.

The seal protecting the cork closure of American fortified wine bottles typically remains the tin, PVC, or polylaminate (polylam) capsule. These products are relatively inexpensive and available in a variety of styles. Producer logos or other custom designs can be readily imprinted on capsules as subtle marketing tactics to foster brand identification. Some of domestic fortified wine makers however, have adopted an alternative protective closure called wax dipping. This product is available as solid blocks of polymer sealing wax in a variety of colors. When the wax is melted to a thick consistency in a heated pot, the winebottle neck is dipped into the wax then cooled in cold water for 10 to 15 seconds. Creative vintners let the wax run down the neck to form artful drips and shapes that draw consumer attention. Running a sharp knife over the top of the wax seal exposes the cork.

The final and often the most compelling expression of vintner art is the bottle label. Consumers are naturally drawn to label designs that stimulate interest, appeal to the senses, or convey a message. In many instances, producers devote as much time, energy, and resources to designing an attention-grabbing label as they do any other phase of the business.

Label design is not without limitations, however. Federal regulations administered by the TTB restrict what can be shown on labels as well as mandate specific information that must appear on all wine bottle labels. American port-style fortified wine producers are uniquely impacted by some of these regulations that date to the original legislation to implement the Repeal of Prohibition in 1933. An example is the TTB prohibition on using the terms "fortified" or "wine/spirits added" on domestic fortified wine labels. All proposed wine labels must be approved by the TTB before they can be applied to bottles. In March of 2006, the United States and the European Union agreed to prohibit the use of "port" on the labels of wines that do not originate in Portugal. However, a grandfather clause allows domestic producers to continue to use the term for labels approved prior to March 10, 2006.

At long last, new American fortified port-style wine is ready for the bottle. Vintners have four options for getting their wine into bottles. Three of these options involve a highly mechanized assembly line process while the fourth requires strength and patience.

Many fortified wine producers will bottle the product using an in-house bottling line. Producers without in-house capability can transport the wine to a facility that will "custom" bottle for a per bottle or per case fee. Such facilities may store the wine for a period prior to bottling and provide pre-bottling stabilization and filtering services.

Medium and small producers can opt to have the bottling line brought to them. Mobile wine bottling lines have been around since the mid-1980s and are now widely utilized in the American wine industry. Compact automated bottling equipment is usually housed in custom-built trailers ranging from 20 to 60 feet long and 8 feet wide. Most mobile lines operate at twenty-five to one hundred bottles per minute and can be configured to fill almost any bottle size and shape. Mobile bottlers also have the ability to apply a wide range of label formats and even print logos on finished wine cases.

With a few individualist twists, most all automated bottling systems operate in a similar manner. Cases of empty bottles are placed on the receiving table where they are aligned to go through the line single file. Empty bottles are normally purged with nitrogen gas to remove oxygen. The bottles then move to the filler that accurately fills each bottle. Next, an automatic corking machine inserts the cork and passes the bottle to either a machine or a person that places a capsule over the neck of the bottle, which is then shrunk by machine. Finally, it's off to the labeler where both front and back pressure-sensitive labels are precisely applied and sent to packers who place the finished bottles in twelve-bottle cases. The cases are tape sealed and any inventory labels such as bar codes are affixed to the cardboard boxes. Finished cases are usually stacked on pallets ready for storage and delivery to the consumer.

Not all American fortified wine producers have access to automated bottling lines. Many small, boutique vintners bottle their wines by hand—one bottle at a time. While the process is essentially the same as automated bottling, hand bottling requires fewer pieces of sophisticated equipment and more intensive labor. Empty bottles are cleaned and sanitized prior to filling. Hand filling can be done with a food grade plastic hose from barrel to bottle or by using a more elaborate four to six spout filler. Some winemakers will do a final filtering as the wine moves to the filler. Corks are inserted with a manual or vacuum corking machine and labels applied manually or with a semiautomatic labeler. There is no standard for the number of cases hand bottled over a period of time. It all depends on how much wine needs to be bottled and the endurance of the bottler(s). A full day for a hand-bottling crew of two to four people would be around one hundred cases.

American port-style fortified wine production has been practiced with a myriad of unique producer deviations for over 250 years. However, port is not the only fortified wine style fashioned by American vintners.

SHERRY-STYLE

Sherry is broadly defined as a fortified wine subjected to controlled oxidation to create a distinctive flavor. More specifically, the special oxidized character of sherry is often describe as baked, nutty, and caramelized. Since the flavors of sherry are derived from complex organic compounds including acetaldehyde, phenyl ethanol, esters, and wood extractives, the aroma and flavor of the original, relatively neutral-flavored grape variety vanishes during production.

The Andalucía region of southwest Spain has been making sherry wines for nearly two millennia from the nondescript white Palomino grape. While the Spanish produce a variety of sherry products, there are essentially two basic types of sherry. Fino sherries derive their light-straw color and hazelnut, light oaky aromas and flavors from flor yeast fermentation. Conversely, Oloroso sherries are darker, more amber in color, generally sweeter, and produced in an oxygen rich environment without flor yeast.

American sherry wines usually fall between the color and aroma extremes of the Fino and Oloroso, ranging from light yellow to medium brown in color. Sugar content of most American sherries ranges from 1.0 to 2.5 percent for dry, from 2.5 to 4.0 percent for standard, and up to 10 percent for cream sherry.

Since Palomino is not widely grown in American vineyards (only 213 acres in California in 2014), domestic sherry wines are produced from an assortment of mostly white grape varieties. In the west, in addition to Palomino, Mission, Grenache, Orange Muscat, and French Colombard are used, while in the east, Chambourcin, Niagara, Delaware, muscadine, and Orange Muscat are the favored varieties for sherry production.

Grapes are normally picked at 22°–24° Brix, then crushed and pressed or pressed immediately upon arrival at the winery, minimizing skin contact. Free-run or lightly pressed juice is often used to make Fino-style sherries, while the juice from further pressing usually creates the Oloroso-style sherries. The pressed juice (called shermat) is then fermented to dryness (no measurable residual sugar) to make the white base wine. The new base wine is racked off the lees, and fortified with grape brandy or wine spirits. The addition of spirits prevents the development of acetic acid (vinegar) bacteria during oxidation.

Following fermentation, sherry winemakers must make a crucial stylistic decision—whether or not to oxidize the base wine with or without yeast. This decision determines the final sherry style: Fino or Oloroso.

Yeast oxidation involves the inoculation of base wine with a special yeast strain called flor, meaning "flower" in Spanish. Flor yeasts produce what looks like thousands of tiny white flowers piled on the surface of the wine. The base wine is fortified to about 15 percent, which allows the development of a flor yeast film. The metabolism of flor yeast is the primary source of the pungent bouquet characteristic of fine sherries. When aged in oak barrels, these unique aromas and flavors combine with yeast autolysis flavors from dying yeast cells to produce a complex, invigorating, fresh, Fino-style sherry.

The surface-film method of making flor sherry can be time-consuming and expensive, so some winemakers have adopted a variation called the "submerged culture" technique. This process, most often applied by larger producers, involves inoculating a 15-percent-alcohol base wine with flor yeast in a stainless steel tank where air or pure oxygen is continuously bubbled through the wine. The tank is regularly stirred or agitated to keep the yeast cells suspended and the development of acetaldehyde is closely monitored. Acetaldehyde is an organic chemical compound that is the key to the sensory definition of sherry. Once the base wine has reached the desired acetaldehyde and flor yeast character, the wine is again fortified to 17–19 percent then racked off the lees. The finished Fino-style sherry is then left to age.

Some vintners elect the non-yeast approach and produce Oloroso-style sherries by either long aging the wine in partially filled oak barrels or by "baking" the base wine. Competitively priced American sherries are often produced by the heating the wine in the presence of air at between 120°F and 140°F for anywhere from 30 to 120 days.

Early California sherry makers would "cook" the base wine by running hot water through a coil placed in a large redwood or oak tank exposed to air. Today's baked sherries utilize a process developed by Cornell University scientist Donald Tressler in 1939. Prior to Tressler's method, making sherry from native labrusca grape varieties was thought impossible due to their "foxy" character. Tressler solved the problem by pumping oxygen through a porous material at the bottom of the fermentation tank, which produced a large number of minute bubbles in a base wine heated to 135°F. The extremely fine air bubbles result in a small volume of oxygen in a large volume of wine that hastened oxidation and removed the foxy component from the wine. The finished sherry is cooled for several days then racked and filtered. Additional fortification with brandy or wine spirits will bring the new Oloroso-style sherry to around 20 percent alcohol. A majority of sherry producers in the eastern United States employ the Tressler method, as do sherry vintners in other areas of the country.

The alternative non-yeast technique of American sherry production is the slow, deliberate oxidation of base wine in partially filled oak barrels under warm conditions. This is an especially appealing process for sherry makers in warm, dry climates like southern California and Texas who allow their sherry barrels to bask under sunny skies for about two years. The young sherry is then racked, fined, and filtered, ready for finishing.

Some sherries improve with age and different styles dictate differing aging schemes ranging from a few months to a few years. Most vintners age sherries in American oak barrels to gain a stronger aroma and drier taste. Traditionally, the solera system is used for storing and blending sherry. This the same technique often used in the fractional blending of port-style wines consisting of stacks of barrels with each row containing a different sherry vintage. The oldest wine in the bottom tier is drawn for bottling and is replaced with wine from the tier above and so on for usually five or more tiers. Few true solera systems are found in American sherry wineries. While fractional blending may still be done, the expense and effort of maintaining the solera is challenging.

Finishing American sherry may involve some blending to adjust sweetness, color, and complexity in order to achieve the vintner's unique stylistic objective. Once the final blend has been achieved, the sherry may be polish filtered, cold stabilized, and finally, bottled.

ANGELICA

Allegedly named for Los Angeles—City of the Angels—in the late eighteenth century, Angelica is America's fortified wine. In fact, Angelica is the only American semi-generic named wine approved by the federal government for use on wine labels.

Traditional Angelica was made from Mission grapes as a mix of 50 percent mission wine and 50 percent mission brandy. Grapes were pressed soon after harvest and the unfermented grape juice was poured into barrels already half-filled with brandy. The brandy arrested the fermentation of the juice while preserving its fruitiness and keeping the wine from going bad. Oxidation in barrels resulted in a dark orange or brown wine with around 20 percent alcohol and 10 percent residual sugar. History asserts that Frenchman Emile Vache documented the 1770 Franciscan friar's recipe that he and his brothers used to make Angelica at their southern California winery in the late eighteenth century.

Only a small handful of American wineries make a fortified wine labeled Angelica. Even fewer vintners make Angelica in more or less the traditional style. As expected, these dedicated Angelica producers are in California where about 700 acres of mission grapes stubbornly cling to commercial viability.

Mission grapes destined for Angelica are picked at peak ripeness, usually around 24° Brix, then destemmed and crushed into open top containers. Some vintners will add about 50 ppm of sulfur dioxide and let the must rest for a day before pressing. While classified as a red grape, the free-run or lightly pressed Mission juice is a light orange color as a result of minimum skin contact. Because federal regulations require all wines to undergo some degree of fermentation, fortification of Mission juice with 185–190 proof neutral brandy occurs about halfway through fermentation. The wines are then racked into neutral oak barrels for aging. A few vintners use a solera system for the fractional blending of old and young Angelica, while other winemakers barrel age their Angelica for two or more years. Finishing Angelica may include a final filtration to clarify the wine and remove any sediment.

Today's mission Angelica is an alluring, light-to-moderate bronze or amber sweet wine with 18–20 percent alcohol and 9–18 percent residual sugar. Berry, toasted nut, caramel, and ripe fig aromas and flavors are often associated with modern Angelica, while some display a captivating sherry or port-like aromatic character.

Not all American fortified wines labeled Angelica are made from Mission grapes, however. Since Angelica is a semi-generic American wine name, domestic producers can apply the name to any "dessert wine (Federal Regulation Title 27, Part 4 Subpart C, Section 4.24(3) in TTB.gov) having the taste, aroma, and characteristics generally attributed to angelica" according to TTB rules. Unfortunately, there does not seem to be a standard definition of such Angelica characteristics. As a result, a few American fortified wines labeled "Angelica" are, in reality, fortified Muscat wines. There may be some precedence for Muscat Angelicas since Muscat grapes could be found in early American "field blend" vineyards. Muscat in a nineteenth century California vineyard of Zinfandel, Alicante Bouchet, and Carignane would serve as a typical example.

Muscat of Alexandria, Orange Muscat, and Muscat Canelli are the three most likely candidates for Muscat Angelica. Their characteristic natural sweetness and floral aromas are well suited for making unique, slightly oxidized fortified wines in the style of traditional Angelica. Fortification of free-run or lightly pressed juice with neutral high-proof brandy and slow oxidation in neutral oak barrels as practiced in making Angelica is similarly applied to the production of Angelica labeled fortified Muscat wines.

MADEIRA

Madeira is a fortified wine originating on the Atlantic island of Madeira in the sixteenth century. America grew fond or Madeira wine in the eighteenth century and became one of the island's biggest customers, buying nearly a quarter of all the wine produced there. Madeira was used to toast the Declaration of Independence in 1776, at the inauguration of George Washington in 1789.

True Madeira is made traditionally from five key grape varieties including the classic Verdelho grape, which is also grown in some areas of California. Traditionally, Madeira is made by a process called estufagem that subjects the brandy-fortified wine to slow heating until it reaches temperatures above 100°F. After "baking" for three months the wine is slowly cooled to ambient temperature. A similar process called canteiro heats the wine in casks where high evaporation helps concentrate the wine. Finished Madeira can age in wood for two to twenty years. Notable California vintner V. Sattui employs an over one hundred- year-old solera aging regiment to maintain consistent quality in their Madeira-style wine.

There are a handful of American vintners making Madeira-style fortified wines. The process closely follows that of white port production with most producers whole-cluster pressing to retain fruitiness and minimize phenolic bitterness. Some vintners will incorporate enzymes prior to fermentation to enhance flavor and juicing. Most producers will use 180-proof wine spirits to stop fermentation at about 8–10 percent residual sugar and 18 percent alcohol. Rather than adding spirits, a few American vintners produce high alcohol concentrations by an enhanced fermentation process (in-situ) fermentation, which produces a more integrated and homogenous blend of the spirits with the natural grape flavors. Following press, producers usually allow for a settling time before filtration. Producers will then initiate their unique heating process at around 110°F for a period of about one year. Vintners will oak-barrel age the "madeiraized" wine to achieve their exclusive style objectives. Prior to bottling, vintners will make any necessary alcohol and acid adjustments to balance the wine then cold stabilize and sterile filter the new wine. Madeira-style wine continues to improve in the barrels, but once bottled it no longer continues to improve. Therefore, most Madeira-style vintners will show both the vintage and bottling dates on the label to indicate the length of barrel aging.

American Madeira-style wines have complex aromas and flavors of toffee, caramel, nuts, marmalade, and raisins supported by bright, fresh acidity.

VERMOUTH

Vermouth may well be America's most unusual and intriguing fortified wine. Simply put, Vermouth is fortified wine infused with herbs and spices. Vermouth is classified by federal regulation as an aperitif wine "having an alcoholic content of not less than 15 percent by volume, compounded from grape wine containing added brandy or alcohol, flavored with herbs and other natural aromatic flavoring materials." (Federal Regulation Title 27, Part 4 Subpart C, Section 4.24(6)(g)(2) in TTB.gov) Aperitif derives from the Latin aperire, which means "to open," in the sense of opening up the appetite.

The base wine for American Vermouth is a neutral-flavored wine often made from a variety of grapes. Production tracks the standard procedures for white port–style wines fortified with high proof neutral wine spirits. Upward of fifty herbs and spices are used in the production Vermouth. Examples of commonly infused ingredients are ginger, marjoram, nutmeg, violet, juniper, allspice, and lavender. The specific types and quantities of infused materials are unique to each producer and usually proprietary. However, under federal regulations, Vermouth is deemed a formula wine and requires TTB approval of each explicit Vermouth formula prior to production.

The extracts for Vermouth often entail soaking the herbs and spices in high-alcohol spirits then adding the extract directly into the wine following fortification. Extraction does not commonly last more than two weeks to avoid the assimilation of unwanted flavors. A darker color can be achieved by adding caramel after the flavor infusion. The wine is then aged for four to six months during which time the flavorants are fully blended. Vermouth is typically fined, cold stabilized, and sterile filtered.

The alcohol content of American Vermouth is normally 14–18 percent with extra dry Vermouth containing about 4 percent sugar while sweet Vermouth has around 16 percent residual sugar.

MARSALA

Marsala is a dry or sweet fortified wine originally produced in the region surrounding the city of Marsala in Sicily. English trader John Woodhouse is generally credited with introducing Marsala to the European wine consumers in 1773 after he discovered the local wine produced in the region, which was aged in wooden casks and tasted similar to the Portuguese and Spanish fortified wines then popular in England. In Europe, both sweet and dry Marsalas are traditionally served as an aperitif between the first and second courses of a meal.

A large eastern wine producer employing high-volume fortified wine production techniques almost exclusively produces American Marsala. Most Americans utilize this wine in cooking such dishes as veal or chicken marsala.

3

ENJOYING AMERICAN FORTIFIED WINES

THE BRITISH TRADITION

The British love tradition and ceremony, especially when it comes to their port. Ever since the English firm of Messrs. Clark, Thornton, and Warre first started shipping fortified wines from Portugal's Alto Douro and the town of Oporto, the British have wrapped drinking in myth and tradition. Probably the most important myth was that port was a wine for gentlemen only. This may not really be a myth since port was an expensive beverage in which only the wealthy and privileged could afford to indulge.

The best-known and most often-followed British tradition is "passing the port." According to legend, British naval officers in the eighteenth century developed the custom of meticulously passing their daily port "from port to port" in a clockwise direction. The English gentry adapted the naval ceremony and cultivated a civilian tradition of passing the port. The ritual involves placing the decanter of port in front of the host who then serves the guest to the right. The host then passes the decanter to the guest on the left and the port is passed to the left until it returns to the host. How quaint.

A related custom involves the almost unforgivable *faux pas* of the port decanter not coming full circle back to the host. According to tradition, it is poor "port-iquette" for the host to directly ask for the decanter. Instead, the host asks the uniformed cretin closest to the decanter if he knows the Bishop of Norwich or some other village in England. This is a rhetorical question not meant to be answered but rather to illicit the action of immediately passing the port. If the offender answers with a "No," they are told that "The bishop is an awfully good fellow, but he never passes the port!"

Always in the mood for a sporting wager, the British gentry often engaged in the custom of "naming the vintage." The practice requires that only the host know what port is in the decanter. Once the port has been properly "passed", the guests are asked to name the vintage and the shipper. More often than not, it was simply the luckiest guesser who won the pot. (Howkins, 2011)

A final old world tradition was that ladies almost never drank port. Women were expected to drink sherry, a light beverage considered more appropriate for the fairer sex.

La Santé Rendue (Health Restored), a late eigh-teenth-century line engraving by Juste Chevil-let after a painting by Gerard Terborch.

AMERICAN TRADITION

Since we had a rag-tag navy with no history, we didn't know any English bish-ops, and few of us could recognize any vintage wine, Americans put port tradi-tions in the baggage when we sent the British packing in 1781. The half-centu-ry-old fortified wines of America were free from any restrictions on production and distribution. This, however, may have been a two-edged sword. Most American fortified wines contained brandy to mask the poor flavor and struc-ture of wines made from native grapes, and the high alcohol made them a fa-vorite intoxicating beverage. Ultimately, free-spirited American fortified wine production contributed to the advent of Prohibition as promoted by newspaper-man and politician Chester Rowell, who proclaimed that "There has never been any excuse for fortified wine except as a booze excuse."(Lukacs, 2000, p.96)

There does, however, seem to be one American tradition inherited from the British. That is the myth that fortified wines are served only after a meal with dessert or as an after-meal beverage. The perpetuation of this misconception reached its pinnacle when the federal regulations enacted following Prohibition defined fortified wines (wines in excess of 14 percent alcohol), including port, sherry, Madeira, Marsala, and Angelica, as "dessert" wines. The dessert wine myth persists to this day and is the foremost fallacy precluding consumers' widespread enjoyment of what are arguably America's most versatile wines.

Getting Started

Enjoying American fortified wine starts with opening the bottle. First, a foil cutter makes exposing the cork as simple as a twist of the wrist and results in the removal of the foil below the lip of the bottle. Exposing the cork of bottles sealed with polymer wax is a bit more labor-intensive. While some producers suggest that wax comes off easily with a sharp knife, running the bottle neck under warm water for twenty to thirty seconds often softens the wax, resulting in a smoother, cleaner knife cut.

A hand-operated screw pull or waiters corkscrew are the favored openers, although variations including the inert gas "poppers" and new-fangled electric corkscrews work well. Avoid the infamous wing-type corkscrew and cheap "T" handle corkscrews whose short, thick augers tend to mangle corks, dumping particles into the wine. A good rule of thumb is to use thin-bladed or long, thin-augered openers. Because fortified wines are aged for some time in bottle, cork integrity can decline over time. The two-pronged or "Ah-So" opener works especially well with older, declining corks. Patiently sliding the prongs between the cork and bottle then gently twisting and pulling will remove the cork intact.

Should your opener of choice fail to remove the whole or partial cork, fear not. Just carefully push the remnants of the cork through the bottle into the wine. Hopefully, there is enough head space between the cork and the wine so the wine doesn't splash back through the neck resulting in port stain. Now grab your handy strainer, unbleached coffee filter, piece of muslin, or nylon stocking and gently funnel the port through the filtering material into a thoroughly cleaned bottle or, better yet, your best crystal decanter. The bit of old cork will remain in the filter. Of course, you can pour the wine back into original bottle if all cork residue has been removed.

Interested in a dynamic way open your port? Next time you want to impress your port-loving friends and family, open the port bottle with port tongs. It seems that port tongs were invented sometime around the eighteenth century and were typically used in Europe as a way to bypass an old port bottle's difficult to remove cork. Port tongs work by creating a drastic temperature change in the glass neck of the port bottle that breaks off the upper neck and cork clean and intact. When done correctly, there are no shards of glass and the break has a clean sharp edge.

WARNING! The use of port tongs—while exciting—is not the safest method of opening a port bottle. In fact, using port tongs makes using a saber to open sparkling wine (sabrage) seem downright tame. The tongs are heated until they are red hot, then clamped around the neck of the bottle just above the shoulder for about two minutes. The tongs are then removed and a wet towel is placed where the tongs were. The rapid change in temperature will result in a clean break below the cork.

Thankfully, port tongs come with instructions and it is prudent to follow these instructions closely. You may want to practice before performing you first public *port tongraphy*. To avoid burning down your house, the use of port tongs should be restricted to the outdoors.

Decanting

Decanting American fortified wines is purely optional. Decanting allows the wine, often locked tightly in the bottle, to get a breath of fresh air. Exposing the aged fortified wine to oxygen during decanting provides time for the wine to aerate and "flesh out."

Over the past couple of centuries it was customary to decant ports aged in bottles to remove the sediment that invariably settles in bottle. This sediment, or "dregs" in vintage and "crusted" ports, is really dead yeast cells and some particulate matter from the grapes. Since these ports were not filtered prior to bottling, as the wine aged, this material would precipitate out of wine and form a crust/sediment inside the bottle. If the harmless but intense sediment was not removed, the port would taste like a bad cup of strong coffee, including the grounds.

Standing the bottle upright for a period prior to opening allows the sediment to settle to the bottom of the bottle. When the cork is removed, the decanting process continues by slowly, steadily pouring the wine from the bottle into the decanter until the sediment reaches the neck of the bottle. A flash light or candle focused on the neck will help determine more precisely when the sediment is about to "breach". A firm hand is required to pour one steady stream to prevent the "wave effect" that can cause the sediment to be stirred back into the wine. The neophyte decanter may employ a port funnel, unbleached coffee filter, cheesecloth, or other suitable material to strain out any sediment during the pour. With a little practice, such aides will be canned.

The time needed in the decanter prior to consumption can vary with the age of the fortified wine. Remember that the purpose of decanting is to expose the wine to oxygen to enhance aerobatic flavors and aromas. While Portuguese ports may age thirty to fifty years or more before opening, few American fortified wines achieve that longevity. Most American port-style wines average ten years or fewer and need less time to blossom. A safe range in decanter is one to two hours before drinking. A pleasant way to monitor the decanter development of your fortified wine is take a "sample" sip every fifteen to thirty minutes. Just make sure you have enough wine left in the decanter to serve.

A few thoughts about decanters: Choose a decanter with the same care you use choosing stemware. Decanters come in a myriad of sizes and shapes, from round, smooth, clear decanters, to exotic, heavy, fluted crystal antiques. Whichever version you choose, the decanter should display the rich color of your wine. However, colored or excessively decorated decanters can distort the wine's true appearance.

Store your decanter in an enclosed cupboard or display case free from dust and odors. Prior to use, rinse the decanter with mineral or distilled water to avoid any chlorine influence from tap water. After each use, clean the decanter by swirling the inside with a mixture of ice and coarse salt. Avoid the use of soaps or detergents that could leave a film or residue inside your decanter. Allow the decanter to thoroughly air dry before storage or reuse.

Earlier, it was stated that decanting American fortified wine was optional, but what indeed are the options? Perhaps the most popular and efficient option is to pop the cork, let the bottle sit open for fifteen minutes, then "pass the port." A slight variation would be to open the bottle and pour an ounce or two in a glass, leaving more space in the bottle to let air react with the wine. After ten to fifteen minutes, drink the wine you poured and serve from the bottle.

Another approach to "quick decanting" is to double decant. Open the bottle and carefully pour the wine into a clean bottle (using an appropriate filter if needed), then pour the second bottle into the original decanter. This double pour exposes the wine to air much like racking wines in barrel.

If opening a bottle of fortified wine is a spur of the moment thought, a new-fangled gadget called a "vinturi wine aerator" is a speedy alternative to decanting. After opening, this devise is placed on the neck of the bottle. As the wine flows through the devise, a small open tube creates a venture effect that sucks air into the wine as it flows into the glass. Proponents of this apparatus suggest that passing the wine through the aerator is equal to about twenty minutes of open-bottle breathing.

Size and Intended Consumption

American fortified wines come in 375, 500, and 750 milliliter bottles. Often, four fortified wine drinkers will consume a 375 ml bottle at one sitting. The sight of 375 milliliters of a bright fortified wine in a 750 ml or larger decanter may appear oddly overwhelming. In such situations, pouring directly from a nicely proportioned bottle may be a better choice. On the other hand, consuming a 750 ml bottle of fortified wine may be too much for one sitting. Pouring the desired measure from a beautiful decanter and knowing you can keep your precious wine for up to a couple of weeks in the stoppered decanter can be quite satisfying. Be sure, however, to keep your decanter in a cool environment out of the light.

The Right Glass

Let's dispel a traditional myth here and now. There is no single "right" glass for fortified wines. Perhaps from the foggy past of our distant relationship with Great Britain, Americans inherited the myth that fortified wines should only be served in special, small stemware with a capacity of about 2.5 to 3 ounces. As a result, we have developed a 2-ounce portion as the standard pour for a glass of fortified wine.

Balderdash! Let's apply a little critical thinking to this issue. Color and aroma are two of the three most appealing characteristics of fortified wines. Appreciation of color requires sufficient viewing area—in this case, the glass—to allow light to interact with pigments in the wine and produce the alluring distinctiveness of port-style, sherry-style, Madeira, and Angelica colors. Port-style vintners are particularly aware of the importance of color and strive to produce wines that realize consumer's color expectations. The tiny glasses rarely have sufficient viewing area to allow for full appreciation of the vivid color of fortified wines. If dry table wines are exposed to light in large glasses to appreciate color, why shouldn't fortified wine color be appreciated in a like manner?

Moving on to aroma, Frenchman Jean Lenoir proved that twelve aromas predominated in port. These aromas are coffee, caramel, blackcurrant, cherry, oak, chocolate or cocoa, raspberry, walnut, plum, liquorice, vanilla, and violet. He goes on to say that the coffee, chocolate, and cinnamon elements in port come from the brandy and from the toasted oak in casks and barrels. That is a lot of interrelated smells just waiting to be released for the pleasure of the wine drinker. Sherry, Madeira, Angelica, and Vermouth have unique combinations of aromas that define their distinctiveness as fortified wines.

Aromas are volatile and nonvolatile organic compounds originating in the skins and pulp of grapes that undergo chemical reactions during fermentation. In addition, odors derived from elements in the winemaking process, such as yeasts, brandy or wine spirits, and aging, what we term bouquet, contributes to the overall aroma of the wine. When exposed to air, these aromatic compounds are vaporized and the nose is filled with a variety of stimuli we relate to a specific type or style of wine.

A glass that is too small to permit sufficient air to react with the wine and release the complex aromatic compounds stifles the ability of fortified wines to fully express themselves. These wines need space to breathe and achieve aromatic balance. Like other wines, fortified wines like to be swirled to get more air-wine interaction. Swirling and sniffing 2 ounces of fortified wine in a 2.5 ounce glass can get pretty messy and detract from the whole experience. Think about this; if brandy—a major component of fortified wines—is served in a large-bowled "snifter" where it can be easily "swirled and sniffed," why do we served fortified wines in tiny, narrow-mouth glasses?

The galaxy of wine glass shapes with the tiny "Vintage" Port glass to the extreme right.

A nonscientific examination of the effects of glass size on consumer perception indicates that the "best" fortified wine glass is a clean, clear vessel that provides you, the drinker, the most satisfying experience. This experience usually involves the full appreciation of the complex aromas and flavors that result from the wine's interaction with air. Therefore, the glass should provide sufficient space for the fortified wine to fully express those wonderful aromas and glorious favors.

A typical white wine glass of 6 or more ounces is great as a fortified wine glass, as is a larger-capacity, rounder bowl red wine. Customarily, wine is poured from one-third to one-half the glass capacity. Consequently, the "traditional" 2-ounce pour of fortified wine in a 6-ounce white wine glass provides for a more rewarding, less messy "swirl and sip." But why only pour two ounces at a time? Larger-capacity red wine glasses afford more wine for a longer, more pleasing experience without have to "pass the port" or other fortified wine.

Please don't take the discussion of fortified wine glasses to mean you should immediately take your expensive set of crystal dessert wine glasses to the nearest Goodwill; quite the contrary! As we have said, the best glass is the one that gives you the most fortified wine drinking pleasure. If that means the petite sipping glasses, by all means, enjoy.

A quick word about "port sippers." These unique glass bowls with a straw-like sipping tube can be interesting and fun, but do nothing to enhance the flavors or aromas of the wine. The bowl is too small to allow much air to react with wine, thus muting the complex aromatics. However, "sippers" can be an innovative way to introduce fortified wines as a fresh wine experience.

FOOD AND AMERICAN FORTIFIED WINE

Fortified wines may well be America's most versatile wine type. This claim is supported by the 250 years of drinking American fortified wine when little else was available. From the British colonies, to the rugged gold fields of the early west, to Prohibition, Americans have washed down their meals or sat beside their fires with a cup or glass of fortified wine. There were no elaborate "food and wine" pairings in those feral days of the developing nation where one ate and drank what was available and affordable. Fortified wine went with every food and quality was in the eye of the beholder.

The myth that fortified wines are "dessert" wines is a product of the Repeal of Prohibition. While it is true that fortified wines were customarily served *after* a complete meal, these sweet, higher alcohol wines were enjoyed before and during meals as well. Since fortified wines were specifically named as a need for Prohibition, it made sense from a political perspective that fortified wines would be penalized in a post-Prohibition America. As a result, Repeal regulations drafted in 1933 arbitrarily established a "dessert wine" classification for grape wines with an alcoholic content in excess of 14 percent but not in excess of 24 percent by volume and having the taste, aroma, and characteristics generally attributed to sherry, port, angelica, and Madeira.

America was in the throes of the Great Depression when Prohibition ended and the government was desperately searching for funds. Taxing alcohol was an obvious source of new revenue. As fortified wines were the majority of American wines following Repeal, lawmakers set a significantly higher tax on so-called dessert wines with alcohol content above 14 percent. In those days, it was unlikely that winemakers could produce unfortified wines that would reach that alcohol level. This proved to be the case until the late 1990s when warm-climate, dry red wines in excess of 14 percent alcohol became fashionable. Today, the federal tax is $1.05 per gallon for wines under 14 percent and $1.57 per gallon for **any** wine over 14 percent. The bottom line? The classification "dessert wine" was created by post-Prohibition federal regulation as a source of tax revenue rather than as a legitimate classification of a wine that was served mainly with desserts.

If not dessert, then what foods are best suited for pairing with America's fortified wines? The answer—all or none. Granted, this may seem like a sweeping contradictory claim, but in truth, it is an affirmation of the versatility of fortified wine.

To help us understand why we can enjoy American fortified wine with practically any food, any time, and for any occasion, we turn to one of the world's leading experts on wine and food, Tim Hanni. A master of wine, and both a professional chef and certified wine educator, Tim is internationally renowned as the "flavor maven." Tim has long been a campaigner for drinking wines you enjoy and not necessarily the wines you are *supposed* to enjoy. In his recent book, *Why You Like the Wines You Like—Changing the Way the World Thinks About Wine*, Tim contends that personal wine preferences are determined by a combination of individual sensory sensitivity and the memories and expectations you have developed through learning, life experiences, cultural or society values, and the like.

Tim advocates a New Wine Fundamental—you should be able to drink your favorite wines with any meal. According to Hanni, the fashionable but passé "metaphorical matching of food and wine weights is based on personal experience, subjective and mostly in the head. The more emotionally you are tied to a wine and food match, the more likely the imaginary wine and food matches you conjure up will work together—a self-fulfilling prophecy" (Hanni 2013, p.25). Here are some of Tim's wine and food principles.

- Match the wine with the diner, not the dinner.
- Drink wines in a flavor or style category you have some capacity to like.
- The more emotionally tied a food and wine match, the more likely it will work.
- Bitterness in wines can be mitigated by "flavor balancing" food with tiny additions of salt or lemon.

To learn more about Tim Hanni's novel approach to understanding personal wine preferences, visit www.timhanni.com/.

If conventional wisdom is that fortified wines are only dessert wines, why is it, as Tim Hanni (also a culinary historian) points out, that "in France fortified wines have been traditionally enjoyed before, and during, the meal. This is a tradition that continues today with France being the leading market for fortified Port wines in the world" (Hanni, 2013, p138).

The time has come for a new wine paradigm: American fortified wines can be enjoyed with or without meals—*anytime, anywhere!*

Before the Meal

An aperitif is simply an alcoholic beverage drunk before a meal. American fortified wines of all types make terrific aperitifs. Whether it is a port-style, sherry-style, Madeira-style, or Vermouth, fortified wine straight up or with a favourite mixer is pleasing way to begin a meal. A glass of chilled white or ruby port-style wine is a great opener, particularly outside on a pleasantly warm day or evening.

Fortified wines are the foundation for some great wine-based cocktails. For a delightful change of pace, mix your favorite port-style wine with equal parts club soda or tonic water and a twist of lemon. Enjoy on or off the rocks. A personal favorite is a fifty-fifty mix of sherry-style wine with ginger ale, ice, and a few drips of fresh lemon juice. Texan Raymond Haak (Haak Winery and Vineyards) recommends triple berry red port sangria as a delicious refresher. Some red port-style wine, local blackberries, raspberries, strawberries, passion-fruit juice, lemonade, and sprite is a hit in the southwest. Another cocktail idea is fill a flute with half port-style wine and half sparkling wine. Just think, bubbles in port!

Of course, Vermouth is the king of fortified wine cocktails. Mixed with a variety of liquors and fruit juices, there is practically no limit to exotic Vermouth creations. A sampling of some of the more popular Vermouth cocktails can be found at www.quadywinery.com.

How about a snack with your favorite American fortified wine? Cheese-based dips or balls are great with port-style wines. Often these concoctions will include a splash or two of the port you will be enjoying with them. Serve with baguette breads or slightly salty crackers. Why not try a port-style wine with potato chips or corn chips and fruit salsa. Bet you can't eat just one.

Main Course Entrees

The extraordinary versatility of American fortified wines may best be displayed when served with and incorporated into main course entrees. Whether meat, fish, fowl, or vegetable dishes, in the words of young Texas chef Tyler Henderson, "the versatility of fortified wines is really limitless."

Fortified wine is to the culinary world what a utility infielder is to baseball. He may not be the star, but he can do just about anything to help the team be successful. Similarly, fortified wine can be key contributors to a vast array of successful soups, sauces, glazes, and marinades.

"Savory" is a term often associated with foods paired with fortified wines. Savory foods are often classified as fare and not inherently sweet, therefore indicative of spicy or tart flavors. Generally, meat and vegetables are considered savory, as are most hors d'oeuvres and even snack foods. Food prepared with minimal sugar and little or no sugary flavor are considered savory. However, people tend to like different flavors in foods so we enjoy both savory and sweet foods since they often complement each other during a meal.

Fortified wines can often be the link between savory and sweet. This connection is frequently achieved when incorporating a fortified wine reduction sauce for meat, poultry, and vegetables dishes. Wine reduction is accomplished by slowly boiling a wine to half its original volume resulting in a thicker, more intensively flavored liquid. In the case of fortified wines, the high alcohol is boiled off leaving a sweet, slightly thickened "sauce" with intense flavors of the wine's grape variety. Often, savory ingredients such as carrots, onions, celery, garlic, and bay leaves are incorporated to enhance the savory/sweet combination. Try a port-style wine instead of red wine to get a very pleasant slightly sweet note in red pasta sauce. Here are some suggestions for exciting fortified wine–enhanced dishes.

Meat
- Roasted Leg of Lamb
- Grilled Tri-tip
- Grilled Steak
- Sausage
- Pork Roast or Shoulder
- Pork Tenderloin
- Braised Brisket
- Meat Ragout

Poultry
- Roasted Chicken and Duck
- Duck and Chicken Breast
- Roasted Cornish Game Hens

Fish
- Baked White Fish (Turbot, Halibut, etc.)
- Salmon with a Port Glaze

Vegetables
- Grilled Mixed Vegetables
- Roasted Root Vegetables

Port-style fortified wines are excellent as a starting ingredient for marinades. An all-purpose red meat marinade would include olive oil, onion, garlic, fresh herbs, a touch lemon or lime juice, and of course, a healthy dose of your favorite American port-style wine.

Gravy is made from combining either corn starch or flour with the pan drippings that contain fat and other savory juices left over from roasting meat. Browning two tablespoons of drippings with two tablespoons of flour in a pan over medium heat until smooth, then whisking in a bit more drippings with a fortified wine will yield a couple of cups of incredibly flavored gravy for meat, potatoes, and vegetables. Add butter, cream, or milk with the wine to get a cream gravy or sauce. Season with salt, pepper, and a touch your favorite herb for a sensational finish.

Almost any soup can benefit from a splash of American fortified wine. A bit of dark wine in dark soups like vegetable beef or a dollop of white port or sherry-style wine in a creamy soup will add a nice touch of flavor.

A well-accepted culinary maxim is to never cook with wine you wouldn't drink. Therefore, if you cook with a fortified wine, why wouldn't you drink it with your meal? It only makes sense that if you enjoy an American fortified wine as an ingredient in your cooking, you would enjoy that same wine with your meal. The old adage "one for the pot and one for the cook" is an appropriate fortified wine and food pairing.

Fortified wines are a fascinating accompaniment to spicy Asian and Latin cuisines. The sweetness of fortified wines can, depending on individual sensitivity, temper the hot burning effect (chemesthesis) of dishes like chili or kung pao chicken. However, if the burn of chemesthesis is your thing, stick to beer.

A great aspect of enjoying fortified wine with food is an inquisitive sense of adventure. In reality, American fortified wines can be enjoyed with practically any cuisine. There are literally thousands of fortified wine recipes and pairing ideas available on the internet. Be adventurous—go for it!

Desserts

American fortified wines and desserts go together in two complementary ways, both in desserts and with desserts. These two approaches are actually enhanced by combining both and having a glass of fortified wine with a "kicked-up" dessert made with a port, sherry, or Madeira-style wine.

Port- and Madeira-style fortified wines can be incorporated into a variety of baked desserts including brownies, chocolate cake, cookies, and various fruit cobblers. For fresh pears poached in port-style wine with a little nutmeg and cinnamon, the pears are steamed in the port with a lid on. The cooked pears are removed and the port is reduced to syrup, then spooned over the pears. A favorite dessert of the author is fresh peaches, pears, or apples sautéed in port-style wine and served over ice cream. Speaking of ice cream, just pouring a bit of fortified wine over ice cream or incorporating a little fortified wine in a homemade ice cream or milkshake really perks up a dessert affair. There are no limits to dessert creativity, especially considering the versatility of America's fortified wines.

A culinary axiom is to not serve a dessert sweeter that the wine. Since American fortified wines have a range of sweetness, they can be enjoyed with a practically endless array of desserts. Of course, the overwhelming favorite is port-style wine and anything chocolate. From truffles to cake, brownies to chocolate chip cookies, and chocolate mousse to fudge sundaes, the sweetness and aromas of port-style wines enhance the flavors of both the dessert and the wine. A definite approach to wine and chocolate is to pair lighter chocolates with lighter port-style wines and darker chocolate with heavier, darker port-style wines.

Fresh berries and tropical fruit desserts match beautifully with American fortified wine. The dark berry notes of varietal port-style wines like Zinfandel, Merlot, Cabernet Sauvignon, and Barbera complement the freshness of the berries while the alcohol tempers any acids and bitterness in the fruit. When served with fresh fruit cobblers or crisps, port, sherry, and Madeira-style wines create a lively conversation between the flavors (and the consumers). Tawny port-style wines may evolve a note of tropical fruit that balances nicely with egg-based desserts such as flan or bread pudding. How about port-style with pumpkin pie—delicious!

Nuts make an interesting and unique match with American fortified wines. Hazelnuts, almonds, and walnuts are particularly good companions to sherry-style wines. Cocoa-dusted almonds or chocolate-covered pecans are a tasty post-meal treat with port or Madeira-style wines or Angelica. Fortified wines are a consistently pleasant escort for most nutty desserts.

There may be no better way to enjoy an American fortified wine than with fresh fruit. Desserts based on strawberries, raspberries, cherries, currants, and full-flavored fruits, are a natural partner with American port-style wines. Try some spice grapes served with a platter of cheeses and nuts and a glass of port-style wine or Angelica.

Cheese

The classic fortified wine combination is port and cheese. This duo most likely predates our nation and is an institution in gastronomic circles to this day. Specific port and cheese pairing have evolved based on traditional European styles of port (ruby, tawny, vintage, late bottled, etc.) that merge seamlessly with European styles of cheese. Since American port-style wines tend not to neatly fit a specific European port style, we can be a bit more liberal in our approach to wine and cheese combinations. We acknowledge that most port-style wines go well with savory foods, and we know that cheese is a savory fare, so a few easy to follow guidelines should suffice to ensure a scrumptious, satisfying cheese and fortified wine experience.

Consider the assertiveness of the cheese and weight of the fortified wine. Is the cheese pungent, salty, or sweet? Look at the texture of the cheese—is it hard, soft, or creamy in texture? The idea is to balance the flavors, aromas, and texture of the fortified wine to the taste , aromas, and texture of the cheese.

Ruby-type port-style wines tend to be a bit lighter in color with a somewhat fresher fruity character that combines effortlessly with robust blue-veined cheeses like Stilton, Roquefort, and Gorgonzola. Port-style wines with higher residual sugar and succulent fruit flavors pair nicely with milder, less-assertive cheeses like Mild Cheddar or Colby Jack.

Tawny-type port-style wines are predisposed to a darker, brownish color with a nose of caramel and complex anise, licorice, blackcurrant, blackberries, and plum flavors. They tend have a mellow, subtle balance of sweetness and alcohol with firm structure and lighter, nuttier finish. The port-style wines can be served chilled with dry, hard, salty cheeses like aged Goat Cheese, Parmesan, and Gouda that balance the sweetness of the wine. More mature tawny-type wines go nicely with Double Gloucester, Berkswell, or Comte.

A word of caution; Brie or Camembert with their soft, creamy textures, are not ideal cheeses for port-style wines as they are too mild and sweet. Velveeta and Cheese Wiz are best left to pair with macaroni and crackers.

While the emphasis has been on port-style American fortified wines, the principles of matching wine and cheese texture and taste apply to sherry-style wines and Angelica as well. The unique nutty character of sherry-style wines make them highly successful matches to a variety of cheese and nut combinations. Remember Tim Hanni's mantra to match the wine to the diner and drink your favorite American fortified wine with whatever dessert you like.

Cigars and Port-style
Although it is difficult to pinpoint the origin of the port-cigar marriage, it seems that the Spanish and Portuguese were smoking the plant leaves discovered during Columbus's journey to the new world at about the same time brandy was added to the wines of the upper Douro. Apparently, it was the British upper class that popularized the habit of enjoying a post-meal cigar with a glass port in the mid-nineteenth century. This fashion caught on in America after the Civil War and became a symbol of wealth and status. It has been said that port and cigars pair well with pretension and old money.

The allure of this combination—which some describe as elegant, others as decadent—is the intense favors contributed by both the tobacco and the wine. Many of the distinctive yet pleasant aromas and flavors experienced in port-style fortified wines are found in cigars. For example, cigar's spicy maduro (dark-brown leaf) wrapper balances the port-style sweetness, providing a satisfying flavor equilibrium.

Tawny-type port-style wines have almond and other nutty flavors that tend to highlight the earthiness of the cigar. Less expensive or younger cigars can sometimes be harsh with off-balance flavors. The sweetness of a ruby-type port-style wine can mask the flaws of these cigars while relaxing the spice. As most American port-style wines mature, they cultivate more complexity and depth, just as a good cigar develops more complexity and mildness with age.

For the past several decades, the health risks of smoking tobacco products have been thoroughly publicized throughout the land. However, these dire warnings of impending doom don't seem to have fazed many of the dedicated men and women who enjoy the elegance and sophistication of a fine cigar and stylish glass of American port-style wine.

In Closing

Perhaps the most significant misconception regarding fortified wines is that once opened, they keep indefinitely. This mistaken belief is based on the (correct) premise that fortified wines don't go "bad" and become vinegar. This is because the high alcohol of fortified wines kill the acetic acid bacteria that causes regular table wines to turn to vinegar when exposed to air.

How long a fortified wine lasts after opening is fundamentally an issue of chemistry and perception. Ideally, an opened bottle of American fortified wine should last as long as the meal. However, there are occasions when the circumstances require stoppering a partial bottle or decanter of fortified wine for later enjoyment. Therefore, whether the saved wine's color and aromas will be the same as the newly opened wine is subject to a number of variables including sugar and alcohol levels, tannic (phenolic) structure, storage conditions, and time.

Oxidation is the common vector driving changes in organic compounds such as those found in both fortified and table wines. As fortified wines are crafted with some degree of oxidation prior to being sealed in bottles, the aging process involves little oxidative reaction. However, when opened and exposed to air, oxidation resumes, modifying key chemical components in the wine. Granted, sugar and alcohol levels moderate these oxidative changes, lengthening the amount of time before sensory perception is affected.

The post-opening longevity of American fortified-style wines depends somewhat of the type of fortified wine. Generally, darker, aged, tawny-type port-style wines will retain color and flavor character longer than younger, ruby-type wines. It is best to drink port-style fortified wines within three days to two weeks after opening. Usually, after a month or more, opened fortified wines will begin to change perceptually and may not have the same character as when the wine was first opened. Drier sherries should be consumed within a few days, while cream sherries will last much longer, usually a couple of months or so. Madeira and Angelica longevity parallels that of American port-style wines.

To minimize the perceptual changes in American fortified wines, opened bottles or decanted wines should be tightly stoppered and placed in the refrigerator. A spritz or two of inert nitrogen gas prior to stoppering will provide a surface barrier to air and minimize further oxidation. Some suggest that if the changes in a fortified make it undesirable to drink, the wine should be used in cooking. There is probably an acceptable end for that last bit of wine, but remember our old axiom: don't cook with wine you wouldn't drink.

That's it! The versatility of America's fortified wines is no longer a mysterious secret.

AMERICAN FORTIFIED WINE INDUSTRY: STATE OF THE ART

AMERICAN FORTIFIED WINE INDUSTRY PROFILE

Some sixty years ago, 70 percent of the wine produced by America's 300 vintners was sweet and most often fortified. Today, according to information gathered by the Sweet and Fortified Wine Association, over one thousand American vintners make approximately 12 million gallons of "dessert" wine, or 2.5 percent of all American wine production. The vast majority (78 percent) of American fortified wine is red port style, while white port-style wines account for 11 percent of production. Sherry-style wines account for 7 percent of America's fortified wine, while Angelica, Madeira, Marsala, and Vermouth make up a meager 4 percent of total production.

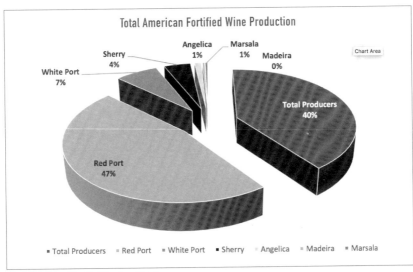

(Source: Sweet and Fortified Wine Association)

Dessert wines made up 8.6 percent of total US wine sales in 2014. This number appears to have remained fairly constant over the past decade and is consistent with California dessert wine shipments made over the same period. What we don't know is specifically how much of total sales are made by American producers, nor do we know the specific types and styles of dessert wines sold.

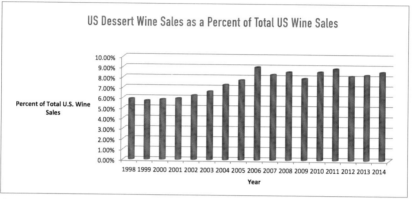

(Source: Wine Institute, Department of Commerce.)

The question is, what happened in the last sixty years to cause such a dramatic shift in fortified (dessert) wine consumption? Like most probing questions about societal change, there is no simple answer. A combination of fact and fiction has conspired over the past six decades to influence wine consumer tastes.

Perhaps the most important influence on the transition from sweet fortified wine drinking to dry wine drinking was the rapid postwar increase in American affluence. More people had money to spend on luxuries, including fine European wines. This new affluence corresponded to the "jet age," which made travel to the wine regions in France, Spain, Italy, Germany, and Portugal quick and relatively easy. Increased affluence also meant that American's could indulge in more sophisticated European culinary styles accompanied by specifically paired wines.

America's wine producers recognized the transitional trend in the early 1960s and began to extensively advertise their dry wines. Almaden, Italian Swiss Colony, and Paul Masson employed a number of advertising gimmicks, including the "Little Old Winemaker" and "No Wine Before It's Time," to promote fashionable dry wines. In 1966 Gallo Hearty Burgundy made from Napa- and Sonoma-grown Petite Sirah was America's number-one selling wine.

The success of America's new line of stylish dry wines spurred a new generation of winemakers, particularly in California. Armed with scientific methodology as taught by University of California, Davis and California State University, Fresno, as well as advanced winemaking technology, young, energetic, innovative vintners took over the sagging California wine industry. These "new world" winemakers of the 1970s and '80s focused on producing sophisticated dry wines made from classic European grape varieties grown in the north coast region of the Golden State.

While America's new affluence was clearly a major factor, the admittedly poor quality of postwar American wine was doubtlessly of equal influence to the decline in fortified wine consumption. Americans in the 1950s and early '60s preferred sweet, often fortified, wine to the harsh, bulk-style wines made from inferior grape varieties grown in the vast vineyards of Central Valley and sold in jugs (hence the name "jug wine"). Perhaps the lowest point in American wine history was the decade between 1955 and 1965 when federal regulations allowed "special natural wine"—wines to which various flavors had been added. Poor-quality spirits were frequently added to these fruit wines to increase the alcohol content, making them "fortified" wines. Large vintners across the nation jumped on this bandwagon as these cheap, sweet, fortified wines flooded the urban areas of the nation. These wines frequently found their way to the lower economic reaches of cities and towns and into the hands of the less fortunate and often addicted populations. Thus were the origins of many popular myths regarding American fortified wine.

FIVE AMERICAN FORTIFIED WINE MYTHS

American Fortified Wines Are Poor Imitations of "Real" European Port and Sherry

Contrary to popular belief, port and sherry are fortified wine styles—not places on a map of Portugal or Spain. While the style originated in these Iberian countries, a small cabal of British producers successfully perpetrated the myth that "real" port and sherry can only be made from native Portuguese and Spanish grape varieties and produced in specific geographical locations using age-old traditional methods.

In reality, these European fortified wines are made by blending brandy during fermentation to retain a degree of sweetness and increase alcohol, just like the fortified wines made in the United States. Granted, aging regimes and product terminology may differ somewhat, but American vintners don't want to imitate European fortified wines. Today, American vintners make port- and sherry-style wines from domestically grown traditional Portuguese and Spanish grape varieties, as well as other classic and hybrid varieties, using methods that result in uniquely American fortified wine—not "knockoff" imitations.

American Fortified Wines Are Cheap, High-Alcohol Wines Favored by "Winos"

Unfortunately, this myth has a basis of truth fostered by the reality of the 1950s American wine industry. Some larger producers made flavored fortified wines that were cheap to make and cheap to buy. A significant portion of these products were consumed by urban populations whose extreme examples were viewed by the public as "winos" drinking cheap port out of a brown paper bag. Even though it has been half a century since this image of American fortified wine emerged, the myth persists, albeit to a lesser degree today. To dispel this myth, we need to address the issues of high alcohol and cheapness.

To begin, most of these 1950s wines were not fortified in the traditional sense. Wine spirits were added to sweet, low-alcohol, still wines after fermentation, bringing the alcohol levels to between 13 percent and 20 percent. Vast quantities of these fruit and "fortified" wine concoctions were produced, and a sort of economy–of–scale made them affordable for everyone. While some of these inexpensive products are still with us, they are not representative of today's American fortified wine enterprise.

Contemporary American fortified wine alcohol levels most often range between 16 percent and 18 percent. These levels are not significantly higher than many highly touted domestic unfortified red table wines with alcohol levels regularly between 14 percent and 16 percent. In addition, unfortified so-called late-harvest red and white wines commonly have alcohol levels in the 14 percent to 20 percent range. Ice wines made from grapes left to freeze on the vine, as well as sweet dessert wines made from grapes infected by the noble rot of botrytis, often have alcohol levels in excess of 20 percent. Therefore, in light of the alcohol levels found in highly acclaimed table and dessert wines, the alcohol intensity of today's domestic fortified wines is not abnormal.

Now, let's examine the issue of "cheapness" related to American fortified wine. Earlier in this chapter we saw that over one thousand American fortified wine producers make around 12 million gallons of fortified wine. According to data compiled by the Sweet and Fortified Wine Association (in an unpublished study done by the association in 2015), the average retail price of American red port-style wine is 5.1 cents per milliliter, or $38.50 for a 750 milliliter bottle. The data also shows the average retail price of American white port-style wine to be 5.3 cents per milliliter or about $39.50 a 750 milliliter bottle. These price averages exclude the "brown bag" fortified flavored wines that typically sell for $3 to $5 a bottle.

(Source: Sweet and Fortified Wine Association.)

While today's American fortified wines are definitely not cheap, their retail prices reflect vintners' commitment to quality standards found in most domestic fine table wines. American vintners often showcase limited-production fortified wines to express their devotion to the art and craft of winemaking. Limited-production fortified wines are expensive to make and most are truly handcrafted. Superior quality grapes, high-end brandy or wine spirits, longer aging periods, and custom bottles and labels all contribute to lofty production costs. There is nothing "cheap" about these world-class American fortified wines.

Fortified Wines Are Just Served After an Evening Meal or With Dessert

There is certainly no argument that American fortified wines are great with chocolate fudge cake dessert or after-dinner Stilton cheese. But, as we saw in Chapter 3, American fortified wines are an "anytime, anywhere" pleasure. The versatility of fortified wines is practically limitless.

Whether chilled or featured in creative cocktails, port- and sherry-style wines, as well as vermouth, make perfect before-meal aperitifs. The incorporation of fortified wines enhances the flavors of soups, sauces, and marinades. Fortified wines liven up even the simplest snacks like mixed nuts, cheese dip, and even potato chips. Served with savory meat, fish, fowl, and vegetable dishes, the unique flavors, aromas, and texture of fortified wines invigorate practically any dining experience. Of course, fortified wine and chocolate desserts are a perfect match, but remember that fruit cobbler, fresh berries, and pumpkin pie go great with a glass of American port-style. Fortified wines may well be America's most versatile beverage.

Fortified Wines Last a Long Time After Opening

There is a kernel of truth to this notion, but in a broad sense, it remains a myth. Fortified wines don't "go bad" in the traditional concept of turning to vinegar. The higher alcohol content of fortified wines inhibits the development of acetic acid bacteria that turn table wines to vinegar with prolonged exposure to air. However, as we saw in Chapter 2, oxidation does drive changes in the complex organic chemistry in fortified wines, which can affect sensory perceptions over time. The fortified wine you first enjoyed when the bottle was opened may not have the same flavors and aromas after months of sitting in a decanter.

American producers make it convenient to enjoy fortified wines when fresh and lively. For those enjoying a glass every couple of days, a 375 milliliter bottle will provide about twelve 2-ounce portions—maybe enough for a week or so. More frequent fortified-wine lovers will find the 500 or 750 milliliter bottles a more convenient option. Whatever your particular pleasure, American fortified wines are best enjoyed within three days to two weeks after opening.

Port Wine Causes Gout—the "Rich Man's Disease"

This urban myth dates to the eighteenth and nineteenth centuries when it was widely believed that drinking port caused gout, an extremely painful flair-up in the innermost joint of the big toe. Because the disease mostly effected upper class sedentary men in their forties and fifties, gout became known as the "rich man's disease". Modern medical science has determined that gout is a form of arthritis caused by excess uric acid in the body and port has been acquitted as the villain.

Origin of the gout, Henry William Bunbury, artist, 1750–1811. The perceived origins of gout may be tied more to the liquor on the table than to the localized work of the devil. (Image courtesy of the National Library of Medicine.)

On a more serious note, a number of medical studies (Nordqvist, Wine: Health Benefits and Health Risks, 2016, medicalnewstoday.com/articles/265635.php) since CBS aired the "French Paradox" on *60 Minutes* in 1990, tend to support the potential health benefits of "moderate" wine consumption (Nordquist, 2016). Ethyl alcohol (ethanol) is the major medically active component of wine, including fortified wines. In addition, wine contains a variety of polyphenolic compounds that are not appreciably found in other alcoholic beverages. One of these phenolic compounds found in grape skins is resveratrol. This compound appears to be a powerful antioxidant with the potential for long-term health benefits. Antioxidant compounds neutralize detrimental oxidative chemical reactions in the body. It appears that antioxidants significantly reduce cardiac risk by preventing the oxidation of LDL or "bad" cholesterol. There is also evidence that antioxidants play a role in cancer protection, and speculation, based on preliminary indications, that the antioxidants in red wine have positive effects on inflammation, lung cancer, cataracts, and the common cold.

A final word on fortified wine and health. There seems to be no information available on how resveratrol is affected by adding wine spirits to red wines (fortification). Since red wine production involves extensive contact between skins and juice, a significantly higher level of resveratrol is extracted into red wines than white wines. Therefore, moderate consumption of red wine will have a higher potential for health benefits than moderate consumption of white wine.

Moderate consumption is based on medical studies involving the liver's ability to metabolize alcohol that suggests 14 ounces of table wine is the safe daily "moderate" consumption level for men. For a number of reasons involving digestive physiology, women's safe or "moderate" consumption level is about half that of men. Remember that fortified wines tend to have about 4 percent more alcohol per serving, so moderate consumption may need to be adjusted depending on a number of variables including body size, gender, habits, medication, and food-influenced alcohol tolerance.

CHALLENGES FACING AMERICAN FORTIFIED WINES

Fortified wines have been at the center of many of the challenges faced, and overcome, by American vintners over the past three centuries. Perhaps the greatest challenge was Prohibition and the crazy quilt of laws and regulations resulting from the Repeal of Prohibition. Chester Rowell's pre-Prohibition battle cry proclaiming "There has never been any excuse for fortified wine except as a booze excuse" set the stage for many of the challenges confronting fortified wine producers today.

The twenty-first century has brought a whole new array of challenges to the American fortified wine industry. International trade, limitations on so-called "semi-generic place names," the internet and direct to consumer marketing, neo-Prohibitionism, and consumer perception are among the most prominent of issues affecting the future of American fortified wines.

Laws and Regulations
As devastating as Prohibition was to the American wine industry, the complex and often confusing web of laws and regulations resulting from Repeal has had a more profound, long-term effect on American vintners. While the Twenty-first Amendment repealed national prohibition, the law reaffirmed the right of each state to regulate the distribution and sale of alcoholic beverages within its boundaries. As a result, vintners not only have to comply with federal regulations on wine production and distribution, but must be conscious of the laws and regulations in each state and individual jurisdiction within the state.

Issues regarding federal wine regulations become even more intricate when considering the arbitrary 14 percent alcohol content threshold and fortified wine. Sometime in the mid-1930s, the Alcohol Tax Unit established in the Treasury Department to regulate post-Prohibition alcohol taxes set 14 percent alcohol content by volume to distinguish between "table wines" and "dessert wines." These arbitrary designations established a significant corresponding tax differentiation. History suggests that this figure was established because only fortified wine contained distilled spirits with alcohol content above 14 percent and therefore should taxed at a higher rate than lower alcohol wines. Over the past eighty years, the Alcohol Tax Unit has been called the Bureau of Alcohol, Tobacco, and Firearms (ATF), and then today's Alcohol and Tobacco Tax and

Trade (TTB) as a result of the Homeland Security Act of 2002. But the 14 percent boundary and the table-dessert wine distinction remains. Current federal wine excise tax rates are $1.07 per gallon for table wines and $1.57 for dessert wines.

Wine labeling is a second area where the capricious regulations dating from the 1930s continue to haunt fortified wine producers. All wine labels require TTB approval and must display certain information regarding alcohol content, vintage, grape sources, and production location as well as mandatory health warnings. However, fortified wine producers are prohibited from using the terms "fortified" or "brandy/wine spirits added" on fortified wine labels. According to Regulation 27 CFR Part 4, Section 4.39(a)(7): "containers of wine, or any label on such containers, or any individual covering, carton, or other wrapper of such container, or any written, printed, graphic, or other matter accompanying such container to the consumer shall not contain any statement, design, device, or representation which tends to create the impression that a wine contains distilled spirits." (Federal Regulation 27 CFR Part 4, Section 4.39(a)(7) in TTB.gov)

Use of the term "fortified wine" was included in the standards of identity for wine in the early version of the Federal Alcohol Administration Act that established the first wine labeling and advertising regulations following the Repeal of Prohibition. The term "fortified wine" was removed by amendment to the act in 1938. Fortified wine producers contend that not permitting labels to fully disclose the contents of a bottle of wine through use of the terms "fortified" or "grape spirits added" on labels can mislead consumers and affect purchasing decisions. TTB argues that "fortified" cannot be used as a wine descriptor since the term "fortified" has a meaning for consumers under the Food and Drug Administration regulations dealing with foods with added vitamins, minerals, or protein. This is a specious argument, however, since Merriam-Webster defines a "fortified wine" as "a wine (as sherry) to which alcohol usually in the form of grape brandy has been added during or after fermentation."

In 2012 the Sweet and Fortified Wine Association filed a petition with TTB for a rule change that would permit the use of "fortified" and "wine (grape) spirits added." After years of review, the agency is considering action to amend the regulation and allow use of "wine (grape) spirits added" on fortified wine labels. However, use of the term "fortified" remains in limbo.

A further labeling challenge involves the prohibition of the use of "port" and "sherry" on domestic wine labels after March 2007. As a result of the 2006 trade agreement with the European Union, domestic fortified wine producers are prohibited from using the term "port" or any terms containing "port" on labels submitted for TTB approval after March of 2007. Regulations adopted to implement the use of so called "semi-generic designations of geographic significance" (Federal Regulation Title 27, Part 4 Subpart C, Section 4.24 (b)(1) in TTB.gov) did, however, include a "grandfather" clause that permitted fortified wine producers to continue the use of "port" and "sherry" on labels approved prior to March 2007. Research by the Sweet and Fortified Wine Association indicates that approximately 45 percent of American port and sherry-style wine producers continue to use the term "port" and "sherry" on labels.

The prohibitive action by the TTB places American producers entering the domestic fortified wine market at a distinct disadvantage. Vintners desiring to add fortified port- or sherry-style wines to their product line are forced to create non-generic, proprietary names and corresponding labels that do not violate TTB label language regulations. While developing proprietary fortified wine labels is sufficiently daunting, producers are unable to accurately communicate on the label that the wine is fortified with the addition of grape or wine spirits.

INTERNATIONAL TRADE

Half a century ago, American wines were consumed by Americans. International wine trade was fairly one-sided. America imported wines from Europe, but there was little American wine going the other way. This all began to change with the 1976 Judgment of Paris tasting that favorably compared California wines with prominent French wines. As a result, the United States became an increasingly important player in the world wine trade. By 2014 the United States was the world's fourth largest wine producer behind France, Italy, and Spain. At the same time, America became the seventh largest wine exporter.

The rapid accession of the United States as a wine producer and exporter did not escape the attention of the wine producing nations in the European Union. In 2006 a bilateral agreement between the United States and the European Union prohibited American wine producers from using semi-generic geographic designations on labels. Among the prohibited label terms are "port" and "sherry."

In late 2014 the European Union placed a number of wine trade issues on the table for forthcoming negotiations. Among the preliminary proposals was revocation of the "grandfather" clause in the 2006 agreement on the use of semi-generic geographic indicators including "port" and "sherry". In response, representatives of the American fortified wine industry strongly opposed any alteration of the 2006 Agreement Between the United States of America and the European Community on Trade in Wine, particularly with respect to the use of semi-generic terms such as "port" on domestic wine labels. In a correspondence to the chief US trade representative, American fortified wine producers wrote:

It has been alleged (in an unpublished letter from the Sweet and Fortified Wine Association to the US Trade Negotiator) that use of a semi-generic term such as "port" misleads consumers. However, there is no basis for this assertion. As noted, semi-generic terms have been used for centuries in the U.S. and they were recognized by the post-prohibition regulatory structure developed in 1935. U.S. law (26 U.S.C. 5388(c)) and regulation (27

CFR 4.34) authorizing those terms require them to be accompanied by an appellation clearly identifying the wine's place of origin. There is simply no evidence that consumers are confused or misled by a semi-generic term used with the required disclosure of the wine origin on the bottle's label.

In addition, the EU Ambassador told Members of Congress in a letter dated May 21, 2014 that, with respect to geographical indications (GIs):

"...The EU legislation on GIs foresees that a name that has become generic cannot be protected and can therefore be freely used by all. We also accept that a name that is protected as a GI in the EU could be considered as generic in another territory such as the US..."

American fortified wine producers have built up considerable consumer goodwill in U.S. wines designated with semi-generic terms and the EU acknowledged our investments in 2006 when it negotiated the Bilateral Agreement. For these reasons, it would be highly inappropriate of TTIP to expropriate the value of these goodwill and intellectual property rights by government action.

Given the long-standing, accepted use of semi-generic terms on U.S. wines and the terms of the Bilateral Agreement, any further restriction on the use of such terms must be the subject of negotiations between interested parties in the EU and the U.S. wineries using those terms. Capitulating to the EU's anti-competitive demands in TTIP will grievously impact a long-standing, highly valued segment of the U.S. wine industry.

As a result of the strong stance taken by fortified wine producers and the American wine industry as a whole, the issue of semi-generic geographic indicators and label terminology has been shelved. However, trade agreement experts expect the issue to resurface in subsequent negotiations with the EU. European wine interests are well-funded and have considerable clout in the arena of international trade. The world's three largest wine-producing nations are EU members. They recognize a rapidly expanding Far East and Pacific Rim market to be exploited, and they seek to strongly influence the export playing field. Elimination of any European wine terminology on non-European wine labels would certainly aid in accomplishing this lofty international trade goal at the expense of other wine exporters, including the United States.

NEO-PROHIBITIONISM

Even though the great social experiment of a national prohibition on the production and sale of alcoholic beverages was unsuccessful, there is a faction of Americans who deem that the consumption of alcoholic beverages can be reduced by restrictive legislation and modifying social norms to diminish the acceptability of drinking. These so-called neo-Prohibitionists tend to believe:

- Alcoholic beverages, including wine and particularly fortified wines, cause drinking problems.

- The easy access to alcoholic beverages in terms of cost and availability leads people to drink.
- Drinking problems are determined by amount and type of alcohol consumed rather than individual environmental factors.
- Problems related to excessive alcohol consumptions should be the focus of public alcohol policy and education.

The vast majority of neo-Prohibitionists are well-meaning people concerned with the impact of irresponsible alcohol consumption. They believe such measures as limiting sales outlets, limiting the alcohol content of beverages, prohibiting alcohol advertising, and the proliferation of warning materials should be adopted as public policy. However, the neo-Prohibition movement sees increasing alcohol taxes as their most potent strategy. We know that the Twenty-First Amendment provided that states could establish their own alcoholic beverage regulations and controls—including taxation beyond the federal excise tax. This has resulted in a staggering myriad of state and local "sin tax" schemes subject to ever-changing political, social, and economic whims. Usually, these taxing policies are based on product alcohol content with higher taxes levied on higher alcohol beverages. Therefore, consumers of fortified wines are more likely to carry a heavier tax burden than table wine and even beer drinkers.

Neo-Prohibitionists tend to focus on cultural influences rather than personal responsibility as the cause for alcohol abuse. There is one area, however, where the interest of the wine industry and neo-Prohibitionist coincide –the elimination of drunk driving. While our strategies may differ, our concern with the tragic effects of drinking and driving are equally strong. Perhaps working together as allies rather than acting as adversaries can effect a more rapid and effective solution to this devastating problem.

PERCEPTION VERSUS REALITY

It is said that over time, perception becomes reality. To a significant degree, this concept can be applied to American fortified wine. For decades there was a persistent perception that American fortified wine was not worthy of consideration by the wine-consuming public. Media coverage of domestic fortified wines was almost always negative. Minimal mention was made of fortified wine production in America's wine-school curriculum. Fortified wines were rarely included in wine competitions and were even less likely to win awards. Even television shows of the 1960s and '70s berated American fortified wine. In a memorable 1966 episode of the popular cop show Dragnet, an intense Sergeant Friday berated a criminal suspect for his behavior due in part to his drinking cheap port wine. Perception became reality.

A recent survey of American restaurant sommeliers revealed that fortified wine sales from all sources accounted for only 2 percent of all restaurant wine sales. Tawny and ruby ports totaled 74 percent of all fortified wine sales and 62 percent of the total were sold after the meal. Even more disturbing is that 63 percent of respondents said they sold little to no fortified wine due to lack of guest interest. Sadly, this information referred only to foreign fortified wines. The only mention of American fortified wines was from one sommelier who said: "Education is the thing holding back fortified wine sales. The public image of every major fortified wine region is still severely tarnished in the US, and it will take continued, patient reminders to reform the idea of what Port, Sherry and Madeira actually are, since the production of cheap California copies continues" (guildsomm.com 2015). To American restaurant sommeliers, perception is reality.

Since the mid-1990s the reality, if not the perception of American fortified wines, has drastically changed. Getting consumer perception to recognize current reality may be the fortified wine industry's greatest challenge. Only through consumer education and information, as well as continuing commitment to quality, will American fortified wine producers meet the challenge of aligning perception and reality.

THE FUTURE

America's fortified wine crystal ball is a bit cloudy. The return to fortified wines as 70 percent of America's total wine production is unlikely. American wineries are very much like any other successful business—they produce only products they can sell. At a recent meeting of California fortified wine vintners, marketing discussions established that the current trend is to produce just enough fortified wine to meet current customer demand. Few producers have extra production that requires aggressive marketing to increase sales. A logical reason for this phenomena is that fortified wines are only a small fraction of many producers' portfolios and most of the marketing efforts are expended on the sale of table wines. Demand is usually driven by consumers tasting fortified wines in the winery tasting room. This situation is reminiscent of the "chicken and egg" dilemma. Should producers increase fortified wine production incrementally to satisfy current demand, or should producers build demand by marketing increased production?

If the future of the American fortified wine relies on building consumer demand, the issue becomes how to go about that process. Producer information provided to the Sweet and Fortified Wine Association suggests that the lack of consumers, as well as a professional knowledge of food and wine, is the greatest barrier to fortified wine sales. Therefore, it appears from a producer prospective that a concerted increase in consumer information and education is the key to the future of American fortified wine.

Developing a comprehensive American fortified wine information and education program will be a daunting task. The wine media would need to devote more space to objectively reviewing domestic fortified wines and doing more features on American fortified wine producers. Wine schools would need to conduct specific classes on fortified wine science and production. Perhaps more scientific research would be focused on the chemistry of fortified wines, as well as more study of consumer preferences with regard to fortified wine characteristics and food. Both amateur and professional wine groups and organizations could sponsor more educational sessions on American fortified wines, including the distinction between "old world" and "new world" fortified wines. More information on American fortified wines would need to be incorporated into mainstream consumer media venues including the various social media and blog sites. Local, state, and national wine associations and societies would need to acknowledge, support, and promote member fortified wine producers. Wine competitions would need to establish a separate category for fortified wines and separate them from non-fortified dessert wines, such as ice wine and late-harvest wines.

Finally, the purpose of this book is to initiate a greater awareness and understanding of American fortified wine. It is intended to inform and educate, as well as dispel misconceptions regarding what might well be America's best-kept wine secrets. Americans have always been proud of their accomplishments. Although American fortified wines have gone through some tough times over the past three centuries, there is ample reason to be proud of quality American fortified wines made in the United States.

THE WINERIES

PARADIGMS OF AMERICAN
FORTIFIED WINE PRODUCTION

PERDIDO VINEYARDS
Perdido, Alabama
perdidovineyards.net
Owners: Jim and Marianne Eddins
Winemaker: Jim Eddins

History
Established in 1972, the 50-acre Perdido vineyard produces muscadine grapes
for Bartels Winery in Florida. In 1979, Perdido Vineyards winery was granted
Alabama Winery Bond Number One as the first farm winery established in the
state since Prohibition. It was not until 2010 that state legislation permitted
fortified wine production in Alabama.

Fortified Wines
Daphne
Port-style blend of muscadine grapes and black currants.
King of Carnival
Red fortified blend of muscadine and blackberries with 16.5 percent alco-
hol.
Queen of Carnival
Blend of muscadine grapes and tart Michigan cherries make a fortified
wine with 16.5 percent alcohol.

BEAR CREEK WINERY

Homer, Alaska
bearcreekwinery.com
Owners: Fry Family
Winemaker: Bill Fry

History
Bill Fry started making homemade wines as a hobby in the mid-1990s. Good reviews from friends and neighbors spurred him to create Bear Creek Winery and a new production facility was completed in 2011.

Fortified Wine
Alaskan Port
Full-bodied, ruby port-style crafted from a variety of lower forty-eight fruit sources.

CALLAGHAN VINEYARDS

Elgin, Arizona
callaghanvineyards.com
Owners: Callaghan Family
Winemaker: Kent Callaghan

History
Harold, Karen, and Kent Callaghan founded the enterprise and produced their first wine in 1990. They found that Mediterranean and Iberian grape varieties do best in the Arizona heat.

Fortified Wine
Cabernet Sauvignon Red Dessert Wine
Estate Cabernet Sauvignon produces a deep, intense, port-style wine.

OAK CREEK VINEYARDS AND WINERY

Cornville, Arizona
oakcreekvineyards.net
Owners: Deb and Florian Wahl
Winemaker: Florian Wahl

History
Oak Creek Vineyards and Winery was initiated in 2003, a year after the purchase of a 10-acre parcel and planting 6 acres of wine grapes south of Sedona at a 3,400-foot elevation. Oak Creek was the first wine tasting room in the Verde

Valley of northern Arizona. Florian became a winemaker through on-the-job training (OJT) and online/extension classes through UC Davis.

Fortified Wines

Arizona Cream Sherry

Crafted in the Jerez cream sherry-style, the fortified sherry is made from Chardonnay and is well balanced with 18 percent alcohol.

Arizona Port Wine

Ruby port-style brandy fortified wine made from estate Zinfandel and aged in medium- plus toast French Oak barrels.

POST FAMILY VINEYARDS & WINERY

Altus, Arkansas

postfamilie.com

Owners: Post Family

Winemaker: Luke Holcomb

History

Five generations of the Post family have grown grapes and made wine in Altus, Arkansas. The tradition began with German immigrant Jacob Post, who came to America in 1872; through Prohibition, when Katherine Post served wine with meals at her restaurant; to great-grandson Mathew, and now his twelve sons and daughters. Post Winery is Arkansas's first and largest vineyard and winery at the foothills of the Ozarks.

Fortified Wines

Altus Port

A blend of classic *vinifera* and muscadine grape varieties grown in the Post Familie vineyard.

Concord

Fortified wine from fresh, grapey Concord grapes with 19 percent alcohol.

Delawine

Pink fortified wine made from Arkansas grapes and 19 percent alcohol.

Sherry

Golden amber–colored sherry-style wine with 19 percent alcohol.

White Port

White port-style fortified wine with 19 percent alcohol.

WIEDERKEHR WINE CELLARS

Wiederkehr Village, Arkansas

wiederkehrwines.com

Owners: Wiederkehr Family

Winemaker: Al Wiederkehr

History

Wiederkehr Wine Cellars is US Bonded Winery Number 8. It all began in 1880 when Johann Andreas Wiederkehr moved his family from Switzerland to the Arkansas Ozarks above the Arkansas River. He selected the site because of its geographical resemblance to the fine European wine regions. Johann dug a wine cave in the property's hillside that became the Weinkeller Restaurant, known today as a National Historic Place.

Fortified Wines

Cabernet Sauvignon Port

Tawny port-style wine fashioned from rare Cabernet Sauvignon and aged in small oak casks.

Tawny Port

Aged port-style wine reflecting the rich, warm flavors and bouquet.

Sherry

Medium dry sherry-style fortified wine with mellow nutty flavor.

Cocktail Sherry

Smooth, nutty character sherry-style fortified wine.

Cream Sherry

Full-bodied, rich, sweet, cream textured sherry-style fortified wine.

MILLIAIRE WINERY/BLACK SHEEP WINERY

Murphys, Calaveras County, California

milliairewinery.com/blacksheepwinery.com

Owner/Winemaker: Steve Milliaire, a graduate of Fresno State University with a degree in enology, Steve Milliaire started his forty-year career in 1975 with the David Bruce Winery in the Santa Cruz Mountains. Steve moved to Murphys in 1982 to work with Brenden Stevenot at Stevenot Winery.

History

Milliaire Winery was founded in 1986 and in 1990 moved into the old "Flying A" gas station building on Main Street in the historic Sierra Foothills town of Murphys. The "Roadside Chateau" remains the Milliaire tasting room.

Founded in 1984, Black Sheep Winery was one of the earliest wineries in Calaveras County. Since 2007, the historic 150-year-old "Yellow Farmhouse" on Main Street in Murphys serves as the Black Sheep tasting room.

Fortified Wines
Black Sheep Winery Fortissimo, Amador County
> Port-style wine crafted from Touriga Nacional, Tinta Cão, and Souzão from the fourty-year-old Amador County Clocksprings Vineyard.

Milliaire Winery Clocksprings Zinfandel Port
> Fortified Zinfandel from Amador County Clocksprings Vineyard.

Awards
> **Fortissimo**, **BRONZE,** Calaveras County Fair
> **Clocksprings Zinfandel Port**, **SILVER,** Calaveras County Fair

BOGLE VINEYARDS/BOGLE FAMILY WINERY
> Clarksburg, Yolo County, California
> boglewinery.com

Owners: Warren Bogle, President; Jody Bogle, Director of Public Relations; Ryan Bogle, Vice President

Winemakers: Eric Aafedt, Director of Winemaking, Eric grew up in Livermore, California, and graduated from Cal Poly San Luis Obispo with a degree in chemistry. He has been with Bogle Family Winery since 1994. Dana Stemmle, Winemaker, A 2005 graduate of UC Davis with degrees in Viticulture and Enology, Dana has been interested in wine since her teenage visit to Italy. She joined Bogle in 2006.

History
The sixth generation of the Bogle family currently farms over 1,500 acres of wine grapes in the Delta region of northern California. The first twenty wine grapes were planted near the tiny Sacramento River town of Clarksburg in 1968. Bogle Family Winery was established in 1978.

Fortified Wine
Bogle Petite Sirah Port
> Ruby-style fortified wine produced from Bogle Vineyard's Quick Ranch grapes. The wine is typically aged for twenty-four months in American oak finishing at 20 percent alcohol and 10.5 percent residual sugar. The intense port-style wine can age comfortably for twenty years.

CEDAR MOUNTAIN WINERY
> Livermore, Alameda County, California
> cedarmountainwinery.com

Owners/Winemaker: Earl and Linda Ault, Earl Ault is the Cedar Mountain winemaker as well as an accomplished sculptor, watercolor artist, and large format photographer. Ault is a physicist who became interested in the business of wine in the mid-1970s.

Linda Ault is a recognized amateur chef who attended the California Culinary Academy and studied with many great chefs at Robert Mondavi winery. Linda's formal education is in the fields of physics and computer science.

History

The Aults purchased the vineyard property on Tesla Road in Livermore in 1988. The original all–Chenin blanc vineyard was grafted to a Chardonnay and Cabernet Sauvignon a year after purchase of the property. Dr. Ault began producing fortified wines in 1993, working with grapes from the Shenandoah Valley of Amador County as well as the Aults's Cabernet Sauvignon vineyard. The Aults's goal is to produce fine fortified wines in the European style by means of quality domestic grapes.

Fortified Wines
Chardonnay del Sol

White port-style wine made from ripe Cedar Mountain estate vineyard Chardonnay.

Reserve Chardonnay del Sol

Ripe estate vineyard Chardonnay grapes produce a white port-style wine aged in toasted oak barrels.

Viognier Port

Intense white port-style from Viognier grapes.

Vintage Port

Full-bodied port-style blend of Tinta Amarelo, Bastardo, Tinta Cão, and estate-grown Cabernet Sauvignon barrel aged twelve years.

Tourtuga Royale

A unique port-style wine produced by co-fermenting estate grown Cabernet Sauvignon with cocoa powder and fortifying it with brandy.

Awards
Tourtuga Royale, BRONZE medal

CHATEAU ROUTON

Fair Play, El Dorado County, California
chateaurouton.com
Owners/Winemaker: Bob and Sheila Routon

History

The Routons purchased their 85-acre ranch in the Sierra Foothills in 1995 primarily to support their stable of Arabian show horses. After studying the wine industry, Bob and Sheila found their niche in producing fortified wines. Portu-

guese varieties as well as Barbera are grown in a 12-acre vineyard on decom-
posed granite soil at an elevation of 2,000 feet. A visit to the tasting features
their unique "port Sundae" and breathtaking views from the Grand Deck.

Fortified Wines
Vintage California Port
>Bottled in 2002 (seventeen years old). Dark garnet color, very complex,
>aged seven and a half years in oak barrels.
>**Cask 99 California Port**
>Dark ruby color, complex, spicy nose, aged forty-two months in oak bar-
>rels.

Sierratage Cask Port/Sierratage Vintage Port
>Blend of estate-grown Portuguese varieties.

Sierrtage Barbera (port)
>An estate-grown Barbera port, smooth and bold.

D'ART WINES

>Lodi, San Joaquin County, California
>dartwines.com

Owners: Dave and Helen Dart
Winemakers: Dave and Jessica Dart

History
Dave and Helen began their wine experience as "gragistes," home winemakers
winning the Best of Show at the Sacramento Home Winemakers wine competition with their 2000 Syrah. The estate Cabernet Sauvignon vineyard was
planted in 1999 on sandy loam valley soil. The d'Art's tasting room exhibits
photo art from Dave and Helen's world travel.

Fortified Wine
Lodi Port
>California port-style wine made from Tempranillo, Cabernet Sauvignon,
>and Petite Sirah.

DEAVER VINEYARDS

>Shenandoah Valley, Amador County, California
>deavervineyards.com

Owners: Deaver Family
Winemaker: Marco Cappelli

History
Joe Davis, grand patriarch of the Deaver family, came to California during the

C
A
L
I
F
O
R
N
I
A

gold rush and settled in the Shenandoah Valley in 1857. For more than one-hundred years the family raised cattle, sheep, and hogs, and grew grain, vegetables, and tree and orchard crops, as well as grapes. Grandpa Joe planted the first 8 acres of Mission grapes in 1858 and the first 14 acres of Zinfandel in the mid-1860s. Both vineyards continue to produce wine grapes to this day. The family sold "old vine" grapes primarily to home winemakers until the mid-1960s when the Trinchero family began buying Amador Zinfandel for their burgeoning Sutter Home winery. Deaver has been producing port-style fortified wines since 1985 from a wide variety of grape varieties grown in Amador County.

Fortified Wines:

Orange Muscat Port

White port-style wine made from Amador County Orange Muscat grapes. Finished with 17.6 percent alcohol with only 5 percent residual sugar.

Alicante Bouschet Port

Unusual port-style fortified wine produced from grapes popular with eastern home winemakers during Prohibition.

Cabernet Sauvignon Port

New to the Deaver stable of port-style wines in 2016.

Angelica Port

This fortified port-style wine comes from Deaver's over one-hundred-year-old Mission vines and is fortified with Mission grape brandy. The generic Angelica "formula" closely mirrors the Angelica wines of the Gold Rush era.

Golden Nectar Port

White fortified wine weighing in at a hefty 21.1 percent alcohol and 18 percent residual sugar.

Petite Sirah Port

The colors of dark chocolate and ruby with a velvety finish

Barbera Port

Often known as Deaver cigar port, this port-style is made from Barbera grapes with a typically spicy finish. A bit higher in alcohol than other Deaver red port-style wines at 18.6 percent.

Zinfandel Port

Deaver has been making port-style wine from estate Zinfandel since 1985. Fortified with Mission grape brandy, the lush, bold wine is aged in neutral oak barrels and finishes with 18 percent alcohol and 8 percent residual sugar.

Awards

Barbera Port, **GOLD**, Amador County Fair

FENESTRA WINERY

Livermore, Alameda County, California
fenestrawinery.com

Owners: Lanny and Fran Replogle

Winemaker: Aaron Luna, a native of Monterey County, Aaron spent ten years with Carmel Valley's Bernardus winery before venturing for a short stint in Western Australia. He graduated from UC Davis with a degree in viticulture and enology and worked at Stags Leap Winery before coming to Fenestra.

History

Starting as Ventana Winery in 1976, the Replogles began winemaking in the Ruby Hill Winery Building in Pleasanton. The original Stony Ridge Winery occupied the historic building where Lanny was the consulting winemaker while teaching organic chemistry full-time at San Jose State University. Following the 1978 name change to Fenestra ("window" in Spanish), winery operations moved in 1980 to the True Winery that had been vacant for two decades. The current winery and tasting room resulted from an eight-month renovation and is the essence of a "no-frills rustic country winery."

Fortified Wines

Port, Lodi, Silvaspoons Vineyards

Classic port-style blend of Touriga Nacional, Tinta Cão, and Souzão.

Tawny Port II

Bold decadent port-style wine fashioned from individual batches of Petite Sirah, Zinfandel, and Souzão ports.

Awards

Port, GOLD
Tawny Port II, GOLD

FICKLIN VINEYARDS

Madera, Madera County, California
ficklin.com

Owners: Ficklin Family

Winemaker: Peter Ficklin

History

Perhaps America's pre-eminent port-style fortified wine producers, three generations of Ficklins have been making handcrafted ports since 1948. The estate vineyards were planted in 1946 to Touriga Nacional, Tinta Madeira, Souzão, and Tinta Cão on advice from UC Davis experts Dr. Albert Winkler and Dr. Maynard Amerine. The Ficklins established perhaps America's oldest existing true solera aging and blending system. Beginning with the first harvest in 1948,

CALIFORNIA

C
A
L
I
F
O
R
N
I
A

the present solera comprises 323 barrels and has never been emptied. According to the Ficklins, "Every barrel and puncheon, and every bottle of the Old Vine Tinta Port has a diminishing percentage of the original 1948 harvest, and every subsequent harvest. It is truly a living history of the wines made at Ficklin."

Fortified Wines

Vintage Ports
1957 Vintage Port
Selected clusters of estate-grown Tinta Madeira grapes showed exceptional promise for a truly extraordinary vintage. Founding owner and winemaker David Ficklin crushed and fermented the marvelous fruit in the traditional port-style manner using pot-still brandy made from the same Tinta Madeira grapes. Bottled in 1960, the nearly sixty-year-old vintage port was first released in 1968.

1983 Vintage Port
Each of Ficklin Vineyard's four estate-grown Portuguese varieties make unique contributions to this vintage port bottled in 1987. Souzão provides deep color and rich, deep flavors while Tinta Madeira furnishes a chocolate flavor with a hint of spice. Touriga Nacional contributes a concentrated fruit flavor and aroma, whereas Tinta Cão furnishes the soft, subtle flavor and delicacy. Released in 1991.

1988 Vintage Port
Tinta Madeira provides the bulk of the grapes for lush, dark, vintage port. Small amounts of the other three Ficklin Portuguese varieties build structure and enhance flavors in this exquisite wine bottled in 1991 and released in 1997.

1996 Vintage Port
Bottled in 1999, the vintage port now has a full seventeen years of traditional aging that soften the young, dark fruit flavors and determines the wine's overall flavor and structure. Made from the four estate Ficklin Portuguese varieties, the wine will benefit from up to twenty years of additional aging.

Aged 10 Year Tawny Port
Crafted from Tinta Madeira and Touriga, this special port was aged ten years in Ficklin's 160-barrel solera of American oak to blend rich fruit flavors with smooth texture and a long finish.

Old Vine Tinta Port
Produced from Ficklin Vineyard's nearly seven-decade-old four Portuguese varieties, this satisfying fortified wine reflects the careful attention to making quality American port-style wine.

Infused Port-style Wines
Chocolate Passport
Almond Passport
Raspberry Passport

All the flavor infused Passport fortified wines are crafted in the ruby style from Ficklin's authentic Portuguese grape varieties blended with natural extracts and essences.

Awards

Numerous medals from wine completions across the nation.

GRAND AMIS

Lodi, San Joaquin County, California
grandsamis.com

Owners/Winemakers: Johnathan and Cathy Wetmore

History

The Wetmores established their Lodi winery in 2002 after nearly twenty-five years of premium vineyard management in the San Joaquin Valley.

Fortified Wine

Grand Amis Port

Aged in oak for twenty-seven months, this Syrah port-style wine is well-structured with a balance of oak and fruit flavors. 17.8 percent alcohol.

Awards

SILVER, California State Fair

GALLEANO WINERY

Mira Loma, Riverside County, California
(Cucamonga Valley AVA)
galleanowinery.com

Owners: Galleano Family
Winemaker: Donald Galleano

History

Donald Galleano's grandfather arrived in California from the Piedmont region of Italy in 1913 and by 1927 was able to purchase the Cantu Ranch in what was once called Wineville in the Cucamonga Valley. This area has been producing wine since 1855 when the first settlers began growing grapes in the near desert of Southern California.

Wineland became Mira Loma in 1930 and, following the repeal of Prohibition, the winery and vineyards expanded. Today, Galleano Winery is a registered California landmark that continues to produce a variety of fortified wines from fruit grown in the 275 acres of "urban" vineyards along the I-15 freeway.

C
A
L
I
F
O
R
N
I
A

Fortified Wines
Sherry
Rose of Peru Sherry
 Pecan, honey and orange zest character.
Sherry Cream Cask Three
 Classic California cream sherry from Cucamonga Valley grapes with an
 aroma of caramel and hazelnut.
Nino's Solera Sherry
 Cucamonga Valley sherry with a dark tawny color and mild tannins.
Galleano Sherry
 Complex flavors and a long finish.
House Cream Sherry
 From Palomino grapes, medium color but a smooth creamy texture.
Port-Style
Alicante Port
 Made from Cucamonga Valley Alicante Bouschet grapes with a deep gar-
 net color, round sweetness, and a long, smooth finish.
Zinfandel Port
 Light red hue with dark fruit flavor and brown sugar sweetness.
Three Friends Port
 Classic aged tawny port-style from Cucamonga Valley fruit.
Galleano Port
 Vintage-style port from Cucamonga Valley uniquely crafted by winemaker
 Don Galleano.

Other Fortified Wines
Angelica
 Brandy-fortified wine from Cucamonga Valley grapes
Sweet Vermouth
 Red Italian-style sweet vermouth from Cucamonga Valley fruit blended
 with herbs.
Marsala
 Made in the amber style, the wine is rich, smoky, and slightly herbaceous.
 Excellent for cooking or sipping.

Awards
 Angelica, Unanimous GOLD, Riverside International Wine Competition
 Alicante Port, SILVER, Long Beach Grand Cru
 Zinfandel Port, GOLD/BEST OF CLASS, Long Beach Grand Cru
 Rose of Peru Sherry, GOLD/BEST OF CLASS/BEST NEW WORLD
  DESSERT WINE/DOUBLE GOLD, Jerry Mead New World Interna-
  tional Wine Competition

GYPSY CANYON

Lompoc, Santa Barbara County, California

gypsycanyon.com

Owner/Winemaker: Deborah Hall has been growing and making wine in the central coast region since 1999. She studied viticulture and enology at UC Davis.

History

Gypsy Canyon Vineyard is a tiny historic vineyard in Santa Barbara County's Santa Rita Hills AVA. Cuttings from the nearby La Purismina Mission were planted in the spring of 1887. During Prohibition, the old vines were hidden under a canopy of sage brush and forgotten for 60 years. In 1994 the Halls purchased the Gypsy Canyon Ranch and discovered the ancient vineyard. It took 5 years to rejuvenate the 3-acre Marcelina's Ancient Mission Vineyard (named for Dona Marcelina Felix Dominguez, the first known woman to grow grapes in California), with the 2001 harvest of the first Mission grapes from the vineyard in 120 years.

Fortified Wine

Ancient Vine Angelica

During her research on Mission vineyards, Deborah discovered notes for producing "California Original Angelica" by 1891 winemaker Emile Vache. Hall chose to duplicate the Vache formula that called for neutral spirits fortification halfway through fermentation. The wine then spends two years in French oak barrels and finishes at 18 percent alcohol and 9 percent residual sugar with an orange/brown color.

HEITZ CELLARS

Saint Helena, Napa County California

heitzcellar.com

Owners: Heitz Family

Winemaker: David Heitz

History

Pioneer Napa vintner Joe Heitz and his wife Alice began the family wine legacy in 1961 with the purchase of eight acres just south of St. Helena. A short three years later, the Heitz family was able to buy a 160-acre vineyard in Spring Valley, east of St. Helen. The following year Joe and Alice met Tom and Martha May who owned a young vineyard in Oakville. For the past fifty years, the extraordinary fruit from Martha's Vineyard produces one of the most renowned Napa Cabernet Sauvignon wines.

In the early 1990s, David Heitz planted eleven classic Portuguese grape varieties including Touriga Nacional, Tinta Roriz, Souzão, Tinta Cão, Tinta Ba-

C
A
L
I
F
O
R
N
I
A

irrada, Tinta Madeira, Tinta Amarela, and Bastardo. The vines flourished in the Napa Valley and in 1994 Heitz introduced Ink Spot Port.

Fortified Wine
Ink Spot Port
An American classic port-style wine is the result blending eight Heitz Vineyard classic Portuguese varieties. Several vintages have been blended to develop a rich, full-bodied fortified wine with lush fruitiness and balanced sweetness. 18.5 percent alcohol.

PEDRONCELLI WINERY
Geyserville, Sonoma County, California
pedroncelli.com
Owners: Pedroncelli Family
Winemaker: Montse Reece, Montse came to the United States to work at Gloria Ferrer Champagne Caves in Sonoma following her 1998 graduation from Rovira i Virgili University in Tarragona, Spain. Following stints at Ferrair-Carano and Rodney Strong, Montse joined the Pedroncelli team in 2007.

History
It was during Prohibition in 1927 that Giovanni and Julia Pedroncelli purchased 25 acres of Sonoma County hillside Zinfandel vineyards. A small Mother Clone block of that original hundred-year-old vineyard still produces budwood for estate Zinfandel replanting. The Pedroncellis sold grapes to home winemakers during Prohibition and with repeal became Bonded Winery Number 113. In 1980 Pedroncelli began replanting the 47-acre Home Ranch vineyard primarily with Zinfandel but the final 2002 mix included four classic Portuguese varieties.

Fortified Wine
Four Grapes Vintage Port
While ripening at slightly different rates, the field blend Tinta Madeira, Tinta Cão, Touriga Nacional, and Souzão are harvested at the same time to provide balance, color and flavor to the port-style wine. Aged four years in neutral American oak barrels, the wine will benefit from bottle aging for ten years. 19 percent alcohol with 9.9 percent residual sugar.

Awards
GOLD, San Francisco Chronicle Wine Competition

JOSEPH FILIPPI WINERY & VINEYARDS
Rancho Cucamonga, San Bernardino County, California
josephfilippiwinery.com

Owners: Filippi Family
Winemaker: Kristina Filippi

History

In 1922 Giovanni Filippi and his son Joseph came to California's Cucamonga Valley from Veneto, Italy to grow premium wine grapes. The 350 acres of new vineyard included Palomino, Grenache, Salvador, Mission, and Golden Chasselas—some of which still populate the smaller urban vineyard today. The Filippi winery moved to the historic Regina Winery where the fourth and fifth generations continue the family tradition of crafting wines from Cucamonga Valley grapes.

Fortified Wines

Alicante Bouschet Dessert Wine

Port-style fortified wine fashioned from Cucamonga Valley old-vine grapes.

Elisa

White port-style wine.

Elana Angelica

Made from Spanish sherry varieties Pedro Ximenez and Palomino, the wine is a combination of creamy baked sweet sherry, dry sherry, and aged sweet Angelica. Seasoned (more than sixty years old) California redwood casts are used for extended aging. 19 percent alcohol.

Crème de la Crème Sherry

Produced from old-vine Palomino, Mission, Grenache, and Pedro Ximenez is a solera-aged blend from baked sherries. 18.5 percent alcohol.

Oloroso

Old-vine Palomino and Mission grapes constitute this dry, nutty, sherry-style fortified wine. Solera aging provides consistency for this aperitif wine reflecting Spanish oloroso sherry.

Fondante Ciello

Chocolate essence port-style wine from Cucamonga Valley grapes. 18.3 percent alcohol.

Ruby Ruby

Young, red fortified wine in the Ruby port-style made from Solera fractional blending of old vine Zinfandel, Alicante Bouchet, Grenache, and Sultana grapes. 19.4 percent alcohol.

Zinfandel Celestiale

Port-style fortified wine from Cucamonga Valley Zinfandel fruit.

Awards

Alicante Bouchet, DOUBLE GOLD, Jerry Mead New World International Wine Competition
Angelica Elena, Multiple-medal winner
Crème del la Crème, Multiple-medal winner
Fondante Ciello, Multiple, **GOLD**

C
A
L
I
F
O
R
N
I
A

MEYER FAMILY CELLARS

Yorkville, Mendocino County, California

Owners: Meyer Family

Winemakers: Matt and Karen Meyer. Matt Meyer is the son of former Silver Oak owners Justin and Bonny Meyer and spent a good deal of his formative years in the vineyards and winery. Matt has a Master of Viticulture from UC Davis. Karen Meyer, born and raised in Perth, Western Australia. Karen has an enology degree from Charles Stuart University. She and Matt met while working together at Oregon's Argyle Winery in 1999.

History

Meyer Family Cellars was founded in 1987 by Justin and Bonny Meyer, who established one of California's iconic Cabernet Sauvignon brands, Silver Oak. Their broad experience in the wine trade built the successful family business which is today under the talented leadership of Matt and Karen Meyer.

Fortified Wine

California Port

A fortified wine using a modified solera-aging system averaging eleven years of Zinfandel port-style wine.

MIRAFLORES WINERY

Placerville, El Dorado County, California

mirafloreswinery.com

Owner: Victor Alvarez

Winemaker: Marco Cappelli. Apprenticing in Italy, France, and Australia after his graduation from UC Davis, Marco worked for Swanson Vineyards for seventeen years prior to coming to Miraflores in 2003.

History

Arizona pathologist Victor Alvarez purchased a 254-acre estate in the Sierra Foothills east of the gold rush town of Placerville in 2003. Some 40 acres of the estate between 2,500 and 3,000 elevation were planted with wine grapes.

Fortified Wines

Angelica

Carefully crafted fortified wine in the tradition of California Angelica made from Mission grapes.

Black Muscat NV

Fortified wine produced as a tribute to early California pioneer Black Muscat field-blend vineyards and rich wines.

Princessa

Brandy-fortified Muscat Canelli wine aged three years in French oak barrels.

NEW CLAIRVAUX VINEYARD

Vina, Tehama County, California

newclairvauxvineyard.com

Owners: Abbey of New Clairvaux Trappist-Cistercian monks

Winemaker: Aimee Sunseri. The fifth generation of the Nichelini wine family, the oldest family-owned winery in Napa, Aimee is a graduate of UC Davis. She also serves as the Nichelini's seventh family winemaker.

History

In 1890, Leland Stanford Great Vina Ranch Winery was the largest in the world, capable of making 1.2 million gallons of wine from over 3,800 acres of Stanford vineyards. Stanford's dream of greatness died with him in 1893 and by Prohibition, most of the land had been sold. In 1955, the 600 remaining acres of the Great Vina Ranch were purchased by the Trappist Cistercian monks who established the Abbey of New Clairvaux. Revitalization of the vineyards began in 2000.

Fortified Wines
Vino Dolce

Meaning "sweet wine" in Italian, Vino Dolce is a ruby port-style wine fortified halfway through fermentation with brandy.

PASOPORT WINE COMPANY

Paso Robles, San Luis Obispo County, California

pasoportwine.com

Owners: Steve and Lola Glossner

Winemaker: Steven Glossner, a graduate of Cornell University with a degree in business, Steve moved to California in 1988 to become a winemaker. After starting as a "cellar rat" in Sonoma, then a harvest in New Zealand, he obtained a graduate degree in enology from Fresno State University and became winemaker at Justin Vineyards and Winery in 1994. Following with Adelaida Cellars and Halter Ranch, he now has his own line of wines and spirits.

History

PasoPort is Steven and Lola's family operated winery focusing on port-style wines made from Paso Robles AVA fruit. In 2013 PasoPort purchased an alembic pot still to produce brandy for their line of fortified, port-style wines.

Fortified Wines
Angelica White Port

A white port-style blend of Verdelho, Muscat and Chenin Blanc grapes barrel aged 7-8 years. The wine finishes with 17% alcohol and 17% residual sugar.

C
A
L
I
F
O
R
N
I
A

Ruby Port

Called "California Style" because the fortified wine is a blend of 50% Zinfandel with Petite Sirah and Syrah and barrel aged for three years. 19% alcohol and 9% residual sugar.

Violeta Port

Portuguese varietal blend of Touriga Nacional, Tinto Cao, and Souzao, the port-style wine is aged three years in neutral oak barrels finishing at 19% alcohol and 9% residual

Tawny Port

Touriga Nacional, Tinto Cao, and Souzao are blended in this tawny port-style wine barrel aged 10 years with 19% alcohol and 9% residual.

Awards

Angelica White Port, **SILVER,** Orange County Wine Competition, **SILVER,** Central Coast Wine Competition

Ruby Port, **GOLD,** Central Coast Fair, **SILVER,** Orange County Fair

California Port, **GOLD,** Central Coast Fair, **SILVER,** 2013 Orange County Fair

Violeta, **BEST FORTIFIED WINE GOLD,** Central Coast Wine Competition, **GOLD,** Orange County Fair Competition:

Tawny, **GOLD,** Central Coast Wine Competition, **GOLD,** Orange County Wine Competition, **SILVER,** San Francisco International Wine Competition

PRAGER WINERY AND PORT WORKS

Saint Helena, Napa County, California

pragerport.com

Owners: Prager Family

Winemaker: Peter Prager

History

Family patriarch Jim Prager's passion for wine motivated him to leave his southern California insurance business and head for Napa wine country. With his wife and seven kids he settled in St. Helena in 1976 and began taking enology classes at UC Davis. After tasting some California ports in the school's wine cellar, Prager was committed to making first-class port-style fortified wines beginning in 1979. Prager's initial focus was on single variety wines from Petite Sirah, Cabernet Sauvignon, and Chardonnay. Being a port house it was inevitable that Prager would make wines from authentic Portuguese varieties so in 1999 the family planted 5.5 acres of Touriga Nacional, Tinta Cão, Tinta Roriz, and Verdelho near Calistoga. Today, three generations of Pragers produce around 3,600 cases of American port-style wines. Prager's tasting room is perhaps the "funkiest" of all in Napa Valley.

Fortified Wines

Royal Escort

    Drier than most ports, Royal Escort is made from 100 percent Napa Valley Petite Sirah grapes. Highly age-worthy at 19 percent alcohol.

Petite Sirah Port

    Produced from Central Valley grown grapes with two years of barrel aging, this ruby-like port-style wine has a light tannin structure and mellow brandy finish.

Noble Companion Tawny Port

    Aged ten years in the traditional tawny port style and made from Cabernet Sauvignon grapes, the wine has a typical golden-orange color and rich creamy texture.

Alyssa

    Dry white port-style wine produced from Verdelho grown in Calistoga and aged two years in French oak barrels.

Aria

    Semi-sweet white port-style wine made from 100 percent Napa Chardonnay. Aged three years in oak barrels.

Prager Port

    Fashioned from Petite Sirah and Tinta Roriz, the combination results in a soft but age- worthy American port-style wine.

Awards

    Noble Companion, DOUBLE GOLD, SF Chronicle Wine Tasting, **DOUBLE GOLD,** American Fine Wines Competition

QUADY WINERY

    Madera, Madera County, California

    quadywinery.com

Owners: Andy and Laurel Quady

Winemakers: Mike Blaylock, Director of Winemaking. Native Californian Mike Blaylock joined Quady in 1984 after a stint with the Peace Corps in the Philippines helping develop new income-generating jobs including a wine production operation. On his return to the United States, Mike enrolled in the graduate enology program at California State University, Fresno, where he received an MS degree in agricultural chemistry.

    Darin Peterson, Winemaker. Originally in the advertising industry working with food stylists, Darin discovered his passion for food and wine. He received his degree in enology from California State University, Fresno, and began his career at Simpson Meadow Winery. After coming to Quady, Darin was promoted to winemaker in 2015.

C
A
L
I
F
O
R
N
I
A

History

Andy and Laurel Quady transitioned from congested southern California to the rural atmosphere of Lodi in 1970. After obtaining his master's degree from UC Davis, Andy worked for a small Lodi vintner as assistant winemaker. He made his first port-style wine from Amador County grapes in 1975. The couple moved to Madera in 1977 and Laurel's flourishing CPA practice helped fund the first decade of Quady Winery production. The current winery was built in 1984 with a unique design featured in *Time* magazine and *Architectural Digest*. Quady is perhaps America's foremost producer of exotic fortified wines.

Fortified Wines

Essensia

Full-bodied, white fortified wine made from Orange Muscat grapes. The variety is known in Italy as Moscato Fior d'Arancio: Orange Blossom Muscat.

Elysium

Originally destined for sacramental wine in 1983, truckloads of Black Muscat grapes had no home until Quady came to the rescue to produce a fortified wine in the manner of the winery's successful Essensia. Violet-crimson color and litchi-rose aromas develop at full maturity.

Batch 88 Starboard

A red port-style wine somewhere between ruby and tawny. Made primarily from Tinta Roriz, the wine is fortified with 190-proof neutral grape spirits. Batch 88 is a blend of several vintages averaging five years in 60 gallon barrcls.

Starboard Vintage 2006

This port-style wine is made from Tinta Cão, Tinta Roriz, Tinta Amarela, Tinta Baroca, and Touriga Nacional from Amador and Madera counties. Fashioned in the traditional vintage style, the wine spent two years in oak barrels and the rest of its life in bottle. Vintage 2006 will age gracefully until around 2024.

Starboard Vintage 1996

Vintage port-style wine crafted from Amador County authentic Portuguese varieties. Bold, rich, and complex supply is limited for the bottle-aged wine.

Palomino Fino

An Amontillado-style fortified wine produced from biodynamically grown Palomino grapes in the San Joaquin Valley. The wine spent five years in barrels under the flor yeast which grows on the surface of young wine to develop richness and flavor.

Vya Sweet Vermouth

A blend of Tinta Roriz, Orange Muscat, and dry white infused with a selection of over 17 herbs and spices.

Vya Extra Dry Vermouth
> Crafted from a blend of San Joaquin Valley Orange Muscat and French Colombard white wine that is carefully infused with a selection over fifteen dried herb leaves and flowers. A powerful, herbaceous, crisp wine.

Vya Whisper Dry Vermouth
> Created ten years after the first Vya Extra Dry, Whisper Dry is a softer, less herbaceous, lighter-style aperitif wine and is designed to pair well with subtle spirits.

Awards
> **Essensia,** Numerous **GOLD** and **BEST OF CLASS**
> **Elysium, DOUBLE GOLD,** San Francisco Chronicle International Wine Competition
> **Batch 88 Starboard, BEST OF SHOW, DOUBLE GOLD, OVERALL TOP WINE,** American Wine Society
> **Starboard Vintage 2006, GOLD,** Orange County Fair
> **Starboard Vintage 1996, GOLD,** Orange County Fair
> **Vya Sweet Vermouth, GOLD**, Winemaker Challenge International Wine Competition
> **Vya Extra Dry Vermount**, **GOLD, RESERVE CLASS** CHAMPION, Rodeo Uncorked International Wine Competition,
> **Vya Whisper Dry Vermouth**, **BEST OF CLASS**, Pacific Rim International Competition

SAN ANTONIO WINERY

> Los Angeles, Los Angeles County, California
> http://sanantoniowinery.com/

Owner: Riboli Family

Winemakers: Anthony Riboli, first of the fourth generation of family winemakers, Anthony received his Master of Viticulture in 1998 from UC Davis. He interned at Groth Vineyards for the 1997 harvest before joining the family business.

Arnaud Debons: The French-born Debons worked in Bordeaux and Cahors following graduation from the University of Toulouse. After moving to the United States he was assistant winemaker at Napa's Newton Vineyards before coming to San Antonio Winery.

History

Santo Cambianica left his home of Berzo San Fermo in Lombardia, Italy, in 1910 to establish his Los Angeles winery in 1917. The fact that the winery was named after Santo's patron saint Anthony may have influenced the archdiocese of Los Angeles to allow Santo's winery to make sacramental wines during Prohibition, allowing San Antonio Winery to flourish as a provider of altar wines.

In 1936, nephew Stefano Riboli began apprenticing under his Uncle Santo, to learn the wine business. Stefano married Maddalena Satragni in 1946 and when Santo died in 1956, Stefano was granted full ownership of San Antonio Winery. The winery currently has vineyards and facilities in Monterey, Napa, and Paso Robles. The Los Angeles Cultural Heritage Board designated the original location on Lamar Street as Cultural Monument Number 42 in the early 1960s.

Fortified Wine
La Quinta Syrah Port
Made exclusively from Paso Robles–grown Syrah grapes, the ruby port-style wine is dark red, rich, and full bodied. California brandy is added when the must reaches 8–10 percent, arresting the fermentation process. The wine is barrel aged a minimum of two years, resulting in a finished wine of 18 percent alcohol.

California Port
Carignane, Ruby Cabernet, and Grenache from California's Central Valley are blended to produce a port-style wine with ruby color and tawny hues. 18.3 percent alcohol.

California Madeira
Produced from rare Mission and Palomino grapes, this Madeira-style wine with oxidized characters of flor yeast is reminiscent of Sercial from the island of Madeira.

California Sherry
Sherry-style wine analogous to the baked Spanish Amontillado, the amber-color wine is vinted from Central Valley Grenache, Palomino, and Mission grapes and aged twelve months to finish at 17.5 percent alcohol

California Marsala
A baked Italian Marsala-style fortified wine made from Grenache and Mission grapes exhibiting traditional deep amber color and rich caramelized flavors. Aged twelve months to finish at 17.5 percent alcohol.

SCOTT HARVEY WINES
Saint Helena, Napa County, California
scottharveywines.com
Owners: Scott and Jana Harvey
Winemaker: Scott Harvery

History
A native of California's Sierra Foothills wine country, Scott first became interested in winemaking as a high school exchange student in Germany. After attending California State University, Sacramento, Scott trained at Amador County's Montevina Winery. His Montevina experience prepared him well for

becoming head winemaker for Story Winery in Amador's Shenandoah Valley in 1978. A year later, Scott's leadership of Santino Winery—later Renwood Winery—and his ownership of the historic original Grandpere vineyard was instrumental in establishing Amador County as a renowned wine-growing area.

In 1996 Scott become partner, winemaker, and president of Napa's Folie a Deux Winery and its line of Menage a Trois wines. The popular brand was acquired by Sutter Home/Trinchero Winery in 2004 and Scott started his own wine venture with partner and wife Jana shortly thereafter.

Fortified Wine
Forte

> Born in the Sierra Foothills, this port-style wine is a blend of Amador County Touriga Nacional, Tinta Cão, Alvarelhão, and Souzão. Flavors of candied red fruit, licorice, and chocolate merge with soft tannins into a long sweet finish. Age-worthy through 2060.

Awards

> **GOLD**, California State Fair
> **GOLD**, Amador County Fair

STEELE WINES

> Kelseyville, Lake County, California
> steelewines.com

Owner: Jed Steel

Winemaker: Jed Steele. For nearly half a century, Jed Steele has been making California wines. Starting as a "cellar rat" with Stony Hill Winery in 1968, to starting Edmeades Winery, and ten years later founding Kendall-Jackson, Jed has produced quality wines from almost every wine region in the state.

History

Steele Wines was established in 1991 when he co-leased a small winery to begin production of Steele and Shooting Star Wines. In 1996, Jed purchased the old Konocti Winery between Lakeport and Kelseyville in Lake County. Today, Steele produces more than thirty individual wines under several different labels.

Fortified Wine
Touriga Nacional

> About half an acre in the Steele Winery vineyard was grafted to Touriga Nacional in order to make this port-style wine. The must is fermented to approximately 7 percent residual sugar before pressing and blending with high proof spirts. The wine spends twenty-four months in a combination of French and American oak before bottling.

C
A
L
I
F
O
R
N
I
A

99

C
A
L
I
F
O
R
N
I
A

TESOURO CELLARS

Saint Helena, Napa County, California
tesourowines.com
Owners: Don McGrath and Rich Auger
Winemaker: Contract winemakers

History

Don McGrath was longtime owner/winemaker of Villa Helen in St. Helena where he made a variety of wines, including a port-style wine made partially from some Cabernet Sauvignon grapes grown by neighbor Rich Auger. Don and his wife sold their winery in 2001 (Auger-Martucci Winery today) but Don and Rich kept thinking about producing a port-style wine from authentic Portuguese varieties. In 2003, the team produced one barrel of port-style wine from grapes grown in the Silvaspoon Vineyard near Galt, Calfiornia, in the San Joaquin Valley. Commercial production began in 2005. Tesouro is the quintessential example of a tiny but laser-focused American fortified wine producer.

Fortified Wine
Vintage California Dessert Wine

Made from a blend of Touriga Nacional, Tinta Francisca, Tinta Roriz, Alvarelhão, Souzão, and Tinta Cão, this is a port-style wine in the Portuguese manner. Fortified with 145-proof French Columbard brandy produced in Mendocino, and aged several years before bottling, the wine finishes at 19 percent alcohol and 11 percent residual sugar.

V. SATTUI WINERY

Saint Helena, Napa County, California
vsattui.com
Owners: Sattui family, Dairo Sattui, President
Winemakers: Brooks Painter, Director of Winemaking.
A graduate of University of California, Santa Cruz, Brooks was born in San Francisco and grew up in northern California. Since joining V. Sattui in 2005, Brooks is responsible for the winery's portfolio of over sixty different wines as well as supervising the estate vineyards.

Jason Moravec, Winemaker. Son of grapegrowers in the Carneros region of Sonoma County, Jason interned at Gloria Ferrer Winery while graduating from UC Davis. Before coming to V. Sattui, Jason gained practical experience working with Patz and Hall in Sonoma, Franciscan in St. Helena, and a stretch in New Zealand with Kim Crawford Winery.

Peter Velleno, Winermaker. Born and raised in San Franciso, Peter received his Bachelor of Fermentation Science from UC Davis in 2003. Following graduation, Peter became assistant winemaker for William Hill Winery, then moved on to the smaller Hartwell Vineyards. Joining V. Sattui in 2008 as associate winemaker, his drive and desire earned him his winemaker title.

History

In 1882, Vittorio and Katerina Sattui settled in San Francisco's North Beach District after arriving in America from their native home in Carsi, Italy, Genoa. The couple began their wine business in 1885 naming the new winery after the source of their grapes, St. Helena. Vittorio renamed the business V. Sattui Wine Company following the purchase of the Rottanzi Winery in the San Francisco Mission District in 1899. Prohibition forced closure of the winery but Vittorio didn't reopen following repeal, opting for retirement.

Fast forward to 1972 when Vittorio's great-grandson Dario returned from a European trip with a unique plan to restart the Sattui wine business. An accounting and finance graduate of San Jose State University with an MBA from UC Berkeley, Dario envisioned a winery modeled after a small Italian village with open grounds and direct-to-consumer sales. The winery building and picnic grounds in St. Helen were completed in 1976. Perhaps Dario's crowning achievement was the 2007 opening of Castello di Amorosa in Calistoga. V. Sattui celebrated its 125th anniversary in 2010.

Fortified Wines

Angelica

Made from the fresh juice from Muscat of Alexandria, Angelica is a full-bodied fortified wine whose roots can be traced to the early days of California wine. Fermentation is arrested with the addition of twenty-year-old pot-still brandy resulting in a light amber/pale salmon color with 18 percent alcohol and 15 percent residual sugar.

Madeira

A complex blend of old port-style wine, Zinfandel, and brandy makes this wine a unique tribute to the original Vittorio Sattui winery. Starting with a "mother" or master blend—over 100-year-old vintage port-style wines aged in a 130-year solera barrel-aging system—provide the foundation for primary, secondary, and tertiary blends of aged Zinfandel that produce a matchless sweet, luscious, almond and caramel flavor wine with 19 percent alcohol and 13.5 percent residual sugar.

130th Anniversary Port

Limited collector's port-style wine to mark a milestone in V. Sattui history. A blended wine in the traditional Portuguese style, the rich, powerful wine was aged a minimum of fifteen years in small barrels.

Vintage Port

Port-style fortified wine made from Tinta Cão, Touriga Nacional, and classic California Zinfadel, this rich, robust wine was aged three years in wood casks prior to bottling,18.5 percent alcohol and 15 percent residual sugar.

CALIFORNIA

101

Awards
Angelica, GOLD, Sommelier Challenge
Madeira, **BEST OF CLASS**, Los Angeles County Fair
Vintage Port, GOLD, Winemaker Challenge
    GOLD, San Francisco Chronicle Wine Competition

SONOMA PORT WORKS
Petaluma, Sonoma County, California
portworks.com
Owners: Bill and Caryn Reading
Winermaker: Bill Reading

History
Sonoma Port Works is one of a tiny handful of America winemakers devoted exclusively to fortified wine production. Reading began his small Sonoma winery twenty-two years ago with the aim to create new styles of fortified dessert wines by nontraditional blending grapes and other ingredients. Petit Verdot and Petite Sirah for Bill's wines are certified organic grown by the Heringer Family in Clarksburg, California. The winery and tasting room are located in the quaint, early 1900s Foundry Building along the Petaluma River.

Fortified Wines
Aris Petite Sirah Port
Rich, brick-red port-style wine fortified with Cabernet Sauvignon wine spirit distilled in a single-batch copper still. Aged six and a half years in small neutral oak barrels and finishing at 19 percent alcohol and 7.5 percent residual sugar.

Aris Petit Verdot
From a grape rarely used for port-style wines, this deep garnet fortified wine is aged two years in oak prior to bottling. 18.3 percent alcohol and 6 percent residual sugar.

Cask Reserve Batch 4
Smooth and rich with delicate favors, the blend of Petite Sirah, Petit Verdot, and other barrel-aged port-style wines is slowly aged to produce a lingering finish. 20 percent alcohol with 6.5 percent residual sugar.

Deco
Petite Sirah and Zinfandel port-style wine infused with natural essence of dark chocolate. 18 percent alcohol and 8 percent residual sugar.

Duet, Sherry
Crafted from Palomino and Mission grapes and blended with natural essence of hazelnut, Duet is a sherry-style fortified wine of amber tone showing traditional vanilla and toasted nutty character. 18 percent alcohol and 8 percent residual sugar.

Dyna Aperitif
> A crisp aperitif with tropical fruit and ginger character, the wine is made from fortified Chardonnay blended with fruit botanical extracts. 17.5 percent alcohol, 3.5 percent residual sugar.

DANIEL GEHRS WINES
Los Olivos, Santa Barbara County, California
danielgehrswines.com
Owner/Winemaker: Daniel Gehrs

History
After his 1973 college graduation, Dan began his wine career at Paul Masson Vineyards in Saratoga, California, in public relations, giving winery tours. Desiring to be a winemaker, Dan and his wife Robin and partner Victor Erikson established Congress Springs Vineyards in the Santa Cruz Mountains. The old winery was in a state of decay in the early 1970s but renovated facility flourished through the 1980s. Gehrs relocated to the Central Coast and from 1993 to 1997 was winemaker at Zaca Mesa Winery. He was a member of the Sunstone Winery team until founding his own enterprise.

Fortified Wines
Tawny Port
> Tawny port-style wine crafted from Madera County Portuguese varieties and aged over ten years in small oak casks. Mellow, smooth texture with distinctive tawny color and flavor.

Fireside Port
> Aged two years in oak barrels, this ruby port-style wine with notes of black fruit is made from Madera County Portuguese grape varieties.

Awards
> Fireside Port, **GOLD/BEST OF CLASS**, New World Wine Competition

PEACHY CANYON
Paso Robles, San Louis Obispo County, California
peachycanyon.com
Owners: Beckett Family
Winemaker: Robert Henson. Following a decade-long stretch in the restaurant business, Robert went back to school in 2002 to obtain his degree in enology from California State University, Fresno. On graduation, he worked as a winemaker in the Santa Cruz Mountains until joining Peachy Canyon in 2015.

History

Doug Beckett was born in West Virginia to a Navy family that finally settled in San Diego California. In 1971 he married Vista California–native Nancy Thibodo and graduated with his degree in business administration. For the next decade, Doug was a multilevel teacher and received his Master of Psychology. The couple and sons Josh and Jake moved to Paso Robles in 1982 where he continued teaching while Nancy put her dance degree to use in 1991 as part owner of a local dance studio. Peachy Canyon was founded in 1988 as a small, 500-case enterprise that grew to its present capacity to ship wines across the nation, Europe, the Pacific Rim, and Canada.

Fortified Wine
Zinfandel Port

> Non-vintage port-style fortified wine made from Paso Robles Zinfandel. The wine is a fraction blend of all prior vintages. Nutty, rich and never cloying, with subtle spice on the finish.

ROXO PORT CELLARS

Paso Robles, San Luis Obispo County, California
roxocellars.com
Owners: Kim and Jeff Steele
Winemaker: Jeff Steele

History

With a passion for traditional port wine, the Steeles established Roxo Port Cellars to make new-world port-style wines using old-world "Methodo Portugues."

Fortified Wines
Ruby Tradicional

> A ruby-style blend of authentic Portuguese varieties Touriga Nacional, Souzão, Tinta Roriz, and Bastardo from Paso Robles and Cienega Valley vineyards. 19.5 percent alcohol and 8.65 percent residual sugar.

Negrette

> Made from 100 percent Calleri Vineyard Negrette (a grape originating in Southwest France), The fortified port-style wine has a classic deep purple color and candied fruit flavors with a final alcohol of 18 percent.

Barbera

> Calleri Vineyard in San Benito County provides the fruit for this 100 percent Barbera port-style wine with elegant color and lively acidity with candied fruit and spice character. 18.5 percent alcohol.

Magia Pret (Black Magic)

> Roxo Port Cellars flagship port-style blend of half Cabernet Sauvignon and half Syrah. Dense and dark with firm tannins and smoked cedar character. 20 percent alcohol and 8.2 percent residual sugar.

Awards
> **Barbera, GOLD,** San Francisco Chronicle Wine Competition
> **Negrette, GOLD,** San Francisco Chronicle Wine Competition
> **Ruby Tradicional, SILVER,** San Francisco Chronicle Wine Competition

SIERRA STARR WINERY
Grass Valley, Nevada County, California
sierrastarr.com
Owners: Phil, Anne, and Jackson Starr
Winemaker: Phil Starr

History

Looking to move their flower nursery business from Monterey in 1995, Phil and Anne found a 5-acre vineyard on the edge of Grass Valley, California. The flowers never did move but the Starrs developed their fledging vineyard and winery business into a thriving 12-acre vineyard with a charming tasting room in a historic downtown brick building purchased in 2003.

Fortified Wine
Five Starr Port

A port-style fortified wine crafted from a blend of Amador County Touriga Nacional, Tinta Cão, Tinta Roriz, and estate Zinfandel and Cabernet Sauvignon. The wine is aged in a 338-gallon German oak cask. The wine is bottled "as needed" and the oak cask is replenished from newer wines aged in small oak barrels. Light tawny character and hints of ruby with 19 percent alcohol and 8 percent residual sugar.

MOUNT PALOMAR WINERY
Temecula, Riverside County, California
mountpalomarwinery.com
Owner: Louidar LLC
Winemaker: James Rutherford. James is a descendant of the first family to settle and produce wine in Napa Valley (Rutherford) who graduated from Cal Poly San Luis Obispo and stayed in the central coast to make wine.

History

John Poole began the 45-acre wine estate in 1969, one of the first to recognize the potential of the Temecula's rolling hills as a fine-wine region. He was a former radio electronics engineer who pioneered radar during World War II and went on to establish Los Angeles radio station KBIG, the first successful LA FM station and first UHF television station. John began making wine in 1975 and his son Peter Poole took over winery operation ten years later. Mount Palomar Winery has been making fortified wines for over thirty years.

C
A

Fortified Wine
Solera Cream Sherry
A truly distinctive fortified cream sherry-style wine made from authentic Palomino grapes, the wine is handcrafted using a unique outdoor fractional blending system. Aged a minimum of five years under the California sun, the wine reflects rich hazelnut and caramel character with 18 percent alcohol and 12 percent residual sugar.

Awards
  GOLD, San Francisco Chronicle Wine Competition

C
O
L
O
R
A
D
O

DEBEQUE CANYON WINERY
  Palisade, Colorado
  Grand Junction Appellation
  debequecanyonwinery.com
Owners: Bennett and Davy Price
Winemaker: Bennett Price

History
Beginning as a home winemaker in the early 1970s, farm-bred geologist Bennett and wife Davy purchased a Colorado vineyard near Grand Junction. While expanding the Chardonnay block, they planted Cabernet Sauvignon and established the Merlot vineyard block in Colorado. After attending viticulture classes at UC Davis, the Prices established DeBeque Canyon in 1997. The winery tasting room is in a fruitpacking building called the "Basket Shed," built in 1903.

Fortified Wines
Fortified Syrah
  Port-style wine from Syrah grapes aged eight years in French oak.
Fortified Merlot
  From estate Merlot grapes and aged nine years in French oak barrels.

GRAYSTONE WINERY
  Clifton, Colorado
  graystonewine.com
Owners/Winemakers: Lynn and Vaughn Goebe

History

Colorado's only dedicated port-style wine producer, the boutique winery was established in 2001 and named for the nearby gray shale bluffs around Grand Valley. A large band of wild horses still roam the bluffs and mesas above the Colorado River.

Fortified Wines

Port

Ruby port-style wines aged in neutral oak barrels finishing at 19 percent alcohol.

Lipizzan

White port-style made from Pinot Gris fermented on the skins for color. 19 percent alcohol.

TALON WINE BRANDS

Palisade, Colorado

talonwinebrands.com

Owners: Foster Family

Winemaker: Glen Foster

History

In 1976, family patriarch Reed Foster co-founded Ravenswood Winery, one of the most acclaimed early Sonoma, California wineries. After nearly thirty years as the Ravenswood CEO, the family relocated to Colorado where they started a small wine shop in Palisade. They named their winemaking venture Talon in recognition of son and winemaker Glenn's passion for falconry.

Fortified Wines

St. Kathryn Cellars (brand) Merlot Port

Crafted from Grand Valley merlot grapes, this wine is rich and sweet.

MOUNTAIN VIEW WINERY

Olathe, Colorado

mountainviewwinery.com

Owners: Michael and Wendy Young

Winemaker: Michael Young

History

Third generation natives of Olathe, a Colorado town on the western slope of the Rockies, Michael and Wendy grow organic grapes and make wine on their vineyard property.

Fortified Wines

Colorado Evening Sherry

A new world version of the old-world Spanish Sherry, this is a robust, brandy-fortified and oak-aged wine.

Precipice Peak Port

A vintage, ruby port-style fortified wine that is smooth and sweet.

CONNECTICUT VALLEY WINERY

New Hartford, Connecticut

ctvalleywinery.com

Owners: Anthony and Judith Ferraro

Winemakers: Anthony and Jason Ferraro

History

The Ferraro's established their picturesque 30-acre vineyard and winery in 2005.

Fortified Wine

Black Bear Port

Smooth, full-bodied, red port-style fortified wine.

Awards

Black Bear Port

Top dessert wine for Eastern States Exposition's Vintner's Harvest.

MIRANDA VINYARDS

Goshen, Connecticut

mirandavineyard.com

Owners: Miranda Family

Winemaker: Manuel "Manny" Miranda

History

A native of Portugal, Manny Miranda modeled his American winery after the old-world family winery. The first vines were planted in 2001 and the winery was opened to the public in 2007. Manny has been making wine since 1970. The former real-estate developer and civil engineer is perhaps one of the most experienced winemakers in Connecticut.

Fortified Wine
Vinho Fino
> White port-style fortified wine made from Seyval and Cayuga hybrid grapes.

Awards
> **Vinho Fino**, **SILVER**, Tasters Guild International Wine Judging

SHARPE HILL VINEYARD
> Pomfret, Connecticut
> sharpehill.com
Owners: Vollweiler Family
Winemaker: Howard Bursen

History
Steven and Catherine Vollweiler established their 25-acre vineyard on the 110-acre Colonial-era estate in 1993. The winery's tasting room and Fireside Tavern are located in a reproduced eighteenth-century American-style building.

Fortified Wine
Pontefract
> Port-style fortified wine made from estate-grown St. Croix grapes.

MURIELLE WINERY
> Clearwater, Florida
> Muriellewinery.com
Owners: Michael and Janine Biglin
Winemaker: Michael Biglin

History
Started in 2000 by former businessman and CEO Michael Biglin, Murielle Winery was named Michael's mother Muriel. Choosing not compete in the over-competitive dry red and white wine market, Biglin elected to work with specialty wines. The winery has no vineyards; rather, Murielle wines are produced from grape juices employing minimally invasive methods.

Fortified Wine
Mad Port
> A port-style blend of Tinta Madera and Tinta Cão juice fortified with eighty proof brandy and aged twenty-two months in oak barrels.

CONNECTICUT

FLORIDA

F
L
O
R
I
D
A

SAN SEBASTIAN WINERY

St. Augustine, Florida
sansebastianwinery.com
Owners: Cox Family
Winemaker: Jeanne Burgess

History
Originally founded in 1983, San Sebastian Winery owns or has contracts with vineyards throughout the state of Florida. San Sebastian grows Florida hybrid bunch grapes as well as native muscadine grapes. San Sebastian is the second largest winery in Florida and is housed in a downtown St. Augustine building constructed in 1923.

Fortified Wines
Port Ruby
Crafted in the ruby port-style, the wine is made from grapes grown in Florida.
Cream Sherry
Full-bodied sweet fortified wine from Florida-grown grapes.

BREWER CELLARS LLC

Winter Springs, Florida
brewercellers.com
Manager: Timothy Brewer
Winemaker: Doug Brewer

History
Founded in 2004, the wines are produced from grape juices and Florida-grown grapes.

Fortified Wine
Chocolate Finale Port
Ruby port-style wine infused with chocolate flavors. 16 percent alcohol.

G
E
O
R
G
I
A

HABERSHAM VINEYARDS & WINERY

Helen, Georgia
habershamvineyards.com
Owner: Tom Slick
Winemaker: Andrew Beaty

110

History
One of Georgia's oldest and largest wineries, Habersham has been producing wine since 1983.

Fortified Wine
Creekstone Georgia Chambourcin
> Bold, fortified port-style wine made from Chambourcin, a French-American hybrid grape.

G
E
O
R
G
I
A

THREE SISTERS VINEYARDS AND WINERY
> Dahlonega, Lumkin County, Georgia
> threesistersvineyards.com
Owners: Paul Family
Winemaker: Family Winemaking Team

History
Billed as "Daholnega's First Farm Winery" Sharon and Doug Paul purchased 184 acres of northeast Georgia property with a view of Three Sisters mountain. The winery was established in 1999 and the tasting room opened in 2001. Three Sisters wines are made from the 20-acre estate vineyard.

Fortified Wine
Georgia Port
> Port-style fortified wine made 100 percent from estate Touriga Nacional.

INDIAN CREEK FARM WINERY
> Kuna, Idaho
> indiancreekwinery.com
Owners: Bill and Mui Stowe
Winemaker: Mike McClure

I
D
A
H
O

History
After his retirement from the Air Force, Bill and wife Mui founded the vineyard and winery in 1982. Bill is an Idaho native and is often referred to as the "grandfather of Idaho wines" who pioneered the state's new wine industry.

Fortified Wine
Ruby Dahlia Port
> A port-style blend of Cabernet Sauvignon Tinta Cão Touriga Nacional, Souzão and Cinsault. Cabernet Sauvignon fortifying brandy is added on

the fourth day of fermentation resulting in a wine with just under 20 percent alcohol and 6 percent residual sugar. The wine is aged about three years in neutral oak barrels.

KOENIG DISTILLERY & WINERY

Caldwell, Idaho
koenigdistilleryandwinery.com
Owners: Andy and Greg Caldwell
Winemaker: Greg Caldwell

History

The Sunny Slope of southwestern Idaho along the Snake River was home to the Caldwell brothers' mother's family who homesteaded in the area and made wine during the Depression. The brothers established the fruit orchard in 1995 and a year later planted a small vineyard which would produce the grapes for their wines and spirits.

Fortified Wine

Two Barrel Reserve Port

Port-style wine produced from estate Merlot and Syrah, fortified with brandy produced in the Koenig Distillery.

FOX VALLEY WINERY

Oswego, Illinois
foxvalleywinery.com
Owners: Faltz Family
Winemaker: Jim Zipper

History

The boutique winery just west of Chicago in the Fox River Valley was started in 2000 when the Faltz family first planted a vineyard that has since grown to its current 25 acres.

Fortified Wines

Amore, American Dessert Wine

Fortified wine made entirely of Frontenac grapes infused with chocolate and raspberry flavors. Aged in French oak barrels with finished alcohol of 19.2 percent.

L'Amour, American Dessert Wine
> Crafted from Frontenac and Noriet grapes infused with chocolate and orange flavorings, the wine is finished by sixteen months of aging in barrels at 19.2 percent alcohol

Vintage Foch, Illinois Dessert Wine
> Port-style fortified wine wholly from Marechal Foch grapes and aged fifty-four months in French oak barriques. 19.8 percent alcohol.

BLUE SKY VINEYARD
> Makanda, Illinois
> blueskyvineyard.com

Owner: Jim Ewers
Winemaker: Karen Hand

History

The first 2.5 acres of 13-acre southern Illinois Shawnee Hills Blue Sky vineyard was planted in 2000. The Tuscan-style winery and tasting room designed by California State University, Fresno's Nancy Karen Brian was completed in 2005.

Fortified Wines
Cream Sherry
> Slowly baked, sweet, sherry-style wine made from Niagara with golden color and rich caramel and roasted nut character.

Renaissance Norton Port
> Powerful, dense, port-style fortified wine crafted from Norton (Cynthiana) grapes.

MASSBACH RIDGE WINERY
> Elizabeth, Illinois
> massbachridge.com

Owners: Peggy and Greg Harmston
Winemaker: Peggy Harmston

History

Farming is in the Harmston family heritage. The Massbach Ridge vineyard was started in 2000 and the Elizabeth tasting room opened shortly thereafter in 2003. The second tasting room in Galena, Illinois, was opened in 2011.

Fortified Wine
Velvet Hour
> Dark, rich fortified wine crafted from Frontenac grapes.

CHATEAU THOMAS

Plainfield, Indiana
chateauthomas.com
Owners: Charles and Jill Thomas
Winemaker: Charles Thomas

History:
In the 1970s, practicing obstetrician and gynecologist Dr. Charles Thomas decided to take his home wine hobby to a commercial enterprise. After careful research and thorough training, Chateau Thomas was launched in 1984 just south of Indianapolis.

Grapes from Chateau Thomas are sourced from California, Oregon, and Washington. Following harvest, the fruit is chilled to 34°F and shipped in refrigerated trucks to the winery.

Fortified Wines
Vintage Port
Crafted from five authentic Portuguese varieties grown in Lodi, California, the port-style wine is aged sixteen months in American oak.
Sweet Sherry
Luscious, sweet, sherry-style fortified wine exhibiting characteristic caramel and nutty flavors.

SIMMONS WINERY

Columbus, Indiana
simmonswinery.com
Owners: Simmons Family
Winemaker: David Simmons

History
Located on the 120-year-old family farm, Simmons Winery opened in 2000. The family began the 12.5-acre vineyard in 1998 and now grows eight hybrid grape varieties.

Fortified Wine
Indiana Ruby Port
Lighter-bodied, port-style wine made from estate French-American hybrid grapes fortified with wine spirits.

OLIVER WINERY

Bloomington, Indiana
oliverwinery.com
Owners: Oliver Winery Employees
Winemaker: Dennis Dunham

History

Indiana University law professor William Oliver started the winery as a hobby in the 1960s. Professor Oliver was instrumental in passing the 1971 Indiana Small Winery Act. Oliver Winery was opened to the public in 1972. Under the guidance of Bill and Kathleen Oliver, growth of the winery through the 2000s places Oliver Winery as one of the largest wineries in the eastern United States.

Fortified Wines
Creekbend Tawny

A unique port-style blend of red Chambourcin and white Vidal Blanc grapes. Fermented separately and fortified with neutral grape spirits, the wine is aged in French oak to develop tawny characteristics.

Maximum Port

Ruby port-style wine crafted from Lodi, California, Petite Sirah grapes. Light press juice is fortified with neutral spirits to arrest fermentation and barrel aged four years to balance fruit, caramel, and nut flavors.

LITTLE SWAN LAKE WINERY

Superior, Iowa
lslwinery.com
Owners: Scott and Diane Benjamin and Family
Winemaker: Scott Benjamin

History

Housed in a remodeled 1920s barn, northeast Iowa's Little Lake Swan Winery was opened in 2002. The 2-acre vineyard grows cold-hardy grapes capable of withstanding Midwest winters.

Fortified Wine
Forte

Fortified port-style wine made from estate Frontenac grapes.

I
O
W
A

SUMMERSET WINERY

Indianola, Iowa
summersetwine.com
Owners: Ronald and Linda Mark
Winemaker: Ronald Mark

History

Located 7 miles south of Des Moines, Ron and Linda began growing grapes on Summerset Ridge above the Middle River in 1989. The winery tasting room was opened in 1997 in the Mark's basement while the wines were produced in the home's modified garage. The entire operation was moved to an upscale barn structure in 2001. The estate vineyard is 12 acres of hardy, cold-climate grape varieties.

Fortified Wine

Ruby LaBelle

Port-style wine crafted from estate Frontenac grapes fortified with home-made brandy to bring the finished wine to 20 percent alcohol.

K
A
N
S
A
S

OZ WINERY

Wanego, Kansas
ozwinerykansas.com
Owners: Noah Wright and Brooke Balderson
Winemaker: Noah Wright

History

Opened in 2007, all Oz wines are crafted in the winery located in the heart of downtown Wamego.

Fortified Wines

Surrender

Sherry-style fortified wine made from Chardonnay grapes.

The Lion's Courage

Sweet, port-style fortified wine fashioned from *vinifera* grape varieties.

SOMERSET RIDGE VINEYARD & WINERY

Paola, Kansas
somersetridge.com
Owners/ Winemakers: Dennis and Cindy Reynolds

History

Pursuing a love of fine wine since their marriage in 1983, the Reynolds established their vineyard on Dennis's parents' limestone ridge ex–cattle ranch property in 1998. The couple bought the adjacent property and in 2001 opened the first winery in Miami County since Kansas prohibition in 1881.

Fortified Wines

Tawny

Tawny port-style wine crafted from a blend of red and white grape varieties fortified with brandy and aged several years in oak barrels.

Ruby Port

Ruby port-style fortified wine made from Norton grapes.

PRODIGY VINEYARDS & WINERY

Frankfort, Kentucky

prodigyvineyards

Owner/Winemaker: Chad Peach

History

The fifteen-year-old vineyard on the Peach Family Farm is located in the heart of thoroughbred race horse country in Woodford County.

PONTCHARTRAIN VINEYARDS

Bush, Louisiana

pontchartrainvineyards.com

Owner/Winemaker: John Seago

History

Pontchartrain Vineyards has been making Louisiana wine since 1991.

Fortified Wine

Port of New Orleans

Port-style fortified wine produced from Mendocino, California Zinfandel.

M
A
I
N
E

SAVAGE OAKS VINEYARD AND WINERY

Union, Maine
savageoakes.com
Owners: Elmer and Holly Savage
Winemaker: Elmer Savage

History

Elmer Savage began farming in 1985 when his parents purchased Barrett Hill Farm. The 95-acre property was purchased from the elder Savages in 2000 and the first 2 acres of wine grapes were planted in 2002. Currently, the vineyard encompasses 4 acres, growing ten grape varieties. Over the past several years, the winery has advanced from a hobby to a successful small commercial producer.

Fortified Wine
Nor'easter

Maine's first and only estate-grown port-style fortified wine made from Frontenac grapes. The wine finishes at 19 percent alcohol and 6 percent residual sugar.

M
A
R
Y
L
A
N
D

ELK RUN VINEYARDS

Mt. Airy, Maryland
elkrun.com
Owners: Fred and Carol Wilson
Winemaker: Fred Wilson

History

On rolling Frederick County, land originally granted to English lord Baltimore from the king of England, the vineyards and winery were established in 1983. The 25 acres of densely spaced vines employ sustainable agricultural practices. Elk River is the only Maryland grower/producer of Gewürztraminer and is first in the state to grow Pinot noir.

Fortified Wine
Lord Baltimore Port

Crafted from estate Cabernet Sauvignon, the port-style fortified wine is aged for three years in old oak barrels and one year in bottle.

Awards

GOLD, Wine Makers Choice Competition
SILVER, International Tasters Guild

TILMON'S ISLAND WINERY

Sudlersville, Maryland
tilmonswine.com
Owner/Winemaker: Hames Don Tilmon

History

Established in 2004, Tilmon's Island was the first winery in Queen Anne's County.

Fortified Wine
Tred Avon's Dessert

Exclusive fortified blend of Chardonnay and blueberry juice.

SERPENT RIDGE VINEYARD

Westminster, Maryland
serpentridge.com
Owners: Hal Roche and Karen Smith
Winemaker: Greg Lambrecht

History

Westminster's first wine enterprise, the winery and vineyards were founded in 2003 and acquired by the present owners in 2013.The 2-acre vineyard produces fruit for small lot, handcrafted wines.

Fortified Wine
Slither

Fortified port-style wine made from Maryland-grown Cabernet Franc, Cabernet Sauvignon, and Sangiovese with 19 percent alcohol and 5 percent residual sugar.

RUNNING BROOK VINEYARDS & WINERY

Dartmouth, Massachusetts
runningbrookwine.com
Owner/Winemaker: Pedro Teixeira

History

Dr. Pedro Teixeira and retired partner Manual Morais founded Running Brook

MASSACHUSETTS

in 1998 to grow classic wine grapes and produce premium wines. Dr. Teixeira grew up in the Azores and Portugal with some time in California before he graduated from The Ohio State University with his Doctor of Dental Surgery. RB Distillery was introduced in 2014.

Fortified Wines
Viva Vidal
> Barrel-aged, white port-style wine made from Vidal blanc fortified with proprietary brandy.

Ruby
> Blend of Cabernet Franc, Merlot, and Petit Verdot crafted into a ruby port-style and oak aged.

WESTPORT RIVERS WINERY
Westport, Massachusetts
westportrivers.com
Owners: Bob and Carol Russell
Winemaker: Bill Russell

History
For years, The Russell's longed to reestablish Carol's family wine legacy created by her German father and grandfather in upstate New York. After an extensive search, the couple settled in Westport in 1982 with the intention of producing New England sparkling wines. They planted their first vines in 1986 and wine production started in 1989.

Fortified Wine
Prodigiosa Vermouth
> A fortified aromatized wine made from quality, estate-grown white grapes blended with various botanicals including wormwood, gentian, bitter orange, and vanilla bean.

MICHIGAN

FLYING OTTER VINEYARD
Adrian, Michigan
flyingotter.com
Owners: Utter Family
Winemaker: Bob Utter

History

The vineyard southwest of Detroit was founded in 2005 with the first harvest in 2007. Hardy, cold-climate hybrid grape varieties were selected and the vineyard employs sustainable agricultural practices.

Fortified Wine

Starboard

> Rich, port-style wine made from Frontenac grapes and fortified with grape wine spirits.

LEELANAU CELLARS

Omena, Michigan

leelanaucellars.com

Owners: Jacobson Family

Winemaker: Michael Jacobson

History

The winery was named for a Native American word meaning "delight of life." The enterprise on the shores of Grand Traverse Bay was founded in 1974 and the first wines were released in 1977. The 90 acres of vineyards produce over thirty varieties of Leelanau wines.

Fortified Wine

Vintage Port

> Made from home vineyard Baco noir grapes, the port-style wine is fortified with brandy and aged in oak barrels.

WARNER VINEYARDS

Paw Paw, Michigan

warnerwines.corecommerce.com

Owner: Patrick Warner

President: James Warner

Operations Manager: William Warner

History

The second oldest Michigan winery was founded by John and James Warner in 1938. Located in heart of Michigan wine country, the Warner "Wine Haus" occupies the historic Paw Paw village water-works building and is a state-designated historical structure.

Fortified Wine
Port
> Fortified port-style wine of deep ruby color and aromatic characteristics of traditional port wines.

CROW RIVER WINERY

Hutchinson, Minnesota
crowriverwinery.com
Owners: McBrady Family
Winemaker: Michael McBrady

History
Crow River Winery and vineyards were established in 2004.

Fortified Wines
Marquette Dessert Wine
> Medium-bodied fortified wine made from Marquette grapes.

Frontenac Dessert Wine
> Deep garnet color, full-bodied fortified wine crafted from Frontenac grapes.

Awards
> **Frontenac Dessert Wine, GOLD, Best Buy, WVWC Best US Fortified Wine**

SAINT CROIX VINEYARDS

Stillwater, Minnesota
scvwines.com
Owners: Paul Quast, Peter Hemstad, and Chris Aamodt
Winemaker: Matthew Scott

History
Founded in 1992, the picturesque Saint Croix vineyard and distinctive one-hundred--year-old rustic barn tasting room is just west of Stillwater.

Fortified Wine
Frontenac Port
> Made entirely from home vineyard grown Frontenac grapes, the fortified port-style wine is barrel-aged, providing rich berry, chocolate, and vanilla character.

INDIAN ISLAND WINERY

Janesville, Minnesota
indianislandwinery.com
Owners: Winter Family
Winemaker: Angie Winter

History
Indian Island Winery is an extension of Winter Haven Vineyard and Nursery established in 2000. The vineyards cover 12 acres and grow seventeen different varieties with a focus on cold-hardy grapes.

Fortified Wines
Dancing Spirit
Fortified white port-style wine made from Frontenac Gris grapes finishing with 18 percent alcohol and 7 percent residual sugar.
Napin-Nagi
Fashioned from home vineyard Frontenac grapes, the port-style fortified wine has 18.5 percent alcohol with 4.25 percent residual sugar.

MINNESOTA

MONTELLE WINERY

Augusta, Missouri
montelle.com
Owner/Winemaker: Tony Kooyumjian

History
Originally established in 1970, Tony Kooyumijan purchased the Augusta property in 1998. Tony is a third-generation grape grower. His Armenian grandmother immigrated to California in 1915 where she established a San Joaquin Valley vineyard. Tony, however, chose a career as an airline pilot. He moved to Augusta in 1988 and established Augusta Winery prior to acquiring Montelle.

Fortified Wine
Cynthiana Port
Full-bodied with a deep burgundy color, this port-style wine is crafted from Cynthiana (Norton) grapes fortified with wine spirits from the Montelle distillery.

MISSOURI

RIVERWOOD WINERY

Weston, Missouri
riverwoodwinery.com
Owners: David Naatz and Ginah Mortensen

History

In 2005, David and Ginah purchased and renovated a 1950s-era school building for their Riverwood Winery tasting room on the scenic Missouri River bluffs. Grapes for Riverwood wines are grown on the 7-acre estate vineyard and purchased from local growers as well.

Fortified Wine

Riverwood Red Eminence

Grape spirits fortified port-style wine made from Chambourcin grapes and aged in Missouri oak barrels.

CHANDLER HILL VINEYARDS

Defiance, Missouri
chandlerhillvineyards.com
Owner: Chuck Gillentine, CSW
Winemaker: Tom Murphy

History

Chandler Hill Vineyards is located on property once owned by freed slave Joseph Chandler who came to Defiance in 1870. In 2007 the present owner began construction of the winery and tasting room on the site of Chandler's original cabin. Chandler Hill has 6 acres of vineyards on the property and 4 acres of vines offsite.

Fortified Wines

Crimson Arrow Dessert Wine

Red fortified wine made from Norton (Cynthiana) grapes — the Missouri state grape

Murphs Vignoles Dessert Wine

White fortified wine produced from estate hybrid Vignoles grapes.

MISSION MOUNTAIN WINERY

Dayton, Montana
missionmountainwinery.com
Owners: Tom Campbell Sr. and Tom Campbell Jr.
Winemaker: Tom Campbell Jr. Trained at UC Davis, Tom worked at Jekel and Shiloh in California as well as Ste. Michelle in Washington.

History

Montana's first bonded winery, Mission Mountain was founded in 1984 by Mr. Campbell and his son. The vineyard on the west shore of Flathead Lakes was first planted in 1979. Winter temperatures as low as -20 degrees and a five-month growing season have narrowed Mission Mountain vineyard grapes to Pinot noir, Pinot gris, Chardonnay, Gewürztraminer and a recent planting of Marquette.

Fortified Wines
Cream Sherry
> Whole berry crushed Orange Muscat grapes fashion this white brandy for-
> tified sherry-like wine.

Port
> Pinot noir grapes crushed whole with stems provide the base for this ruby/
> vintage port-style wine fortified with high-proof brandy. Aged in old
> French Limousin oak barrels, the wine has a firm, tannic backbone and
> dark, rich color.

Cocoa Vin
> Port-style wine blended with chocolate extract.

M
O
N
T
A
N
A

SOARING WINGS VINEYARD

> Springfield, Nebraska
> soaringwingswine.com

Owners: Jim and Sharon Shaw
Winemaker: Jim Shaw

History
Soaring Wings Vineyard was first planted in 2001 and the winery was opened in 2004. Jim is a pilot and the vineyards and winery are his retirement plan. Sharon keeps the business going while Jim is "soaring."

Fortified Wine
Cap'N Jim's AirPORT
> Ruby port-style wine crafted from Frontenac grapes and aged at least one
> year in oak barrels, the wine finishes at 22 percent alcohol.

N
E
B
R
A
S
K
A

PAHRUMP VALLEY WINERY

> Pahrump, Nevada
> pahrumpwinery.com

Owners/Winemakers: Bill and Gretchen Loken

N
E
V
A
D
A

History

In 2002 Bill and Gretchen Loken discovered the Pahrump Valley Winery, established in 1990. After taking control of the vineyards and winery in 2003, the couple began renovating the property. Their first harvest of Nevada Zinfandel was in 2005. The complete upgrade and renovation included a state-of-the-art kitchen and fine-dining restaurant called Symphony, a mere 55-minute drive from the Las Vegas strip.

Fortified Wine:
Crème Sherry
> Fortified sherry-style wine produced from California grown Palomino and Grenache gris grapes and aged at least four years in neutral oak barrels. The unique wine finishes with 17 percent alcohol and 17 percent residual sugar.

FLAG HILL WINERY & DISTILLERY

South Hampton, New Hampshire
flaghill.com
Owner/Winemaker: Brian Ferguson

History

Flag Hill farm, New Hampshire's largest vineyard, was founded in 1990. In 1950 Reinhold Farm was established by Frank Reinhold Sr., and the property managed as a dairy farm until 1964. The property remained unused until Linda and Frank Reinhold Jr. returned to farming and renamed the farm Flag Hill Farm. The first Flag Hill wines were produced in 1995 and all Flag Hill Winery wines are made from 100 percent New Hampshire fruit.

Fortified Wine
North River Port
> New Hampshire's first class port-style wine. Oak aged with balanced sweetness and warmth.

JEWELL TOWNE VINEYARDS

South Hampton, New Hampshire
jewelltownevineyards.com
Owners: Peter and Brenda Oldak
Winemaker: Peter Oldak

History

A pioneer in New Hampshire viticulture and winemaking, physician Dr. Peter Oldak and his clinical specialist Brenda, established Jewell Towne Vineyards in 1990. The winery was constructed in 1998 as an eighteenth-century post-and-beam barn reproduction.

Fortified Wine

New Hampshire Port

Medium-bodied, port-style fortified wine produced from 100 percent New Hampshire–grown Chancellor grapes with balanced sweetness and complex flavors.

HOPEWELL VALLEY VINEYARDS

Pennington, New Jersey

hopewellvalleyvineyards.com

Owner/Winemaker: Sergio Nen

History

Founded in 2001, the 20 acres of vineyard at the base of the Sourland Mountains near the Delaware Valley produces both *vinifera* and North Atlantic hybrid grapes for handcrafted Hopewell Valley wines.

Fortified Wines

Porto Rosso

Fortified, port-style wine made from estate Chambourcin grapes.

Chocolate Porto Rosso

Chocolate infused, port-style fortified wine with short barrel aging made from estate Chambourcin.

Porto Bianco

White port-style wine made from Vidal blanc and brandy and fortified during fermentation, resulting in 9 percent residual sugar.

RENAULT WINERY

Egg Harbor, New Jersey

renaultwinery.com

Owner: MCC Presidential

Winemaker: Marco Bucchi

History

The story of one of America's oldest continuously operating winery begins with the destruction of French master vintner Louis Nicholas Renault's Rheim vineyards by the evil phylloxera aphid. Renault relocated to California in 1855, only to find the bug devastating California wine grapes as well. Learning that native American grapes on the east coast were resistant to phylloxera, Renault purchased land near Egg Harbor in 1864 and introduced New Jersey Champagne in 1870. John D'Agostino purchased the winery on the eve of Prohibition and flourished as the producer of sacramental and medicinal wines. John's sister Maria took over the winery after his death in 1949 and made the old winery a New Jersey showplace, adding a wineglass museum in 1966. Universal Foods purchased the property in 1968, operating the winery until the 1974 acquisition by the New Jersey investment group MCC Presidential.

Fortified Wines
Cream Sherry
> Sherry-style fortified wine with sweet toasted almond and butterscotch character finishing at 18.5 percent alcohol.

American Port
> Port-style blend of red grape varieties with 20 percent alcohol.

White Port
> White port-style fortified wine with pineapple and citrus character and 18.5 percent alcohol.

VALENZANO WINERY

Shamong, New Jersey
valenzanowine.com
Owners/Winemakers: Anthony and Mark Valenzano

History
One of the east coast's largest wine producers, the Valenzanos started making wine as a hobby in 1996. Located in the New Jersey Pine Barrens, Valenzano farms include 88 acres of vineyards. The winery also sources wine grapes locally and nationally for its epitomes wines.

Fortified Wine
Jersey Devil Port
> Deep, velvety, port-style brandy fortified wine made from Cynthiana grapes and aged three years in oak barrels. Named for the legendary creature from the Pine Barrens.

LA CHIRIPADA WINERY & VINEYARD

Dixon, New Mexico
lachiripada.com
Owners: Michael and Patrick Johnson
Winemaker: Joshua Johnson

History
La Chiripada (meaning "a stroke of luck" or "a lucky fluke") was established in the Rio Embudo Valley of northern New Mexico in 1977. The southwest-style winery was built in 1981, the same year as the first commercial vineyard harvest. The estate vineyard's 6,100-foot elevation limits viticulture to cold climate and short season varieties, so La Chiripada purchases some varieties from Mimbres Valley in southern New Mexico.

Fortified Wines
New Mexico Port
Made from 100 percent Ruby Cabernet grapes, the port-style wine is fortified with brandy and aged in Hungarian oak barrels.

Vino De Oro
Fashioned from Orange Muscat grapes and oak barrel aged for six months, the white port-style brandy fortified wine has a characteristic Muscat bouquet.

Awards
New Mexico Port, **GOLD,** Finger Lakes International Wine Competition, **GOLD**, New Mexico State Fair

BARNSTORMER WINERY

Rock Stream, New York
barnstormerwinery.com
Owner: Scott Bronstein
Winemakers: Consultant Team

History
Barnstormer Winery opened in 2013 in the 170-year-old historic barn on Seneca Lake. The owner is a native of Syracuse who pursued a wine business career in California's Napa Valley before returning to his home state in 2012. The property originally housed the Arcadian Estate winery started in the 1970s.

Fortified Wine
Nosedive Port
Merlot port-style fortified wine with 20 percent alcohol and 12 percent residual sugar.

BROTHERHOOD WINERY
Washingtonville, New York
brotherhood-winery.com
Owners: Cesar Baeza, Castro Family, Chadwick Family
Winemaker: Robert Barrow

History
There is no doubt that Brotherhood is America's oldest existing winery. In 1837, French Huguenot émigré Jean Jaques planted grapes on a plot of land in Washington, NY. Mr. Jaques's first wine was made in his underground cellars dug in 1839. The cellars are still in use today. After almost sixty years of Jaques family operation, the winery was purchased and run by the Emerson brothers until Prohibition. Louis Farrell bought the winery and its sacramental wine, eventually turning the facility into a tourist destination. Cesar Baeza, a prominent international wine authority, became a member of the partnership1987, determined to make premium New York wines. However, a 1999 fire set the enterprise back until Mr. Baeza formed a new partnership in 2005, one that undertook restoration and renovation of the winery, thus retained claim to the oldest American winery.

Fortified Wines
Ruby Port
Heavy-bodied, ruby port-style wine with a velvety-smooth character.
Cream Sherry
Sweet, amber-colored sherry-style fortified wine.

JOHNSON ESTATE
Westfield, New York
johnsonwinery.com
Owners: Frederick and Jennifer Johnson
Winemaker: Jeffery Murphy

History
In 1908 English orphan and Canadian immigrant Frederick Johnson purchased a circa1822 home and farm in Westfield, NY that he named Sunnyslope Fruit Farm. He built an apple cold storage facility in 1920 that survives as the estate's tasting room. Frederick Johnson Jr., son of Frederick Johnson, took over farm

operation after the passing of his father. He replaced the orchards and Concord grape vineyard with French-American hybrid and native American grape varieties. Sunnyslope Fruit Farm was established as the oldest New York estate winery in 1961 with all the winery's grapes grown on the property. The three Johnson children inherited the estate in 1998, continuing to operate the enterprise until Frederick Jr. and Jennifer became the sole owners in 2010.

Fortified Wines
Ruby Port
   Crafted from Chancellor grapes, fermentation for the ruby port-style wine was stopped at eight brix and fortified with wine spirits to finish at 18 percent alcohol and 6 percent residual sugar.
Cream Sherry
   Aged in American oak barrels, the wine is made from white Delaware grapes providing raisin and nut character. 17 percent alcohol and 8 percent residual sugar.

PLEASANT VALLEY WINE COMPANY
Hammonsport, New York
pleasantvalleywine.com
Owners: Doyle Family
Winemaker: Michael Doyle

History
Founded in 1860 and designated US Bonded Winery No. 1, Pleasant Valley Wine Company was started by Charles Davenport Champlin and twelve local area businessmen. The facilities still in use today were constructed of wood and stone with a cellar cut into the property's hillside. The first crush was of 18 tons of Isabella and Catawba grapes. The winery started producing sparkling wine in 1865 and by 1870 Pleasant Valley was dubbed "Rheims of America". Pleasant Valley survived Prohibition by making sacramental wine. Davenport's grandson, Charles II, became the dean of American sparkling wine until his passing in 1950. The family sold the business to Marne Obernauer in 1955, who then sold it to the neighboring Taylor Wine Company in 1961. Coca-Cola Company acquired Taylor in 1977 which was in turn acquired by Joseph E. Seagram & Sons in 1983, and finally Vintners International Company in 1987. The local Doyle family purchased the historic wine operation in 1995. The winery is popularly known today as the Great Western Winery.

Fortified Wines
Solera Dry Sherry
   Using the solera "fractional" aging and blending system, this fortified sherry-style wine finishes with a crisp, light-nutty character and only 5.4 percent residual sugar.

Solera Sherry

Sweeter at 9 percent residual sugar than the dry sherry-style, this wine exhibits more complex aromas and flavors.

Vanilla Cream Sherry

The sweetest of all solera sherry-style wines at 13.25 percent residual sugar, the wine has a pronounced smooth fresh-vanilla character.

Maderia

Sweet fortified wine made in the style of wine from the Island of Madeira. 7.4 percent residual sugar.

Marsala

Wood aged, medium-bodied fortified wine in the classic Italian style.

PORTS OF NEW YORK

Ithaca, New York

portsofnewyork.com

Owner/Winemaker: Frederic Bouche

History

Frederic comes from a rich history of French winemakers going back to his great, great grandfather from Bordeaux. He trained in winemaking as a small boy in his grandfather's winery in the Calvados appellation of Normandy and started his own Finger Lakes region winery nine years after coming to the United States.

Fortified Wines

Meleau (pronounced "mellow") is a distinctive category of port-style wines. Grape wine spirits are used to arrest fermentation and are aged a minimum of four years in a neutral oak solera system. Meleau wines are unique in that a small amount of honey ("mel" meaning nectar) is used to grow yeast prior to fermentation.

Red Meleau

A blended, port-style wine made from Cabernet Franc, Merlot, and Noiret grapes fortified 6 percent with 175 proof grape spirits.

White Meleau

Full-bodied, white port-style wine fashioned from Muscat Ottonel and Vignole grapes fortified with 175 proof spirits.

GOOSE WATCH WINERY

Romulus, New York

goosewatch.com

Owners: Peterson Family

Winemaker: Derek Wilber

History
Established in 1997 by the Petersons, owners of Swedish Hill Winery, the Goose Watch 21-acre vineyard overlooking Cayuga Lake grows six grape varieties. The winery tasting room is a restored century-old barn.

Fortified Wines
Finale White Port
> Balanced, white port-style wine with exotic tropical fruit character crafted from a blend of Vidal blanc juice, Riesling, and Valvin Muscat grapes.

Classic Cream Sherry
> Rich, complex, sherry-style blend of Concord, Delaware, Chardonnay, Cayuga White, Vidal blanc, Niagara, and Catawba fruit aged in oak for smoothness.

Awards
> Finale White Port GOLD, Jefferson Cup Invitational, SILVER, New York State Fair
>
> Classic Cream Sherry, GOLD & BEST DESSERT WINE, Florida State International, DOUBLE GOLD, Monterey Wine Competition, GOLD, San Francisco Chronicle

DUPLIN WINERY
Rose Hill, North Carolina
duplinwinery.com
Owners: Fussell Family
Winemaker: Jason Bryan

History
D. J. Fussell and his two sons began growing muscadine grapes in the 1970s and started Duplin Winery as a market for the fruit. The next decade proved successful as the venture grew rapidly until 1983, when tax law and other legislation stymied progress. However, the family persisted and the third generation of Fussells assumed leadership in the early 2000s. Today, the 1.4 million gallon winery is the largest in the South.

Fortified Wine
American Port
> Port-style wine crafted from estate grown Noble grapes fortified with Noble grape wine spirits and aged in barrel for five years.

N
O
R
T
H

C
A
R
O
L
I
N
A

BRUSHY MOUNTAIN WINERY
St. Elkin, North Carolina
brushymountainwine.com
Owners: Jason Wiseman and Amy Euliss
Winemaker: Jason Wiseman

History
Ann and Matthew Mayberry established Brushy Mountain in 2005 in the old Elkin Canning Company building in downtown Elkin, NC. Jason is an experienced winemaker and he and Amy have long-time roots in western North Carolina.

Fortified Wine
Pour Mon Amour Dessert Wine
Chambourcin grapes from Yadkin Valley create the port-style wine aged two years in oak barrels.

Awards
BRONZE, Mid-Atlantic SE Wine Competition

NONI BACCA WINERY
Wilmington, North Carolina
nbwinery.com
Owners: Toni and Ken Incorvaia
Winemaker: Ken Incorvaia

History:
Fascinating family linages provide the background for the eastern North Carolina winery founded in 2007. Originally from Buffalo, NY, Toni and Ken are descendants of European families. Ken's family , Carmelo and Concetta Incorvaia, emigrated to the United States from Sicily in the early 1900s. Toni's family is from Bansko, Bulgaria. The winery name originated from Toni's early childhood when she mispronounced "Noni" for Toni. "Bacca" just came along with the nickname.

Fortified Wines
Dock at the Bay
Full-bodied, red wine crafted in the classic ruby port-style using Tempranillo grapes.
Porta Caffe
Port-style wine flavored with coffee beans. The "invigorating elixir" has medium roast coffee character with a vanilla finish.

FIRELANDS WINERY
Sandusky, Ohio
firelandswinery.com
Owners: Lonz, Inc. John Kronberg and Claudio Salvador
Winemaker: Claudio Salvador

History
Fireside Winery is the vanguard producer of Lonz, Inc., owners of Mon Ami, Lonz, Mantey, and Dover wines. The Edward Manty family built the original Fireside wine cellar in 1880. The name was derived from the area in north–central Ohio allotted to Connecticut families whose homes were burned by the British during the American Revolution. Mantey Winery was acquired by Paramount Distillers in 1979, and Lonz Inc. purchased the winery from Paramount in 2002.

Fortified Wine
Threesome Dessert Wine
Touriga Nacional, Tinta Cão, and Bastardo grapes are blended in this enduring port-style wine.

MEIER'S WINE CELLARS
Cincinnati, Ohio
meierswinecellars.com
Owner: Paramount Distillers, Inc.
Winemaker: Robert Distler

History
Meier's Wine Cellars has been making Ohio wines and fruit juices for over 120 years. It was established in 1890 by John Conrad Meier as the John C. Meier Grape Juice Company, Inc. The business survived Prohibition by making Catawba grape juice and the company was renamed Meier's Wine Cellars in 1938. Cleveland-based Paramount Distillers purchased the operation in 1976 and it is today Ohio's largest producer of wine and juice from native American grapes. Winery fruit is purchased from independent growers in Ohio, New York, and Pennsylvania.

Fortified Wines
Meier's Dry Vermouth
Dry fortified white wine flavored with imported botanicals.
Meier's #11 Pale Dry Sherry
The driest of Meier's sherry-style wines, the sherry material ("shermat") base wine is made from Niagara grapes. The shermat is fortified and aged until the wine exhibits typical sherry, nutty, and caramel character.

135

Meier's #22 Golden Sherry

Made the same way as #11, this sherry-style wine is blended to produce a darker golden color and bit more body.

Meier's #33 Cream Sherry

A sherry-style blend of Niagara and Muscat grapes with a hint of oak.

Meier's #44 Cream Sherry

The winery's premier sherry-style wine. Grape spirits are added to a blend of Niagara and Muscat wines then aged in 50 gallon barrels for three summers.

Meier's #44 Red Port

Made from a blend of *vinifera* grapes, the port-style wine is aged in oak barrels.

Meier's Ruby Red Port

A blend of fortified Concord wine and oak aged ruby port-style wine, the complex dessert wine is fruitier than the #44 port-style.

Meier's Tawny Port

Longer aging in oak barrels provides the tawny color for this port-style wine that starts as a ruby port-style. More complex and smoother finish than ruby style.

Meier's Marsala

Semi-sweet fortified marsala-style blend of white wine and unfermented grape juice that is aged in new and old oak barrels and casks.

VALLEY VINEYARDS

Morrow, Ohio
valleyvineyards.com
Owners: Schuchter Family
Winemaker: Greg Pallman

History

Located between Dayton and Cincinnati in the Ohio River Valley Appellation, the Schuchter family has been producing estate wines since 1970.

Fortified Wine
Vintage Port

A proprietary blend of estate grown French-American hybrid grapes fermented on skins until 7.5 percent residual sugar when natural grape spirits are added to arrest fermentation. Aged three years in French and American oak barrels, the port-style wine finishes at 18.7 percent alcohol.

WOODSTONE CREEK WINERY AND DISTILLERY

Cincinnati, Ohio
woodstonecreek.com
Owner/Winemaker: Donald Outterson

History

Perhaps Ohio's smallest artisan winery and boutique distillery offering season-al wines, spirits, and meads produced entirely from Ohio-grown fruit. Don-ald Outterson is an unusual combination of winemaker, certified brewmaster, meadmaker, and master distiller.

Fortified Wines
Ambiance

White port-style wine made from Niagara grapes with tawny color finish-ing at 21 percent alcohol and 9 percent residual sugar.

Laureate

Meaning "worthy of praise," Laureate is a ruby port-style wine crafted from a Meritage blend of Ohio Cabernet Franc, Cabernet Sauvignon, and Merlot. Aged in an oak sherry cask, the wine finishes with 21 percent alco-hol and 9 percent residual sugar.

STABLERIDGE VINEYARDS

Stroud, Oklahoma
stableridgevineyards.com
Owners: Don and Annetta Neal
Winemaker: Annetta Neal

History

Likely the only winery and vineyard located on America's Historic Route 66, StableRidge Vineyards was founded in the wake of two devastating 1999 tor-nados that hit the Neal home and adjoining property. Undeterred, the Neals were able to restore their home and purchase the neighboring property for the vineyard where grapes were first planted in 2000. The winery tasting room is the restored downtown Stroud Catholic Church built in 1898. Annetta, a citizen of the Cherokee Nation, retired from teaching in 2004 while Don spent twen-ty-three years as a corporate recruiter.

Fortified Wine
RidgePort Select

Blended port-style fortified wine aged in cask four years to develop a full flavor.

CHAMPOEG WINE CELLARS

Aurora, Oregon

champoegwine.com

Owners: Louanna and Chuck Eggert

Winemaker: Ted Ottmar

History

Boutique Champoeg Wine Cellars is situated southwest of Portland in the historic Champoeg State Park area of the north Willamette River Valley. While the winery was constructed in 1992, the vineyards are not new to the Champoeg hillside. In 1858, French immigrant Jean Mathiot planted a portion of his 139-acre "La Butte" property from cuttings purchased in California. Mathiot's community was named Butteville, and by 1880 the area was referred to as the wine capital of the Oregon Territory.

Fortified Wines

Dessert Wine

White port-style wine made from late harvest estate Riesling.

Willamette Port

Crafted from estate Pinot noir and barrel aged six years, the port-style wine exhibits cherry and plum character.

Oregon Port

Spicy chocolate and cherry notes mark this port-style wine produced from estate Pinot Noir.

Chardonnay Port

Barrel aged five years and made from estate Chardonnay, the white port-style wine has notes of soft caramel and subtle citrus.

EOLA HILLS CELLARS

Rickreall, Oregon

eolahillswinery.com

Founder/General Manager: Tom Huggins

Winemaker: Steve Anderson

History

Located a short ten-minute drive west of Salem, former agricultural insurance expert Tom Huggins constructed the winery in 1987 to turn his Eola Hills vineyards into fine Oregon wines.

Fortified Wine

Reserve LBV Cabernet Port

Fashioned from Cabernet Sauvignon grapes grown in the Willamette, Applegate, Umpqua, and Columbia Valleys, the LBV port-style wine was barrel aged six years for the tawny hue and well-balanced candied nut and brandy character.

Awards
PLATINUM, San Diego International Competition

OSWEGO HILLS
West Linn, Oregon
oswegohills.com
Owners: Jerry Marshall Family
Winemaker: Derek Lawrence

History
The site of Oswego Hills Winery was originally settled by Ohioans Sarah and Richard Whitten in 1852. Following Richard's death, Sarah married Franklin Ford and the family farmed the property until it was purchased by Czech immigrant James Spousta in the late 1910s. Spousta worked at a foundry in Portland and the owner, K. B. Hall, purchased the farm in the early 1940s. Hall turned the property into a 125-acre equestrian center that was purchased by the Morley family in the 1950s.

Airline pilot Jerry Marshal and his family lived within half a mile of the much admired property for twenty-five years and finally purchased 36 acres of farm in 1996, planting the vineyard in 1997. The seven structures on the property were in disrepair, and the Marshall family continue to rehabilitate the buildings that will be integrated into the completed winery facility.

Fortified Wine
Tempranillo Port
Port-style wine made entirely from Tempranillo (Tinta Roriz) grown in the Rattlesnake Hills appellation of Washington. Aged twenty months in French oak, the fortified wine finishes with 18 percent alcohol and 8 percent residual sugar.

SCHMIDT FAMILY VINEYARDS
Grants Pass, Oregon
sfvineyards.com
Owners: Judy and Cal Schmidt
Winemaker: Cal Schmidt

History
Fulfilling a life-long dream, Cal purchased the old Bennett Ranch near Grants Pass in 2000 and began the vineyard by planting Merlot, Syrah, and Cabernet

Sauvignon in 2001. He took viticulture and enology classes in his spare time while operating a successful business.

Fortified Wines:

Doce Nectar

A blend of Merlot and Cabernet Sauvignon, the dryer, port-style fortified wine was barrel aged two years.

Tout Suite

White port-style fortified wine made from Viognier grapes.

Vermillion

Port-style red wine blended from Touriga Nacional and Tempranillo.

DAVID HILL VINEYARDS & WINERY

Forest Grove, Oregon
davidhillwinery.com
Owners: Milan and Jean Stoyanov
Winemaker: Jason Bull

History

Milan and Jean acquired the property in 1992, naming the winery after a site with a history going back to the 1880s. The vines planted by the homesteading Rueter family were pulled in favor of fruit trees with the advent of Prohibition. Half a century later, UC Davis graduate Charles Coury came to northern Oregon and was instrumental in the new Oregon wine industry when he planted vines on Rueter's David's Hill property. Milan, a retiring lumberman, turned his vineyard/winery investment into a thriving business with the introduction of the David Hill label in 2000. Today, the 1883 Reuter farmhouse is the David Hill tasting room.

Fortified Wines

Estate Muscat Port

White port-style fortified wine fashioned from Muscat grapes planted by Charles Coury in 1965. The wine is aged six years in French Oak barrels and finishes with 19 percent alcohol with 7.8 percent residual sugar.

Estate Pinot Noir Port

Crafted from David Hill Pinot noir grapes, the port-style wine is aged five years in a 132-gallon French oak puncheon. 18.2 percent alcohol and 8 percent residual sugar.

VALLEY VIEW WINERY

Jacksonville, Oregon
valleyviewwinery.com

Owners: Ann, Mark, and Michael Winsovsky and Family
Winemaker: John F. Guerrero

History

Oregon pioneer Peter Britt originally established the Rogue Valley winery in the 1850s. However, Britt's passing in 1906 ended the enterprise until 1972, when the Winsovsky family restored the Valley View name with their vineyards and winery in Applegate Valley.

Fortified Wine
Anna Maria Port

Port-style fortified blend of estate Merlot and Tempranillo grapes.

EDENVALE WINERY

Roseburg, Oregon
edenvalewines.com

Owner: Anne Root
Winemaker: Ashley Campanella

History

In 1885 Joseph H. Stewart established a pear orchard that went on to be known as the birthplace of Oregon's pear industry. Known as Eden Valley Orchards, the enterprise grew to over 700 acres by 1932 under the direction of Colonel Gordon Voorhies. Unfortunately, the Depression heralded the gradual decline of the southern Oregon production. Today EdenVale Winery occupies the historic orchard property, producing their first wine in 2001.

Fortified Wines
Diamante Bianco

White port-style wine made from Pinot noir and fermented with no skin contact and fortified with Viognier brandy.

Rosso Rubino

Red port-style fortified wine crafted from late harvested Merlot grapes.

BOYD'S CARDINAL HOLLOW WINERY

North Wales, Pennsylvania
cardinalhollowwinery.com
Owner/Winemaker: Christopher Boyd

History
Chris developed his wine interest as a result of his job-related travels in the mid-1990s. He started reading about wine during his time in airplanes and became a home winemaker in 1995 which evolved into a commercial enterprise.

Fortified Wines
Nutty Sailor Port
Made from Tinta Madeira grapes, the port-style fortified wine has 21 percent alcohol and 10 percent residual sugar.
Merlot Ruby Port
Ruby port-style wine crafted from Merlot grapes finishing at 16.7 percent alcohol and 10 percent residual sugar.
Tawny Port
Blended from three different vintages, the tawny port-style wine is brandy fortified and barrel aged in French oak for six years. 19.5 percent alcohol, 10 percent residual sugar.

SPYGLASS RIDGE WINERY

Sunbury, Pennsylvania
spyglassridgewinery.com
Owners: Tom and Tammy Webb
Winemaker: Tom Webb

History
Tom Webb became interested in winemaking while in college, and worked for a time at a Lehigh Valley winery. Approximately fifteen years ago when Tammy's family farm became available, the couple purchased the property and planted twenty thousand grape vines. The farm had a barn built in 1814 that was renovated for the winery and tasting room. What started as hobby has now become a fully functioning commercial winery.

Fortified Wine
Cab-Berry Port
Tawny, port-style wine crafted from Cabernet Franc blended with blueberries and blackberries. Fortified with grape spirits, the wine was aged in French oak barrels.

HERITAGE WINE CELLARS

North East, Pennsylvania

heritagewine.biz

Owners: Matthew and Joshua Bostwick

Winemaker: Matthew Bostwick

History

The Bostwick Family tradition goes back 150-plus years to the original 100-acre fruit farm started by Harry Hall in 1805. Since then the heritage has been maintained by seven generations of grape growers and three generations of vintners. Heritage Wine Cellars is in the fourth largest Concord grape region in the United States.

Fortified Wine

Flagship Red

Port-style fortified wine made from estate-grown Concord grapes.

PRESQUE ISLE WINE CELLARS

North East, Pennsylvania

piwine.com

Owner: Marlene Moorhead

Winemaker: Kris Kane

History

Presque Isle Winery has been producing a wide array of wines made from classic, French-American hybrid, and native *labrusca* grape varieties purchased from regional growers since 1969.

Fortified Wine

Touriga Nacional Port

Vintage port-style fortified wine made from rare Touriga Nacional and Cabernet Sauvignon grapes. Fermented and aged twelve to twenty-four months in American oak barrels, the wine finishes at 19.6 percent alcohol with 8 percent residual sugar.

MANATAWNY CREEK WINERY

Douglassville, Pennsylvania

manatawnycreekwinery.com

Owners: Levengood Family

Winemakers: Darvin and Joanne Levengood

P
E
N
N
S
Y
L
V
A
N
I
A

History

The Levengoods have been making wine at Manatawny Creek since the early 1990s. Darvin was a mechanical engineer who got started in wine as a home winemaker while daughter Joanne left her environmental engineering career to study enology at UC Davis. She worked at several California wineries before returning to the family farm in 1997. Manatawny Creek has three separate vineyards totaling 10 acres. The 5 acres of hybrid varieties was planted in 1991.

Fortified Wine
Cabernet Franc Port
> Ruby port-style fortified wine made from Cabernet Franc grapes providing 18–20 percent and some residual sugar sweetness.

NEWPORT VINEYARD & WINERY
Middletown, Rhode Island
newportvineyards.com

Owners: John and Paul Nunes
Winemaker: John Nunes

History

In 1917 the great-grand patriarch of the Nunes family acquired the Bailey farm and planted 30 acres of stone wall to protect the vineyards. Almost three-quarters of a century later, the Nunes family and retired Captain Richard Alexander established the Vineyard Wine Company a bit north of Newport. The winery was acquired by John and Paul Nunes in 1995, establishing the Newport Vineyards brand.

Fortified Wines
White Cap Port
> A blend of white grape varieties produce this white port-style fortified wine.

Port
> Several wine vintages dating to near ten years are blended to make this ruby port-style fortified wine.

VALLEY VINEYARDS WINERY

Vermillion, South Dakota

buffalorunwinery.com

Owners: Eldon and Sherry Nygaard

Winemaker: Leif Nygaard

History

Legitimately billed as the "first and oldest" South Dakota Winery, the Nygaards started growing grapes in 1993, then opened their winery "as a hobby that got out of hand."

Fortified Wine

Wild Grape Port

Self-proclaimed as the only port-style wine in the world made from wild American grapes *(Vitis riparia)*, the fortified wine is barrel aged for fourteen years.

ARRINGTON VINEYARDS

Arrington, Tennessee

arringtonvineyards.com

Owners: Kix Brooks, Kip Summers, and John Russell

Winemaker: Kip Summers

History

Originally named Firefly Vineyards, Kip Summers and a fellow oenophile purchased a 25-acre hog farm in hills of central Tennessee and began planting grape vines. A year later, the adjacent farm was acquired to expand the vineyard. The first two vintages of Kip's wines were made at Beachaven Winery before construction began on the Arrington facility in 2006. The tasting room was opened in 2007 in the property's renovated farmhouse.

Fortified Wine

Encore

Vintage port-style wine made from home vineyard Chambourcin and fortified with brandy. Aged in American oak barrels for two years to finish with 18.5 percent alocohol and 7.5 percent residual sugar.

BEANS CREEK WINERY
Manchester, Tennessee
beanscreekwinery.com
Owner/Winemaker: Tom Brown

History
Opened in 2004, nine local families are involved in the winery. Principle owner Tom Brown made his first wine in his mother's kitchen in 1976 to keep the local grapes from going to the birds. He was a home winemaker until Beans Creek in 2004.

Fortified Wines
Apropos
Full-bodied, port-style fortified wine made from Tennessee Cynthiana grapes. 18.9 percent alcohol.
Amore
Sherry-style fortified, oxidized blend of Cayuga and Vidal blanc white grapes finishing with 19.1 percent alcohol.

OLD MILLINGTON VINEYARD & WINERY
Millington, Tennessee
oldmillingtonwinery.com
Owner: Carrie Marcinko
Winemaker: Perry Welch

History
The boutique family winery in the hills 14 miles north of Memphis was established in 2000.

Fortified Wine
Red Port
Lightly oaked port-style fortified wine made from Tennessee Chambourcin.

DRY COMAL CREEK VINEYARDS
New Braunfels, Texas
drycomalcreek.com
Owners: Franklin and Bonnie Houser
Winemaker: Franklin Houser

History

In the 1970s, the Housers purchased a 103-acre parcel of land as a get-away spot for the family. The first wine grapes were planted in 1992 by the "retired" attorney and a year later 4,000 *vinifera* vines were established. Dry Comal Creek Vineyards first opened their tasting room in 1998; however, floods in 1998 and 2002 wiped out both vineyards and winery. Pierce's disease struck in 2000 but the undeterred Housers discovered the disease-resistant grape Black Spanish (Lenoir) and became pioneers in making Black Spanish Wines.

Fortified Wines:
Port
>   Port-style fortified wine made from Texas Black Spanish grapes with 18 percent alcohol and 6.5 percent residual sugar
White Port
>   Crafted from a French Colombard foundation, the white port-style wine is aged in small oak casks to finish at 18 percent alcohol and 4.5 percent residual sugar.

HAAK VINEYARDS & WINERY

>   Santa Fe, Texas
>   haakwine.com
Owners: Raymond and Gladys Haak
Winemaker: Raymond Haak

History

It all started in 1969 with an anniversary gift of a few grape vines that Raymond planted on the Haak's Galveston County property. Some time later, Raymond discovered that the Florida hybrid Blanc du Bois did well along the gulf coast and planted cuttings in his vineyard. His homemade wines were well received by friends and the response to his amateur winemaking was so encouraging that Ray established the commercial enterprise Haak Winery in 2000.

Fortified Wines
Blanc du Bois
>   White port-style wine crafted entirely from estate Blanc du Bois grapes barrel aged thirty-two months.
Madeira Blanc du Bois
>   White Madeira-style wine fashioned from Blanc du Bois grapes using the heating or Estufagem process that produces the characteristic Madeira brownish tea color.
Reserve Tawny Port
>   Made entirely of Texas Black Spanish grapes, the fortified port-style wine is aged three years in American oak.

147

Madeira, Jacquez

Distinctive Madeira-style fortified wine made from Jacquez (Lenoir/Black Spanish) grapes aged at least six months in the unique Portuguese-inspired estuafa ("oven") at between 105 and 115 degrees resulting a dark brown coffee color.

Madeira, Jacquez 10 Year

Crafted in the same manner as the Madeira-Jacquez wine but barrel aged in American oak for ten years.

Madeira, Jacquez (Thomas Jefferson)

Fashioned in the consistent Haak Madeira-style using Jaquez grapes with fortified wine, this Madeira-Jacquez is aged three years in American oak barrels and appropriately named for America's most prominent Madeira wine connoisseur.

Awards

Madeira Blanc du Bois, GOLD, San Francisco Chronicle Wine Competition

Reserve Tawny Port, SILVER, Houston Livestock Show & Rodeo Wine Competition

Madeira, Jacquez, GOLD, San Antonio Stock Show & Rodeo Wine Competition

Madeira, Jaquez (Thomas Jefferson), GOLD, Texsom Dallas Morning News Wine Competition

FLAT CREEK ESTATE

Marble Falls, Texas
flatcreekestate.com
Owners: Rick and Madelyn Naber
Winemaker: Tim Drake

History

The 80-acre Flat Creek Estate was purchased in the Central Texas Hill Country property in 1998. The first 6 acres of vines were planted on April Fool's Day in 2000 and the vineyard has steadily expanded to today's 20-acre vineyard. The winery was completed in 2001 and doubled in capacity in 2009. The Flat Creek Bristro and Event Center was constructed in 2005.

Fortified Wines
Port

A traditional blend of estate-grown Portuguese varieties Tinta Madeira, Tinta Cão, and Touriga Nacional, the port-style wine is aged in a rare Texas solera system. The wine is fortified with grape brandy and finishes at 19 percent alcohol.

MESSINA HOF WINERY

Bryan, Texas
messinahof.com
Owners: Bonarrigo Family
Winemaker: Paul Bonarrigo

History

The Bonarrigo family began making wine in their native Messina, Sicily, in the 1800s. Paul and Merrill Bonarrigo planted the first vineyard in 1977 and shortly thereafter established Messina Hof as the fourth winery in Texas.

Fortified Wine
Glory
> Made entirely from Texas-grown Muscat Canelli, the brandy-fortified white port-style finishes at 16 percent alcohol and 9.5 percent residual sugar.

Awards
> **Double Gold Medal, Class Champion and TexasClass Champion,** Houston Livestock Show and Rodeo
> **GOLD,** San Francisco Chronicle Wine Competition

PEDERNALES CELLARS

Stonewall, Texas
pedernalescellars.com
Owners: Kuhlken Family
Winemaker: David Kuhlken

History

The original 17-acre Kuhlken Estate Vineyard was planted in the early 1990s in the first Texas AVA—Bell Mountain. In 2005 the family developed Pedernales as a boutique winery focused on small lot wines crafted from Texas Hill Country grapes.

Fortified Wines
Texas Ruby
> Blend of Texas-grown Iberian grape varieties, the fortified port-style is nearly tawny in character with longer aging to produce a wine with 18 percent alcohol and 3.5 percent residual sugar.

Texas Dulce
> White port-style fortified wine blended from different vintages and aged several years in neutral oak barrels.

T E X A S

WILLIAM CHRIS VINEYARDS
Fredericksburg, Texas
williamchriswines.com
Owners/Winemakers: Bill Blackmon and Chris Brundrett

History
Bill and Chris, founders of the namesake vineyard/winery have over thirty-five years of combined hands-on "winegrowing" experience. Texas Tech graduate Bill Blackmon has three decades of experience planting and managing Texas High Plains and Hill County wine operations while Texas A&M graduate Chris Brundrett has quickly acquired a range of vineyard and winery experience. The first William Chris wine was bottled in 2008 and the team acquired the historic Deike farmhouse in Hye 2009. The farmhouse renovation to the winery and tasting room was completed in 2010 and the new Hye Estate Vineyards adjacent to the winery were planted in 2012.

Fortified Wines
Fortified Roussanne
Crafted from 100 percent Roussanne grapes, this Madeira-style fortified wine was baked in neutral oak barrels and aged eighteen months. 21 percent alcohol.
Jacquez
Made from Texas Jacquez (Black Spanish/Lenoir) grapes this red fortified port-style is full-bodied at 19 percent alcohol.

V I R G I N I A

DESERT ROSE RANCH AND WINERY
Hume, Virginia
desertrosewinery.com
Owners/ Winemakers: Bob and Linda Claymier

History
With roots in the eastern Oregon high desert ranch country, the Claymiers have traveled the world to finally retire in Virginia to raise horses, grows grapes, and make wine. Retired from the federal government, the Claymiers were home winemakers for more than forty years before establishing the commercial venture on the property of their equally successful horse breeding, training, and boarding operation.

Fortified Wine
Starboard
Port-style fortified wine with 8 percent residual sugar made from 100 percent Norton grapes and aged in both oak and used whiskey barrels.

150

HORTON VINEYARDS

Gordonsville, Virginia
hortonwine.com
Owners: Dennis and Sharon Horton, Joan Bieda
Winemaker: Michael Heny

History

Dennis Horton began his venture as a home winemaker with a small vineyard in 1983. In 1988, the Hortons and business partner Joan Bieda purchased 55 acres and planted both *vinifera* and native Norton grape varieties. The first small crop was harvested in 1991 and wines made at Montdomaine Cellars. Dennis took over management of the noted producers in 1992 and construction was begun on the stone underground cellars looking out on the Blue Ridge Mountains. The first Horton cellars crush was in 1993 and the vineyards were expanded in 1994.

Fortified Wine
Vintage Port

> The 1995 vintage was the first commercial port-style wine produced in Virginia since Prohibition. A blend of estate Touriga Nacional and Tinta Cão.

TRUMP WINERY

Charlottesville, Virginia
trumpwinery.com
Owner: Eric Trump
Winemakers: Katell Griaud, Jonathan Wheeler

History

Situated on 1,800 acres a few miles from Thomas Jefferson's historic Monticello property, Trump Winery has near 200 acres of French vinifera vineyards, the largest planting of classic European vines on the east coast. The 50,000 square foot winery includes a 750-barrel aging cave that was opened in 2011.

Fortified Wine
Cru

> Fortified white port-styled fashioned from 100 percent estate grown Chardonnay grapes. The Chardonnay juice is blended with grape brandy and is aged more than a year in American oak bourbon barrels finishing with 18 percent alcohol and 14 percent residual sugar.

ATHENA VINEYARDS & WINERY

Heathsville, Virginia
athenavineyards.com

Owners: Carol Spengler, Ada Jacox, Ruth Harris
Winemaker: Tom Payette

History

Named for Pallas Athena, the favorite daughter of Greek god Zeus, Athena Vineyards was established by three nurses in 2002. The winery constructed in 2005 was the first commercial vineyard and winery in Northumberland County, Virginia. Athena's 15-acre vineyard, with over twenty varieties, overlooks the Great Wicomico River. The winery and vineyards follow environmentally safe, best production management practices.

Fortified Wine
Safe Harbor

Port-style fortified made from Chambourcin grapes with shorter barrel aging than with traditional ports. The 18 percent alcohol wine is distinctively bottled in the shape of a caravel ship that brought the first English settlers to Jamestown in 1607.

BLUESTONE VINEYARD

Bridgewater, Virginia
bluestonevineyard.com

Owners: Curt and Jackie Hartman
Winemaker: Curt Hartman

History

The Hartmans have lived on a hill above Jordan Stretch in the Shenandoah Valley of Virginia since 1995. With the help of neighbors, the first vines were planted on the hill to produce grapes for home winemaking. The vineyard went commercial in 2007 with the planting of an additional four thousand red grape variety vines. The winery was built in 2010.

Fortified Wine
Dry Dock

Fortified to complete dryness, the wine is then blended with wine spirits to 18 percent and stored in whiskey barrels for two years.

RAPPAHANNOCK CELLARS

Huntly, Virginia
rappahannockcellars.com

Owner: Delmare Family
Winemaker: Theo Smith

History
The Delmare family wine history begins over twenty-five years ago at Saratoga Vineyards in California's Santa Cruz Mountains (now Savannah Channel Vineyards) where John and Marialisa made wine in a one-hundred-year-old redwood winery. The Delmares relocated to the Virginia piedmont at the base of Blue Ridge Mountains in 1998. The 30 acres of the family's Glenway Farm vineyard supplies about half the grapes for Rappahannock Cellars so the operation leases vineyards from like-minded Virginia growers. The winery was established over fifteen years ago to make old world–style wines from grapes best suited to the Virginia environment.

Fortified Wine
Port
> Port-style red wine fashioned from 100 percent Norton grapes, fortified with brandy and aged in new whiskey casks. 17.9 percent alcohol.

FIRST COLONY WINERY
> Charlottesville, Virginia
> firstcolonywinery.com

Owners: Heather and Bruce Spiess, Jeffrey W. Miller
Winemaker: Jason Hayman

History
Originally established by a previous owner, First Colony Winery has undergone substantial change under the current administration. In 2013, 4.5 acres of classic *vinifera* grapes were added to the vineyard with the ultimate goal to reach 20–25 acres of vines. October 2013 saw the transformation of the existing winery building with the construction of a thatched roof made of imported Turkish water reed—the only thatched roof winery in America.

Fortified Wine
Thatch
> Port-style wine made on the dryer side with only 5 percent residual sugar. Crafted from Virginia-grown Touriga Nacional and Chambourcin, the wine is fortified with 168-proof neutral grape spirits and aged in neutral oak barrels for fourteen to forty months. 17 percent alcohol.

Awards
> **GOLD**, Jefferson Cup Medal of American Excellence

KING FAMILY VINEYARDS

Crozet, Virginia
kingfamilyvineyards.com

Owners: King Family
Winemaker: Matthieu Finot

History

It all started in 1998 with a knock on the door from a young man inquiring about leasing 10 acres of the King family's 327-acre farm for a vineyard. The family had relocated to Virginia from Houston, Texas, in 1996. After doing some research, the first 8 acres of vine were planted in the new vineyard with the idea of making a little wine and selling the rest of the fruit to local wineries. The King Family decided to go commercial in 2002 and sketched out their winery design on the back of a napkin. Continued vineyard and winery growth resulted in the new state-of-the-art winery in 2013.

Fortified Wine

Seven

Named for the "7th Chukker" in polo, the 100 percent Petit Verdot portstyle fortified wine is aged two years in Kentucky bourbon barrels.

BONAIR WINERY

Zillah, Washington
bonairwine.com

Owners: Shirley and Gail Puryear
Winemaker: Bill Mechem

History

Yakima Valley's Rattlesnake Hills is home to Bonair Winery's 40 acres of estate vineyards. Chateau Puryear Vineyard is the home vineyard planted in 1980 while the Morrison Vineyard to the north was planted by Joe and Sid Morrison in 1968 and acquired by Bonair in 2001. The Puryears met at Washington State University and Gail became a teacher in California while Shirley was a social worker. The couple moved back to Washington in 1979 and started the winery in 1985. Gail left education in 1992 to become a full–time Bonair winemaker until turning the vintner duties over to Bill Mechem in 2007.

Fortified Wine

Touriga Port

Vintage port-style fortified wine made from classic estate grown Touriga Nacional grapes with 18.5 percent alcohol.

ENGLISH ESTATE WINERY

Vancouver, Washington
englishestatewinery.com
Owners: Carl and Gail English
Winemaker: Carl English

History:
Vancouver Washington's first vineyard and winery, the English family has farmed the property for well over a century. The first crops on the land were potatoes, grain, and prunes, but it wasn't until 1980 that the vineyard was established. The winery building is a big red barn constructed in 1915, and the farm's craftsman-style house was built in 1917. The refurbished barn winery and Pump House tasting room were opened to the public in 2000.

Fortified Wines
All the English Estate Fort Sweet Nectars are wines fortified with estate brandy.
Baillies Folly, Late Harvest Riesling
Gewurztraminer
La Modeste, Sauvignon blanc
NV Pinot, Pinot Noir
Sweet Autumn Gold, Oak-aged Pinot Noir
Sweet Ruby Red, Ruby port-style aged Pinot Noir

HINZERLING WINERY

Prosser, Washington
hinzerling.com

Owners: Wallace Family
Winemaker: Mike Wallace

History
Former Seattle PD Detective Lieutenant Jerry Wallace planted the first vines in the family's 23-acre Prosser vineyard in 1972, making Hinzerling the oldest family-owned–and-operated winery in Yakima Valley.

Fortified Wines
Angelica
Crafted from estate Gewürztraminer that is crushed then pressed after being left overnight on the skins. The fortifying brandy is added at the beginning of fermentation and placed in stainless steel barrels to be chilled outside for eight to ten months prior to bottling. The finished Angelica has 18 percent alcohol and 18 percent residual sugar.

W
A
S
H
I
N
G
T
O
N

155

Collage

White port-style brandy fortified wine made from a blend of three Muscat varieties—early Muscat, Orange Muscat, and Muscat Canelli. 10 percent residual sugar.

Pale Dry Cocktail Sherry

Fino sherry-style fortified wine fashioned from Riesling grapes, inoculated with flor Sherry yeast and allowed to slowly oxidize, resulting in the nutty character of sherry.

Rainy Day Fine Tawny Port

This tawny, port-style wine was first assembled in 1989 from a solera fractional blending system of Cabernet Sauvignon, Merlot, and Lemberger wines. The solera now consists of three tiers totaling fifteen barrels. During November of each year, half the barrels of the oldest tier are blended and drawn off for bottling.

Three Muses Ruby Port

Ruby port-style wine constructed in much the same manner as the Rainy Day Port, but using only two solera tiers.

Wallace Vintage Port

Declared "Vintage" in 1989, 1990, and 1994, this vintage-style fortified wine embraces the concept of exceptional single-vintage wines with a heavier body and darker color than either ruby or tawny-style port wines.

KNIPPRATH CELLARS

Spokane, Washington
knipprath-cellars.com
Owners: Knipprath Family
Winemaker: Henning Knipprath

History

Established in 1999, this boutique winery focuses on fortified port-style wines made from Pacific Northwest–grown Iberian grape varieties.

Fortified Wines

La V!

Madagascar bourbon vanilla bean infused port-style wine made from Merlot grapes.

Spanish Nudge

Syrah-based port-style fortified wine aged with coffee and cinnamon to recreate the Spanish coffee experience.

Au Chocolat!

Small lots of port-style wine from Cabernet Sauvignon aged with 100 percent natural cocoa bean essence.

Matrix Reserva Especial Ruby Port Reserve

Crafted from Touriga Nacional and Tinta Roriz grapes, the fortified wine has the character of classic port style.

Chocolate Truffle Port

A four-year process in which select lots of Au Chocolat! are aged in oak barrels previously used for vanilla port-style wines.

Oloroso

Fashioned from Washington State grapes, this Oloroso sherry-style is a product of Knipprath's solera fractional blending system providing traditional cask-aged flavor and character.

PARADISOS DEL SOL

Zilah, Washington

paradisosdelsol.com

Owner/Winemaker: Paul Vandenberg

History

One of Washington State's most experienced enologists, Paul began his wine career in 1983 and has worked at ten Pacific Northwest wineries. He considers himself a practicing terroirist winegrower who allows the wine grapes and wines to develop naturally. Paul was with the first Washington vineyard to be certified organic and worked at the first Washington winery to produce organic wines. His wife Barbara Sherman and son Kevin are intimately involved in the tasting room and winery.

Fortified Wines
Zort

Based on estate grown Zinfandel, the fortified wine is made in the ruby Angelica style.

Angelica SR

Uniquely American Angelica crafted from Semillon and Riesling with un-aged grape brandy fortification aged for twenty-two months in mature barrels.

SWAKANE WINERY

Wenatchee, Washington

swakanewinery.com

Owner: Mike and Donna Franks

Winemaker: Mike Franks

History

Making wine at home from Washington blackberries and classic wine grapes in 2000 inspired Mike to earn a degree in enology in 2004. He gained hands-on experience at Tildio Winery while finding a vineyard site on the Columbia River, thus beginning a six-year winery development adventure. The Franks opened their doors in 2009 bringing life to their dream.

Fortified Wine
Woohoo Pink Dessert Wine
Limited skin contact during early fermentation produces a deep rose colored fortified port-style wine made from estate Cabernet Franc grapes. 16.4 percent alcohol and 14.3 percent residual sugar.

TANJULI WINERY
Zilah, Washington
tanjuli.com
Owner/Winemaker: Tom Campbell

History
Washington wine pioneer Tom Campbell came to Rattlesnake Hills area in 1981 and with UC Davis classmate Stan Clarke, created the white wine program for Quail Run Winery in 1982. Tom and wife Hema settled in Zilah in 1984 and established Horizon's Edge Winery, which they sold in 1999 to pursue other ventures. In 2005 the couple returned to Rattlesnake Hills to plant a 7-acre vineyard and make estate wines.

Fortified Wines
Orange Muscat Sherry
Sherry-style fortified wine made from estate Orange Muscat grapes.
Black Muscat Port
Sweet, spicy fortified port-style wine crafted from estate Muscat of Hamburg.

THURSTON WOLFE WINERY
Prosser, Washington
thurstonwolfe.com
Owners: Dr. Wade Wolfe and Rebecca Yeaman
Winemaker: Dr. Wade Wolfe

History
The winery was founded in 1987 to produce small lots of finely crafted wines from the best vineyards in Washington State.

Fortified Wine
Touriga Nacional Port
Single variety Touriga Nacional port-style wine Crafted from Yakima Valley Lonesome Spring Vineyard grapes.

TUCKER CELLARS WINERY

Sunnyside, Washington
tuckercellars.net
Owners: Randy and Debbie Tucker
Winemaker: Randy Tucker

History

The Tuckers were among the first to realize the 1980 Yakima Valley wine boom by opening their winery in 1981. At that time, Chenin blanc and Riesling were the only two wine grape varieties grown in the region. But, vineyards and wineries were not new to Yakima Valley. In the early twentieth century, William Bridgman pioneered the early Yakima Valley wine industry, planting a vineyard in 1914 and helping to establish Washington State's wine laws and regulations. Melvin and Vera Tucker moved from Nebraska to share crop grapes for Bridgman after the repeal of Prohibition. Second-generation Dean and Clifford Tucker continued working in the postwar Bridgman wine business with Randy and wife Debbie, thus continuing the family wine tradition.

Fortified Wines
Syrah Ruby Port

Fortified ruby port-style wine crafted from Washington Syrah grapes. 6.5 percent residual sugar.

Syrah Tawny Port

Crafted from estate Syrah grapes, this fortified tawny port-style wine is aged in French oak barrels finishing with 6 percent residual sugar.

COUGAR CREST ESTATE WINERY

Walla Walla, Washington
cougarcrestwinery.com
Owners: Deborah and David Hansen
Winemaker: Deborah Hansen

History

The Hansens's first developed an appreciation for fine domestic wines in northern California wine country. Following graduation from Washington State University, the couple moved to San Francisco in pursuit of their professional careers and to become California wine tourists. After eighteen years in the Bay Area, the Hanson family returned to Washington in 1996 after purchasing a 125-acre apple orchard in the Walla Walla Valley. The 1997 planting of wine grapes in the orchard was a great success and today the vineyards cover a total of 60 acres. David and Deborah started making frequent trips to UC Davis for viticulture and enology classes in 1999 and established their Walla Walla airport winery in 2001. The new Cougar Crest wine facility was completed in 2008.

WASHINGTON

Fortified Wine

Estate Grown Port

A classic blend of estate-grown Tinta Cão, Touriga Nacional, and Souzão the fortified port-style wine has deep red color with dark fruit and chocolate characteristics.

DANIEL VINEYARD

Crab Orchard, West Virginia

danielvineyards.com

Owner/Winemaker: Dr. C. Richard Daniel

History

Since converting a 192-acre golf course into a 20-acre vineyard in 1990, Dr. Daniel has experimented with 114 different grape varieties. He currently propagates 14 "cold hardy" wine grape varieties including 5 red and 9 white varieties.

Fortified Wine

Port

Semi-sweet port-style fortified wine.

WOLLERSHEIM WINERY

Du Sac, Wisconsin

wollersheim.com

Owners: Robert and JoAnn Wollersheim

Winemaker: Philippe Coquard

History

Hungarian count Agoston Haraszthy settled on a sloped Wisconsin hillside and began growing grapes in 1840. A short time later the flamboyant count incorporated the state's first town, Sauk City, across the Wisconsin River from Prairie du Sac. Gold fever struck the young immigrant and in December 1849, Haraszthy headed for California. He went on to be one of the most influential and controversial figures in the early California wine industry. Wollersheim Winery currently sits on the site of the infamous count's original vineyard. Peter Kehl took over Haraszthy's property, which remained in the Kehl family until it was purchased by the Wollersheims in 1972. The family planted new vineyards, refurbished the limestone cellars, and rehabbed the old carriage house into a store. French-born vintner Philippe Coquard became the Wollersheim's winemaker in 1985. Coquard continued to expand with new facilities constructed in 1994 and 2008. Many of Haraszthy's original structures still stand today and the original winery is now a National Historical Site.

Fortified Wines
Port
> Made from 100 percent New York–grown Marechal Foch grapes, the brandy-fortified port-style wine is aged thirteen months in older American oak barrels to finish with 20 percent alcohol.

White Port
> Muscat grapes from New York are used to craft this white port-style wine using brandy to arrest the short on-skin fermentation. The new wine is aged six months in older French barrels and finishes with 20 percent alcohol.

Aged Tawny Port Wine
> Tawny port-style fortified wine made from New York Marechal fruit, the wine is aged in American oak barrels for forty-eight to sixty months prior to bottling. 20 percent alcohol.

CAPTAIN'S WALK WINERY
> Green Bay, Wisconsin
> captainswalkwinery.com

Owners: Aric and Brad Schmiling
Winemaker: Aric Schmiling

History
The Schmiling brothers first experienced the wine business at the ripe age of eight and six when their parents purchased the old von Stiehl Winery in 1981. The brothers purchased the winery from the parents in 2003 and then went on to establish Captain's Walk in 2007. The winery is located in the heart of downtown Green Bay in the pre-Civil War Italianate Victorian home of Wisconsin pioneer Elisha Morrow.

Fortified Wine
Captain's Mistress
> Fashioned from northeast Wisconsin's estate-grown Marquette grapes, this bold, velvety port-style fortified wine finishes with 6 percent residual sugar.

GLOSSARY OF
FORTIFIED WINE GRAPES

Essentially, any grape wine can be fortified. While this is quite a broad statement, research indicates that American winemakers employ over 60 grape varieties to produce domestic fortified wines. There seems to be no limit to the creativity of American producers to fashion both red and white port-style wines as well as Sherries from traditional Portuguese and Spanish varieties, all the way to French-American hybrid and native grape varieties.

Depth of color, ability to develop high sugars while retaining balanced acidity at harvest, aging potential, and sufficient structure to retain varietal character when blended with wine spirits are preferred attributes of fortified wine grapes. Each variety can exhibit an exclusive combination of these attributes and it is the vintner's distinctive style that determines the ultimate amalgamation of character elements in American fortified wines.

Vitis Vinifera

The world's greatest wines are derived from *Vitis* (bunch grape) *vinifera* species. Commonly referred to as "European vines," the exact origin of *vinifera* is still shrouded in uncertainty. What is a bit more certain is that domestication of *vinifera* began near the Transcaucasia region some six thousand years ago and spread throughout the Mediterranean basin. Phoenicians, Greeks, and Romans are credited with bringing *vinifera* to Europe where it often morphed with native grape vines to produce the multitude of classic wine grape varieties we revere today. *Vinifera* grapes include the noble grapes of France, Italy, Germany, and Eastern Europe as well as the port grapes of Portugal's Douro River region.

PORTUGUESE PORT GRAPE VARIETIES

Alvarelhao

Alvarelhao is a red-skinned grape grown in the upper reaches of the Douro Valley that plays a minor role in some port blends. Thought to be a native Portugal's Dao region, across the border in Spain, the grape is called Brancellao.

While not overly vigorous, Alvarelhao is a hearty variety resistant to temperature extremes and inclement weather. A rarity in the United States, a bit of Alvarelhao is grown in California, but because of vine wood misidentification, some of the vines may in fact be Touriga Nacional.

Bastardo
The Portuguese name for the **Trousseau**, a dark-skinned wine grape originally from northeastern France that has migrated over the centuries to vineyards in northwestern Spain and Portugal. Wines made from Trousseau typically have a deep cherry-red color and flavors redolent of dark red berries and other forest fruits. They also tend to be powerfully alcoholic, thanks to the prolific natural sugars of the Trousseau berry and their correspondingly high potential alcohol. The Bastardo grape is generally not as highly regarded as other port varieties but the vine's greatest virtue is the high natural sugar content of its grapes.

Souzão
The Souzão is a dark red grape grown to give color to Douro Valley port. Although this red-wine grape is indigenous to northern Portugal, it's not widely grown there. Souzão has met with greater success in California where Paul Masson made a Souzão port-style wine in 1968. Its vigorous vines produce one of the only grapes in which the juice contains pigment resulting in brilliant, rich-colored port-style wines with luscious fruit flavors. The grape is known for the deep color it produces in a wine as well as its coarse and raisiny taste.

Tinta Amarela
Also known as Trincadeira, Tinta Amarela is deep purple–skinned grape that is blended in port wines to enhance color and deepen flavor. The grape is native to the Alentejo region of Portugal and a notoriously finicky variety that is subject to rot when grown in moist climates. Harvest can also be challenging as the fruit has a very narrow window of optimum ripeness. Most of the rare American Tinta Amarela is growing in California's Central Valley.

Tinta Roriz
Tinta Roriz is the finest Spanish red grape variety, with delicate strawberry, red cherry, and spice nuances with tobacco notes and deep color with lively character. Vigorous upright shoots produces mid-size, compact, cylindrical bunches of spherical, deep blue-black, think-skinned fruit subject to powdery and downy mildew. Called Tempranillo in California, the name, from *temprana*, or "early," refers to its trait of ripening early. High in vigor, moderate in productivity and highly resistant to heat and aridity, it grows best on hot, dry, south-facing, well-drained slopes, away from water, with shelter from wind. Such siting helps curb the vine's vigor and also helps it avoid rot, to which it is susceptible. The Tinta Roriz produces masculine wines of firm tannic structure, excellent complexity, and distinctive raisiny fragrance, with flavors of plum and strawberry.

Tinta Madeira/Tinta Negra Mole

Tinta Madeira is a dark-skinned wine grape best known as the dominant grape of Madeira. Negra Mole literally means "black soft," and the name perhaps derives from the belief that the variety is a crossing of black Grenache and soft Pinot Noir. Tinta means "dark" or "pigmented."

Tinta Cao

A native of Portugal, Tinta Cao is one of the oldest Douro varieties, having been cultivated there since at least the sixteenth century. One of the highest quality port varietals, the low yielding vines produce tiny, compact bunches of small berries that add finesse, complexity, and a bit of spiciness to ports. Of moderately high vigor, it thrives in cooler areas, and the thick skin of the berries contributes to its resistance to disease. The vine's name means "red dog," a grape that bites when not ripe.

Touriga Francesa

Touriga Francesa is related to the Touriga Nacional vine, though more fragile. Moderately vigorous and low yielding, it thrives in warm climates and relatively fertile soils. The thick-skinned grapes grow in delicate clusters that may not survive drought conditions. Very high in tannin and highly scented, it is an important contributor of structure and balance.

Touriga Nacional

Touriga Nacional is widely recognized as the finest grape for making traditional port. The grape calls the northern Douro Valley home and is probably related to Touriga Francesa with links to Moscetel Galego and the Tinta Negra Mole of Madeira. The grape grows on vigorous vines that thrive in warm, dry climates. Grapes mature early and have intense color and aroma. The vines bear tight clusters of thick-skinned, concentrated, tiny blue-black berries that have a high skin-to-pulp ratio, which heightens the amount of extract in wines. Touriga Nacional provides structure and body to wine, with high tannins and concentrated flavors of black fruits. It has excellent acid balance and aromatic components but because of its relatively low yield it is blended with other varieties to make traditional port-style wines to provide deep color and rich flavors.

CLASSIC VINIFERA GRAPE VARIETIES

Alicante Bouchet

Born in France in 1865 as the offspring of the marriage between Petit Bouschet and Grenache, Alicante was groomed to add color and body to southern French *vin ordinare*. It is one of few red viniferous grapes to produce red-pigmented free-run juice. Charles McIver imported the first Alicante Bouschet to his Mission San Jose nursery in the early 1880s. The grape variety was widely planted in the 1890s, and by 1919 Alicante was the most widely planted red-juice grape in California. During Prohibition, Alicante Bouschet attained star status with home winemakers in the east because of its heavy skin, high sugar content, and deep color.

Barbera

The second most grown grape in Italy behind Sangiovese, Barbera is the everyday wine in the Piedmont region of northwestern Italy. The highest quality grapes are grown under strict government regulation in the Barbera d'Alba and Barbera d'Asti regions. A vigorous vine that grows particularly well in warm climates and poor soils, Barbera produces moderately sized, tight bunches of small, black berries. The vine is hearty but somewhat susceptible to leaf role virus.

Black Muscat

Muscat is a family of *Vitis vinifera* with over two hundred different varieties grown around the world. No one knows for sure, but Muscat is probably the oldest cultivated grape variety, most likely originating in ancient Greece. Scientists have discovered that Muscat wine seems to have been the beverage of choice for funeral feasts dating to the eighth century BCE. Eventually, Muscat vines made their way to Rome, Egypt, and Gaul. Eventually, Muscat migrated to the New World, Australia, and South Africa. Black Muscat is a red grape derived from the crossing of the Schiava Grossa and Muscat of Alexandria. It is also known as Golden Hamburg, and Black Hamburg. Black Muscat has been used to make a richly colored, highly aromatic fortified wine for over one hundred years in California.

Cabernet Sauvignon

Cabernet Sauvignon is acknowledged as the king of the noble grapes. The offspring of Sauvignon blanc and Cabernet Franc and a native of the Bordeaux region of France, Cabernet Sauvignon is the most widely planted and important grape of the five dominant varieties in the great wines of the Medoc.

While Cabernet Sauvignon can thrive in a variety of settings, the vines do best in moderately warm, semi-arid regions with long growing seasons. The grapes like well-drained but not-too-fertile soils and are quick to reflect their environment in the wines they produce. Cabernet Sauvignon berries are small and spherical with thick black skins that makes them resistant to disease and spoilage. It is the tannins in the thick skins and the high solids-to-juice ratio that give Cabernet Sauvignon its distinctive flavors and reputation for longevity.

Carignane

The Carignane grape variety is one of the most widely planted grapes in the world. In fact, it is the most widely planted grape in France, principally in the southern Rhone, Midi, and Languedoc regions. Carignane probably originated in northeastern Spain in the province of Aragon and moved to southern France in the twelfth century. Called Carinena in Catalonia, it is blended with Grenache, Monastrell (Mourvedre) and Tempranillo.

The grape grows well in warm "Mediterranean" climates. It is a late ripening variety that is susceptible to mildew and rot, making it highly suited for regions with long, hot, dry growing seasons. Carignane is a prolific producer of high crop yields.

Counoise

Originating in the south of France, Counoise is a black-skinned grape famous as a component of the Châteauneuf-du-Pape. Low-yielding Counoise vines produce late ripening, large round grapes but short on deep color and tannin. However, the grape's lively acidity and spicy character make the variety a blending favorite. Grown in small quantities in California and Washington, Counoise is sometimes blended in Syrah-based fortified wines.

Grenache

Grenache is the favored grape in the brilliant rosés of France's Rhone Valley. One of the best grape varieties on both sides of the Pyrenees, Grenache has its origins in the Aragon region of northeastern Spain. From the twelfth to the fourteenth century, Grenache (Carnacha or Garnacha tinta in Spain) spread from Roussillon in France to Sardinia, where it was called Cannonau.

Grenache is a vigorous variety with the potential of between 10 and 14 tons per acre. The hearty vines thrive in a warm, dry climate and require little if any irrigation through the growing season. The strong, sturdy vines don't need staking or trellising and are often head pruned in a "goblet" shape.

Lemberger

The German name for the Central European for the Blaufrankisch grape, Lemberger is a blue-skinned, late ripening variety grown in limited quantities across the United States. The name derives from the vines imported to Germany from the city of Lemberg in what was the Austro-Hungarian Empire during the nineteenth century. Lemberger is a vine of medium-high vigor with early bud break, making it susceptible to frost. Lemberger tends to make intensely colored, spicy wines with rich tannins that add color and structure to blends.

Merlot

Merlot is derived from Cabernet Sauvignon which probably has its origins in the prehistoric Middle East as a distant descendant of a grapevine known as Balisca. The vine migrated from the Greek wine region of Dyrrachium on the Adriatic Sea to Bordeaux well before the Roman Columella wrote of Balisca in 71 CE. For centuries, Merlot has been a blending grape in the classic wines of Bordeaux.

Merlot is a fairly vigorous vine that can produce 3 to 6 tons of grapes per acre. Vines like low-fertility locations with warm (not hot) days, cool nights, and enough moisture to sustain fruit development during the summer growing season. Merlot ripens earlier than Cabernet Sauvignon but the early bud break makes it susceptible to spring frost. Grapes are reddish black in color and form medium-sized, fairly tight clusters.

Malbec
Malbec's early history found it growing side-by-side with Merlot and Cabernet Sauvignon in the famed vineyards of Bordeaux and used in as a minor grape in classic claret blends. In 1956, a severe spring frost killed three-quarters of Bordeaux's Malbec, ending the grapes utility in the region.

Malbec is a thin-skinned, black grape that needs lots of sun to reach full maturity. The vines produce moderate yields of large, round berries in large, loose bunches. Malbec can produce uneven crops and is susceptible to rot in cooler, wet locations. Grapes ripen mid-season but the vines are particularly sensitive to frosts. While Malbec loves the sun, vineyards planted on northern and eastern exposures provide the evening cooldown period that retains acid and flavor components.

Mission
No one knows just when the name "Mission" was given to the grapes brought from Mexico to Baja then to Alta California and finally to the American southwest by the Jesuits and Franciscans who established the Spanish missions in the new world. Spanish researchers have recently found that a little known Spanish grape called Lista Prieto is identical to the Mission grape. Mission vines are strong and vigorous with thick trunks and stout canes supporting large, dark green leaves and loose bunches of red-skinned grapes.

Nebbiolo
Nebbiolo is the royal grape of the Piedmont region of northwestern Italy where it originated. While written references to the grape date to the ninth century, Nebbiolo was first cultivated in the fourteenth century in the Valtellina Valley of the neighboring Lombardy region at the foot of the Italian Alps north of Lake Como.

Nebbiolo can be a challenging grape for growers as well as vintners. It is highly sensitive to environmental and climatic conditions including soil and sun exposure. Nebbiolo is a relatively late ripening variety that does best when cultivated on south- or southwest-facing hillsides with calcareous (limestone-based) soils. The vines prefer climates that feature warm-to-hot summers and long autumns that allow the berries to fully mature and ripen. While thin-skinned, Nebbiolo is remarkably tough and resistant to most vineyard diseases.

Syrah
Syrah and Shiraz are the same grape, indigenous to the northern Rhone region of southeastern France. Syrah is an early ripening grape prone to heat stress and

overripe fruit can result in flat, flabby wines with a "burnt" character. Syrah vines need vigilant vineyard practices to produce quality grapes. Syrah can be a vigorous vine so many growers are careful to manage vine canopy to allow for plenty of stippled sunlight on the grapes without sunburning.

Petite Sirah

In 1880 Dr. Francois Durif developed a new grape variety he piously named for himself. Durif came to California in 1884 and in fact may have been labeled as Petite Sirah. By 1897, phylloxera had destroyed the last of the true Syrah and what growers had taken to calling Petite Sirah (Durif) was widely planted as a replacement for Mission vines.

The vines are sturdy and thrive in many soils producing big clusters of small, thick-skinned black grapes. Favoring warm climates, the grapes are somewhat prone to sunburn and the fairly tight clusters are subject to rot when damp. Petite Sirah's high skin-to-juice ratio produces wines with high tannins and acidity, thus the ability to age.

Petit Verdot

While there are records of Petit Verdot in Bordeaux by the early eighteenth century, the variety predates Cabernet Sauvignon and may well have come to the region with the Romans. Grape scientists have determined Petit Verdot to be a parent of the infamous Portuguese port blend grape Trousseau (Bastardo).

Petit Verdot grows best where days are hot and sunny, nights cool and crisp. Vines like shallow, well-drained soils and produce relatively small, loose clusters of round, dark-colored, thick-skinned berries. Ripening as much as two weeks after Cabernet Sauvignon, Petit Verdot is vulnerable to late season frosts.

Ruby Cabernet

Professor Harold Olmo started a grape-breeding program at UC Davis in 1931 with the goal of developing wine grape varieties that combined high productivity with superior fruit quality that could be commercially grown in Central Valley. In 1936 Professor Olmo successfully crossed Cabernet Sauvignon with Carignane to produce Ruby Cabernet. Following exhaustive testing in the1940s, Ruby Cabernet was released commercially in 1948. While there were high hopes for the grape statewide, Ruby Cabernet's acidity, high yield, and Cabernet-like flavors made it most suitable for California's hot Central Valley.

Ruby Cabernet vines are highly drought resistant, stand up well to high winds, and are very vigorous in deep clay loam soils. Vines can be spaced 7 to 8 feet apart for optimum vertical shoot positioning and easy machine harvesting, or divided horizontally on a quadrilateral trellis.

Sangiovese

Sangiovese is the predominant red grape of Italy. Thought to be a native of the Tuscan region, the use of the grape to make wine probably predates Roman times. Sangiovese grows best in hot, dry climates at elevations between 500 and

1,500 feet. The vines are vigorous and produce highly variable yields. Grapes are medium to medium-large in size with a relatively thin, purplish black skin. Slow to mature and late to ripen, Sangiovese is fairly disease resistant, although it is subject to raisining when overexposed to the sun and rot when exposed to late season moisture.

Zinfandel
Research by Dr. Carole Meredith and Croatian scientists has determined that Zinfandel and the indigenous Croatian grape Crljenak are the same. Zinfandel vines produce large, reddish-black, neutrally flavored berries that form medium-to-large compact clusters. Able to adapt to a variety of soils, Zinfandel vines are of medium vigor and can yield 4 to 9 tons of fruit per acre. Characteristically, Zinfandel berries ripen unevenly and tend to raisin.

NATIVE AND HYBRID VARIETIES

Native American Varieties

Vitis
Vitis are grapevines in the genus of about sixty species of vining plants in the flowering plant family Vitaceae. The *vitis* genus consists of the eight species of grapes, six of which are native to North America, and were growing in the New World long before the arrival of European colonists. When pioneering viticulturists finally determined that most efforts to grow European *vinifera* vines was futile, they turned to native American grape species in their attempt to establish an American wine commerce.

Vitis rotundifolia is a species of muscadine grape and the first species in North America to be heavily cultivated as a wine grape. After four hundred years of viticultural history, over three hundred improved muscadine varieties are currently growing throughout the southeastern United States. The most famous of these is known as the scuppernong. Occasionally the term scuppernong is misused as a synonym for muscadine, but muscadine is the broader term encompassing all *rotundifolia*.

Vitis rupestris (the sand grape) is more common in France than anywhere else in the world because American *rupestris* cultivars are used as phylloxera-resistant rootstock for European *vinifera*. Deep rooting makes *rupestris* well adapted to sunny, well-drained environments throughout the southwestern United States.

Vitis labrusca (fox grape) is most well known for producing wines with classic foxy or musky flavors and aromas. Concord and Niagara are the two generally recognized V. *labrusca* varieties producing "grapy" sweet and fortified wines. The species is well suited to the cold northern regions of the United States.

Vitis riparia (frost grape) is considered by viticulturists to be the most commercially viable native American species for rootstock hybridization with *vinifera*. *Riparia* has an expansive growing range from New England to Oregon to Texas. The species is fairly disease and pest resistant and cold hardy to well below freezing.

Vitis aestivalis (summer grape) wine profiles are probably more closely related to *vinifera* wines than other native American species. The best known *aestivalis* cultivar is Norton, one of America's oldest known variety and the official grape in the state of Missouri. The grape is also popular with grower in the other states including Arkansas and Virginia. *Aestivalis* is pest resistant and cold-hardy but difficult to propagate through dormant cuttings.

Vitis mustangensis (Mustang grape), has little commercial wine production value. Limited to growing conditions in Texas, Oklahoma, and parts of Louisiana, the mustang grape is highly acidic and bitter tasting.

Muscadine Grapes

Welder is a bronze muscadine grape introduced by Henry Welder of Tavares, Florida, in 1972. Discovered in 1957, the origin of the open pollinated Welder seedling is unknown. Welder berries are a bit smaller than Carlos, but have a higher sugar content and better fruit rot resistance. Yield is moderate, and the berry ripening period can be quite extensive.

Noble is the primary red muscadine grape used in wine production in the southeast. It is a highly productive, vigorous, self-fertile cultivar with medium-sized fruit in large clusters. The grape ripens mid-season and is cold hardy as well as disease resistant. Released in 1973 by W. Nesbitt, D. Carroll, and V. Underwood of the North Carolina Agricultural Experiment Station, Noble is a juice grape whose purple pigments are more stable than most muscadines, which tend to brown over time.

Carlos is a vigorous, productive, self-fertile grape bred in North Carolina where uniform ripening facilitates mechanical harvesting of this cultivar. The medium-sized bronze-colored grape is a very vigorous producers of high yields and is one of the most cold-tolerant cultivars when completely dormant in the winter. However, it is prone to early bud break and may experience cold damage from late spring freezes or frosts. Carlos was released by W. Nesbitt, V. Underwood, and D. Carroll in 1970 from the North Carolina Agricultural Experiment Station in Raleigh.

The *Concord* grape was developed in 1849 by Ephraim Wales Bull in Concord, Massachusetts. Bull planted thousands seeds from wild *Vitis labrusca* before finding what he believed to be the perfect grape. However, the parent pollen is unidentified. The hermaphrodite flowers suggest at least a small amount of *Vitis vinifera* in its lineage, and indeed, recent genetic testing confirmed that Concord has roughly one-third *Vitis vinifera* parentage. The skin of a Concord grape is typically dark blue or purple, and often is covered with a lighter-colored "bloom" that can be rubbed off. It is a slip-skin variety, meaning that the skin is easily separated from the fruit. Concord grapes have large seeds and are highly aromatic. The Concord grape is particularly prone to the physiological disorder Black Leaf. Wines are strongly "foxy" in flavor and structure.

Norton/Cynthiana, a grape believed to be largely derived from *Vitis aestivalis*, is grown in the Midwestern and Mid-Atlantic states and northeastern Georgia. It was introduced by Dr. Daniel Norborne Norton of Richmond, Virginia, who selected it from among what he believed were seedlings of a long forgotten grape variety called Bland. Dr. Norton's propagation of the grape between 1817 and 1824 may make Norton the oldest native American grape now in wide cultivation. Norton was available for sale commercially by 1830.

This grape lacks most of the distinct "foxy" flavors that are typical of native American *Vitis labrusca* grapes, and is hearty, cold tolerant, and fairly resistant to pests and diseases. Norton has a deep purple color with high acidy that exhibits red and black fruit character with a touch of coffee and bittersweet chocolate. Cynthiana is genetically identical to Norton and may be a mutation of the original grape.

HYBRID VARIETIES

Crossing two or more *Vitis* species produces a hybrid grape variety. Hybridization can be accomplished by either grafting bud wood and rootstock or pollinating one species with the flower of another species. A third hybridization process introduced in the twenty-first century involves altering *vitis* species at the genetic level.

The purpose of hybridization is to overcome many of the environmental and pathological challenges associated with viticulture as well as produce unique new wine products. Disease resistance, climate variations, and wine characteristics are among the concerns addressed by development of hybrid wine grape varieties.

Grape hybridization has evolved in three somewhat overlapping stages. Initially, interspecific hybrid grapes were developed in the 1860s by the French, who placed *vitus vinifera* grape cultivars on resistant native American rootstock to combat the devastation of French vineyards by the phylloxera root louse. The second stage of hybridization occurred during the turn of the century when vine breeders used crosses between hybrids developed during the first stage to introduce new interspecific American-French hybrid varieties. Stage three is the modern evolution of hybridization where hybrid crosses from the second stage are melded with *V. vinifera* to address specific issues of grape production and wine quality.

Baco noir is a hybrid red wine grape variety produced from a cross of *Vitis vinifera var. Folle blanche*, a French wine grape, and an unknown variety of *Vitis riparia* indigenous to North America. French grape breeder François Baco propagated the grape in 1894 but it wasn't until 1951 that the variety was introduced to the cooler viticulture regions of North America. Baco noir has fine acidity and prefers cooler climates. Baco is an extremely vigorous variety that is best grown on heavy soils. The fruit is usually high in acid, producing wines of good quality that are deeply pigmented and fruit forward. Baco noir wines do not exhibit the distinctive foxy aromas and flavors of other *Vitis riparia* varieties, but shows rich fruit tones of blueberry and plum.

Chancellor is a hybrid grape created by French botanist Albert Seibel in the 1860s, who named it Seibel 7053. At one time, the vine was the most widely planted hybrid in France, but was never really used to produce commercial wines. It was introduced into the United States in the 1940s and into Canada in 1946, becoming an important grape in some of the cooler regions of those countries. In 1970, the Finger Lakes Wine Growers Association decided to rename it Chancellor. It is considered a cold-hardy variety, but does have early bud break that can be problematic in areas with late spring frosts. The vine is also susceptible to a handful of vine diseases, but it is thought that its susceptibility to both downy and powdery mildew has limited its plantings, especially in damp, humid climates.

Wines have an inky, opaque purple-black color with a thin crimson rim. The nose is fairly intense with aromas of raisins, dried blueberries, and dried figs. On the palate, the wine is on the fuller side of medium with medium acidity and high alcohol. It is medium sweet with velvety dried blueberry, blackberry jam, prune, raisin, and fig flavors.

Chambourcin is a French-American hybrid variety of uncertain parentage. The grape has only been available since 1963. It is a late ripening grape and has a good resistance to fungal disease. Chambourcin requires a long growing season and a site less subject to low winter temperatures. The large, moderately loose bunches set medium-sized blue berries. The vine is very productive and cluster thinning is required. The grape produces a deep-colored and aromatic wine. It can be made into a dry style or one with a moderate residual sugar level. Chambourcin is a teinturie grape whose juice is pink or red rather than clear like most *vitis vinifera* cultivars.

Corot noir is a hybrid red grape variety developed by grape breeder Bruce Reisch of the Cornell University New York State Agricultural Experiment Station. Released in 2006, Corot noir is the result of a cross between hybrids Seyve Villard and Steuben in 1970. It ripens mid- to late season and cluster thinning is usually required to avoid over-cropping. Vines are vigorous and productive with good powdery mildew and botrytis fruit rot resistance. Corot noir wines are usually dry with medium color, big soft tannins, and marked cherry and berry fruit aromas.

De Chaunac is a French-American hybrid grape variety developed in the 1860s by Dr. Albert Seibel to combat the devastation of phylloxera in France. Named for Canadian enologist Adhemar de Chaunac, the variety was introduced in Ontario, Canada in 1947 and migrated to the United States in the 1950s. De Chaunac is a very vigorous vine whose small, round, blue-black berries ripen in mid-season. Grown primarily in the northeast, De Chaunac is fairly cold tolerant with good resistance to mildew. Fruity, mild tanning De Chaunac wines are often blended with tannin-thick wine and smoothly fortified.

Frontenac is a dark-skinned, hybrid French-American grape variety, the result of a crossing made by the University of Minnesota in 1978 between Landot

Noir and a native *Vitis riparia* vine noted for its resistance to the cold. Vines produce loose clusters of dark, highly acidic, small, high-sugar berries. Frontenac is an extremely cold-hardy, vigorous vine resistant to downy and powdery mildew. Wines have a deep garnet color, with cherry aromas and flavors of blackcurrant, plum, and sometimes chocolate. Complex and low in tannin, winemakers can be challenged by the grape's high natural acidity.

Lenoir/Black Spanish is the probable result of a natural cross between American *Vitis aestivalis* and an unknown *Vitis vinifera* variety. Lenoir was named for a man who cultivated the grape in South Carolina. Sometime time in the late eighteenth century, the grape migrated to Texas and was christened Black Spanish and often used to make communion wine. The disease-resistant, black-skinned grape is favored by Texas port-style vintners for its dark color and earthy aroma.

Léon Millot is a dark-skinned French-American sister hybrid grape to Marechal Foch. Born of the same *riparia-rupestris* hybrid and the *vinifera* variety, Millot shares Foch's cold resistance but is a more productive than its sibling. Leon Millot ripens early in the vineyard, making it appropriate for marginal regions where the growing season is limited. Viticulturist Philip Wagner brought cuttings of Léon Millot he had obtained from Gerard Marot's vineyard in France to the United States in the early 1950s. Vines are vigorous producers of small clusters of small, black, round, juicy berries. Léon Millot wines exhibit distinct berry aroma and a hint of chocolate that blends well with Marechal Foch.

Marechal Foch is an interspecific hybrid French red grape variety that has proven to be a prolific producer in cold weather wine growing regions of North America. Marechal Foch was first bred as Kuhlmann 188 in 1910 by Alsatian Hans Kuhlmann, who crossed a *riparia-rupestris* hybrid and the *vinifera* variety Goldriesling—Riesling combined with Courtiller Musque, an early-maturing Muscat. The grape came to the United States in 1946 where it was named for famous French World War I general Ferdinand Foch.

Foch is a cold-hardy and disease-resistant hybrid that avoids the "foxy" character prevalent in many American hybrids. The variety classified as a teinturier, a red grape variety where both the skin and pulp are a deep red color. This characteristic makes for deeply colored wines, an essential for classic red port-style fortified wines. It is a cousin of the familiar French American hybrid Frontenac, and grandson of the widely admired Pinot Noir.

Marquette is a dark blue variety crossed by the University of Minnesota in 1989. The complex hybrid released in 2006 was developed for cold-climate vineyards with resistance to powdery mildew and black rot. Moderately vigorous vines produce small to medium-sized clusters of round, medium-sized berries with light pink flesh. With high sugar and medium acidity, Marquette grapes produce ruby-colored wines with red and black berry flavors and firm tannins. The brilliant color andbalanced structure makes Marquette an attractive candidate for northeastern fortified wines.

Cornell University and the New York State Agricultural Experiment Station developed **Noiret** as a cold-climate hybrid grape for the northeastern United States. The grape is the result of complex breeding beginning in 1973. Its parents are Steuben and Chancellor. Released to growers in 2006, the vines are quite productive with moderately large berries that ripen mid-season. Noiret makes richly colored, somewhat herbaceous, fruit-forward wines with soft tannins. Lacking the "foxy" character of other hybrids, Noiret is a strong candidate for blended fortified wines.

Created in 1967 by Professor Gerhardt Alleweldt at the Institute for Grape Breeding in Geilweilerhof, Germany, the **Regent** grape is a cross between Silvaner, Chambourcin, and Muller-Thargau. Regent is a late-ripening, cool-climate grape that is highly resistant to most vine diseases. Vines produce good yields of medium-sized, dark, thick-skinned, red-stained fleshy grapes. Wines are densely colored with red fruit flavors and soft tannins that are ideal for fortification. While quite new to the United States, small quantities of Regent are grown in the Pacific Northwest.

Rougeon is a French-American hybrid grape obtained by crossing Munson and Seibel varieties. Cold-hardy vines produce medium-sized clusters of bright red grapes somewhat susceptible to mildew. Rougeon produces brilliant red wines that are often blended with Chambourcin or Baco Noir to make deeply colored port-style wine.

Valiant is a cold-hardy, vigorous grape developed by South Dakota State University as a cross between Fredonia and the *Vitis riparia* Wild Montana vine. The high-yielding vines can survive temperatures of –35°F and produce round, blue, early ripening grapes. While the tart fruit is best suited for jelly and grape juice, Valiant can produce a low-acid, sweet wine.

WHITE FORTIFIED WINE GRAPES

Classic Varieties

Recent UC Davis DNA fingerprinting studies have determined that in fact Chardonnay is the result of a cross between Pinot and Gouais blanc varieties. Now, the theory of origin is that the Romans brought Gouais blanc from Croatia to France, where it was widely planted by French peasants.

Chardonnay is a relatively easy vine to cultivate and has the ability to adapt to differing growing conditions. Highly vigorous, Chardonnay thrives in regions with moderately long growing seasons and favors chalk, clay, and limestone soils. Chardonnay vines can yield up to 5 tons per acre but wine quality can suffer at such a high yield. A thin-skinned, early-ripening grape, Chardonnay is susceptible to spring frosts and problems related to millerandage, coulure, and powdery mildew. Berries are relatively small, fragile, and prone to oxidation.

Palomino is the predominant white grape in the Andalusian region of Spain, which produces the great sherry wines of Europe. The grape came to California in the 1850s as a table grape from New England. In addition, the

Russians grew Palomino grapes imported from Peru in the 1860s at their Fort Ross vineyard on the Sonoma coast.

Palomino is a high-yielding, easy to grow grape that thrives in the warm dry climate of California's Central Valley. It was used extensively in pre-Prohibition sweet wines and was revived by the sweet wine demand of the 1940s and '50s. While Palomino acreage has declined dramatically since the 1990s, the grape is used almost exclusively to make fine domestic sherries.

The "other" white grape that produces the fine sherries of Spain, the **Pedro Ximenez** is native to the Andalusia region of Southern Spain. Grown since at least the seventeenth century, vigorous vines produce thick-skinned, mid- to late-ripening grapes in large clusters. However, Pedro Ximenez is susceptible to a variety of hazards including bunch rot and downy mildew. The grape's high sugar and acidity make it ideal for the production of sweet wines and sherry. Contrary to popular folklore, the grape was most likely not brought to Germany from the Canary Islands or Madeira by a Spanish soldier named Pedro Ximenez.

Riesling is the white wine grape most associated with the German wines from the Mosel and Rhine regions. It produces wine with fresh floral aromas characteristic of roses. The naturally cold-hardy variety is grown from coast to coast—New York to Washington and California. The small to medium-sized fruit clusters are sensitive to powdery mildew and bunch rot. Rieslings produce a moderate yield of slow-maturing fruit. Cuttings were brought to Sonoma California by Emil Dresel in 1859 from his home town of Griesheim, Germany. Riesling was referred to as Johannesburg Riesling in the 1870s in honor of the famous Rheingau estate; however, BATF (United States Bureau of Alcohol, Tocacco, and Firearms) ruled in 1996 that "Johannesburg" cannot appear on California labels. Small to medium-size fruit clusters are sensitive to powdery mildew and bunch rot. Fortunately, Reisling is susceptible to the "noble rot," *Botrytis cinerea*, which can result in phenomenal late-harvest sweet dessert wines and fortified white port-style wine.

Sauvignon blanc is an indigenous grape of Bordeaux whose name (*sauvage*, "wild") reflects its ancient origin; it is acknowledged to be a parent of royalty. Sauvignon blanc's marriage to Cabernet Franc produced the king of reds—Cabernet Sauvignon. Sauvignon blanc grapes infected by the "noble rot" (*Botrytis cinerea*) are blended with Semillon to produce the famous, and expensive, Sauternes dessert wines. Sauvignon blanc is highly site-sensitive and small variations in climate, water, slope, and sun exposure have significant effects on the grapes. Sauvignon blancs from cool-climate vines tend to be high in acidity, with a floral aroma, robust fruitiness, and streak of herbal grassiness. Grapes hidden from the sun by a thick canopy of leaves will exhibit a more pronounced grassiness.

The story of **Gewürztraminer** goes back to Roman times when a green-skinned grape was cultivated in the village of Termeno in the northeastern Italian region of Alto Adige at the base of the Tyrolean Alps. The origin of Traminer—named for the village—is unclear and the grape appears to be closely related to Sauvignon blanc.

Gewürztraminer was first brought to California by the flamboyant wine pioneer Agoston Haraszthy in 1862. Gewürztraminer is a fussy vine to grow. It prefers cooler climates but likes dry, warm summers. Vines are moderately vigorous producers but as an early ripener, Gewürztraminer can be the victim of spring frosts. Vines produce moderately sized clusters of small, loosely packed, pink to light red oval berries. Dessert-style Gewürztraminer wines can be late harvest or fortified.

Muscat, in California, there is historic evidence of Muscat being "field-blended" in some early Mission vineyards. By the mid-1850s, California vineyards were being planted with red and white Muscat varieties shipped from East Coast nurseries. Early California winemakers would blend Muscat wine with harsher Palomino or Berger wines to produce a "Germanic" floral character. Following prohibition, Muscat was unfortunately associated with cheap, fortified sweet wines like muscatel.

Of the two hundred Muscat varieties, only three white-skinned grapes are of major importance to California winemakers. Muscat blanc was originally used by California winemakers for small qualities of sweet dessert wine and blending in fortified wine.

Muscat of Alexandria is officially a raisin grape. Although an excellent table grape, the variety has been an important part of the California wine industry for almost 150 years. Nurseryman Antoine Delmas of San Jose is credited with importing the first Muscat of Alexandria into the state in 1852. The first wines produced from the variety were sweet, fortified muscatels.

Little is really known about the Orange Muscat grape but it is definitely a member of the Muscat family. The "orange" comes from the grape's orange-blossom aroma that is particularly evident in the vineyard during the growing season. Orange Muscat makes a delightfully sweet fortified dessert wine with brilliant orange-gold color and aromas of orange and apricot

In 1878, Sutter County, California, rancher William Thompson ordered a group of grape vine cuttings from a nursery in New York. Among the cultivars Thompson received were vines that produced prodigious yields of seedless, medium-sized, greenish white to golden berries that ripened early in mid-August. It was grower John Onstott who realized the commercial potential of the grape (which he named *Thompson Seedless* for his neighbor) and shipped cuttings and rootstock throughout California in 1892.

Originating in Turkey as the Sultana, Thompson Seedless is the most widely planted grape variety in California. Although a true *vinifera* variety, about 70 percent of the annual crop is devoted to raisin production while another 15 percent is marketed as fresh table grapes. The remaining 15 percent of Thompson Seedless are crushed for grape juice concentrate, wine, and grape spirits.

The origin of the once-common *Viognier* grape on the terraced slopes of the northern Rhone Valley in the Condrieu region of France is steeped in misty legend. Perhaps the most widely favored tale finds Viognier's ancient ancestors cultivated on the island of Vis in Dalmatia. DNA research at UC Davis indicates that the grape is closely related to the northwest Italian Piedmont grapes Freisa and Nebbiolo Grown on hearty but low-yielding vines, the soft-skinned, deep yellow Viognier can be prone to powdery mildew and other vineyard diseases. Vines thrive in terroir with well-drained soils and warm, long growing seasons.

Verdelho is one of the three traditional varieties grown in the Azores that was exported to mainland Europe before the variety was all but wiped out in the phylloxera plague. When Verdelho first came to California is undocumented but in 1963 the University of California Experiment Station recommended the variety for "high-quality sweet wines." (Sullivan, 1998 p.381) Verdelho is a moderately vigorous vine that produces small bunches of small oval berries with a high skin-to-juice ratio. The grapes ripen early but can be prone to powdery mildew. The vines can also be susceptible to frost during the spring. Wines are usually aromatic and high in alcohol and acid, with rich, herbaceous, spicy, and nutty tropical fruit flavors.

WHITE HYBRID VARIETIES

In 1953, the New York State Agricultural Experiment State crossed the French American hybrid Seyval and the classic Chardonnay to produce what is now called *Chardonel.* The vigorous, cold- and disease-resistant hybrid vines bare large clusters of green or amber berries that ripen mid to late season. Chardonel reflects more of its Chardonnay parentage, producing wines with rich fruit flavors and solid structure that can support port-style fortification.

Niagara is the most common grape grown for grape juice production in North America. A product of Niagara County, New York, residents C. L. Hoag and B. W. Clark crossing Concord and Cassady varieties in 1868, the large, juicy, round, pale-green grape retains the "foxy" character of native *Vitis labrusca*. The grapy aroma of Niagara is a positive attribute for white wines that can be enhanced by fortification with bandy or distilled spirits.

Developed by Bertille Seyve and Victor Villard in the early to mid-1900s, the green-skinned *Seyval blanc* grape is the most successful of French hybrids. A result of the complex classical breeding process, the grape is a cross of two varieties developed by French viticulturist Albert Seibel. In his work to develop phylloxera-resistant vines, Seibel produced over sixteen thousand hybrid grape varieties. Fairly cool-hardy, Seyval blanc vines produce small berries in large clusters that ripen early in the season. The variety is susceptible to powdery mildew and botrytis. Seyval blanc wines have flavor characteristics between Chardonnay and Sauvignon blanc, with sufficient structure for fortification.

Wisconsin grape breeder Elmer Swenson developed *Brianna* in 1983 as a vigorous variety that could withstand the harsh cold climates of the upper midwestern United States. An interspecific hybrid of *V. labrusca* and *V. riparia*, the Muscat-like grapes have thick, greenish-gold berries in medium to large clusters. Vines are slightly susceptible to mildew but moderately susceptible to black rot and *botrytis*. Originally bred as a table grape, Brianna was available as a wine grape in 2001, producing dry or sweet wines with tropical fruit flavors that enhance white wine blends.

Frontenac gris is the white version of the University of Minnesota's dark-skinned, French-American Frontenac hybrid. According the university, Frontenac gris is a single bud mutation that yields a gray (gris) grape with amber-colored juice. The variety was released for propagation in 2003. Moderately high vigor vines produce loose, medium-sized clusters of small to medium-sized grayish-amber berries. Ripening mid to late season, Frontenac gris produces wines with unique and complex flavors with excellent potential for fortification. An important variety grown primarily in southwestern France, *Petit Manseng* migrated to the Basque region of Spain then to Australia and eventually to Virginia. Low-yielding vines produce loose bunches of thick-skinned, small berries that can achieve high sugar levels while retaining balanced acidity. The fortunate combination of sugar and acid levels, along with a long ripening season, results in distinctive late harvest wines that can be readily tailored to fortification.

Vignoles is a complex white grape interspecific hybrid named by the Finger Lakes Wine Growers Association in 1970. Originally thought to have developed by J. F. Ravat in 1930 as a Seibel–Pinot Noir clone cross, genetic testing indicates that Vignoles does not have the genetic markers of either variety, making the grape's parentage unknown. Vignoles is a moderately vigorous vine with moderate yields of small, compact bunches of small, thick-skinned, light green berries susceptible to *botrytis* and prone to cracking prior to harvest. With moderate cold hardiness, Vignoles ripens mid-season and produces balanced, fruity, late harvest–style sweet wines with ample fortification potential.

John A. Mortensen created the American hybrid *Blanc du Bois* grape at the University of Florida's Central Florida Research and Education Center in 1968 with the goal of producing a grape variety resistant to Pierce's disease. A bacterial infection spread by the Glassy Wing Sharpshooter insect, Pierce's disease can quickly devastate large areas of grape vines. Named for grape grower Emile DuBois, who emigrated from France in 1882, Blanc du Bois is a cross of Florida's hybrid Muscadine and California's Cardinal table grape. Vines are moderate to highly vigorous, producing medium-sized amber-green berries. Since its release in 1987, Blanc du Bois has been particularly successful in Texas producing superbly balanced Madeira and port-style wines. Blanc du Bois is becoming an increasingly popular variety along the southeast coast.

The Florida Agriculture Experiment Station specifically bred the *Lake Emerald* grape for compatibility with the warm-winter climate of the southern coast. In 1944, the university crossed the white Pixiola with the yellow Golden Muscat to produce the hybrid resistant to most vine diseased affecting Florida-grown grapes including Pierce's disease. Vigorous vines produce medium-size, tough-skinned, light green to light golden berries that ripen in mid to late July. Originally intended as a garden variety arbor grape, Lake Emerald's distinctive aromatics, tropical fruit flavors, and light color make it a pleasant lightly fortified wine.

In the 1930s, French grape breeder Jean-Louis Vidal crossed Ugni blanc (Trebbiano) with Rayond'Or (Seibel 4986) to produce a hybrid variety for brandy production in cold, maritime climates. The result was a very winter-hardy grape that can produce high levels of sugar while maintaining good acidity. *Vidal blanc* came to Ontario, Canada, in the late 1940s and has become one of the most versatile white grape varieties in North America. Vines produce large clusters of thick-skinned grapes that are moderately resistant to downy mildew but susceptible to a number of other vine related afflictions. Vidal blanc makes golden-hued ice wine or a highly flavored fortified wine.

BIBLIOGRAPHY

2016 Directory and Buyers Guide. Wines and Vines. San Rafael, CA: 2016

Adams, Leon D. *The Wines of America*. Boston: Houghton Mifflin Company, 1973.

The American Wine Society. *The Complete Handbook of Winemaking*. Ann Arbor, MI. G.W. Kent, Inc. 1993.

Amerine, Maynard A. and Roessler, Edward B. Wines—Their Sensory Evaluation. San Francisco, CA: W.H. Freeman and Company, 1971.

Atime4wine.com. " California Port Wine" Retrieved from www.atime4wine.com/port-ca. 2007.

Baldy, Marian W., PhD. *The University Wine Course*. San Francisco: The Wine Appreciation Guild, 1993.

Brenneman, Chik. Norton-New World Nobility. *WineMaker*. June/July 2010 (p.19–22).

Book of California Wine. Berkeley: University of California Press/Southeby Publications, 1984.

Costa, Eric J. *Old Vines—A History of Winegrowing in Amador County*. Jackson, CA: Cenotto Publications, 1994.

Cox, Jeff. *From Vines to Wines*. New York: Harper & Row, 1985.

De Groot, Roy. *The Wines of California—The Pacific Northwest & New York*. New York: Summit Books, 1982.

Domine', Andre'. *Wine*. Cologne, Germany: Konemann, 2001.

Fermentation Handbook. Petaluma, CA: Scott Labs: 2006.

Ficklin, David. *Making California Port Wine: Ficklin Vineyards from 1948-1992*. Oral History Office, Bancroft Library, 1992.

Ficklin Vineyards. Retrieved from www.ficklin.com.

Galet, Pierre. *Grape Varieties*. London: Cassell Illustrated. 2002.

The Global Encyclopedia of Wine. Willoughby, Australia: Global Book Publishing, 2000.

Hanni, Tim. *Why You Like the Wines You Like: Changing the way the world thinks about wine*. Napa, CA: HanniCo LLC, 2013.

Hartung, Alexis. Chambourcin. *WineMaker*. October-November 2004 (p.17–20).

Hartung, Alexis. Vignoles. *WineMaker*. February/March 2007 (p.19-21).

Hartung, Alexis. Vidal Blanc. *WineMaker*. October/November 2005 (p.18–19).

Heintz, William F. *Wine Country: A History of Napa Valley, the Early Years 1838-1920*. Santa Barbara CA: Capra Press.

Howkins, Ben. *Real Men Drink Port …and ladies too!*. Shrewsbury, UK: Quiller Publishing Ltd., 2011.

Into Wine. "Enjoying Port." Retrieved from www.intowine.com/port. 2006.

Jackisch, Philip. *Modern Winemaking*. Ithaca, NY: Cornell University Press. 1985.

Jackson, Ron S. *Wine Science—Principles, Practice, Perspective* – 2nd Edition. London: Academic Press, 2000.

Johnson, Hugh. *Story of Wine*. London: Mitchell Beazley, 2002.

Johnson, Hugh. *Wine Companion*. London: Mitchell Beazley, 2001.

Keller, Jack. Taming the Wild Mustang. WineMaker. June/July 2004 (p.48-52).

Kramer, Matt. *Making Sense of California Wine*. New York: William Morrow and Company, 1989.

Lukacs, Paul. *American Vintage—The Rise of American Wine*. New York: W. W. Norton & Company, 2005.

Margalit, Yair. PhD. *Winery Technology and Operations—A Handbook for Small Wineries*. San Francisco, CA: The Wine Appreciation Guild, 1996.

Mendelson, Richard. *From Demon to Darling—A Legal History of Wine in America*. Berkeley, CA: University of California Press, 2009.

Millner, Cork. "Sherry." *Sante' Food & Beverage Guide* (April/May, 2000)

Musings on the Vine. "Dessert Wines" Retrieved from www.musingsonthevine.com. 2007.

Nordqvist, *Wine: Health Benefits and Health Risks*, Retrieved from: medicalnewstoday.com/articles/265635.php, 2016.

Okrent, Daniel. *Last Call*. New York: Scribner, 2010.

Patterson, Tim. "Muscat—The Power of Aromatics." *WineMaker*. June/July, 2003. (p.22-29).

Peninou, Ernest P. *Leland Stanford's Great Vina Ranch*. 1881–1919. (n.d)

Pinney, Thomas. *A History of Wine in America—From Prohibition to the Present*. Berkeley: University of California Press, 2005.

Pinney, Thomas. *A History of Wine in America—From The Beginning to Prohibition*. Berkeley: University of California Press, 1989.

Pombianchi, Daniel. "Luscious Port." *WineMaker*. 5,6 (December 2002-January 2003): (p.36-41).

Port and Sherry. London: Geo. G. Sandeman Sons & Co., 1955.

Robinson, Janice. *Guide to Wine Grapes*. Oxford: Oxford University Press, 1996.

Robinson, J., ed. The Oxford Companion to Wine (Third ed.), Oxford: Oxford University Press, 2006.

Sharp, Andrew. *WineTaster's Secrets*. Los Angeles, CA: Warwick Publishers, 1995.

Sullivan, Charles L. *A Companion to California Wine*. Berkeley: University of California Press, 1998.

Teiser, Ruth and Harroun, Catherine. *Winemaking in California*. New York: McGraw-Hill Book Company, 1983.

Wagner, Philip M. *A Wine-Growers Guide*. San Francisco: The Wine Appreciation Guild, 1996.

Wine Laws, Regulations, and Public Guidance. Retrieved from: www.ttb.gov/wine/wine_regs.shtml.

Why Use Enzymes in Winemaking. Retrieved from: vintessential.com.au/resources/articles/why-use-enzymes-in-winemaking.html.

WINE PRODUCERS INDEX